Running on Empty in Central America?

Canadian, Mexican, and US Integrative Efforts

A. Imtiaz Hussain

UNIVERSITY PRESS OF AMERICA,® INC.
Lanham • Boulder • New York • Toronto • Oxford

Copyright © 2006 by
University Press of America,® Inc.
4501 Forbes Boulevard
Suite 200
Lanham, Maryland 20706
UPA Acquisitions Department (301) 459-3366

PO Box 317
Oxford
OX2 9RU, UK

British Library Cataloging in Publication Information Available

Library of Congress Control Number: 2005933173

ISBN: 978-0-7618-3285-0

∞™ The paper used in this publication meets the minimum
requirements of American National Standard for Information
Sciences—Permanence of Paper for Printed Library Materials,
ANSI Z39.48—1992

To
Lyle McGeoch, Jack Nagel,
. . . and the memory of Alvin Rubinstein . . .
reasons why I remain on my toes still!

Table of Contents

Illustrations

Figures

Abstract

What led Canada, Mexico, and the US to deepen economic integration with Central American countries? Since all are members of NAFTA and FTAA, why did one succeed, another fail, and a third struggle in between? Could *how* they negotiated be as important as *what* they were negotiating?

A structured focused analysis (George 1979) of Canada's Central American Four Free Trade Agreement (CA4FTA), Mexico's Plan Puebla-Panama (PPP), and the US Central American Free Trade Agreement (CAFTA) reveals, in spite of a common Washington Consensus thrust, diverging domestic interests shaped disparate outcomes: (a) Canada was driven by development, Mexico restructuration, and US strategic imperatives; (b) relative economic size and deeper trading history partly explain why the US succeeded, Canada failed, and Mexico continues sputtering; (c) while lesser developed Central American (CA) countries embraced *maquiladorization*, developed Costa Rica found its corporatist networks threatened; and (d) while no single negotiations paradigms accounted for the complex dynamics, those accounting for asymmetry (Habeeb 1988) proved more useful than those ignoring it (Feinberg 1997).

Among the implications: (a) Canada and Mexico may be better off free-riding US initiatives; (b) CA liberalization may be irreversible, but widens gaps with sustainable society; and (c) anticipated CAFTA ratification strengthens FTAA momentum at Brazil's expense.

Meant primarily for students/scholars of international political economy, North, Central, and Latin America, as well as comparativists and negotiation theorists, the book reports on unfolding developments affecting transitional societies at large, whether in the western hemisphere or elsewhere.

Acknowledgment

This book profited from two fellowships: the annual CONACYT awards for individual scholars (#39667 under the 2002–01 SEP-CONACYT Convocation), and a Canada-Latin America-Central America award from the International Council of Canadian Studies. I am grateful to the Mexican government for the former, and to the Canadian government for the latter. My appreciation to Gaëtan Vallieres and Pierre Sved for steering me through the second fellowship, and to Sofía Gallardo Calva, Guillermo Ibarra Escobar, and Alejandro Mercado Celis for supporting me in its pursuit. One portion of the manuscript previously appeared in the May 2004 issue of *Revista Mexicana de Estudios Canadienses*, and I am grateful to Miriam Alfie Cohen and the editors of the publication for furnishing the permission to borrow from that article. Several portions have also been presented in various conferences, where others on the panel offered useful comments. My appreciation extends to them as well. A final note of thanks goes to Donald Mackay and Sharon O'Regan of FOCAL in Ottawa, Canada, for interviews; Gustavo Acua Popocatl and Marlene Oechler Solana for technical assistance; and Alejandra Santoyo Mora for bailing me out countless times. At University Press of America, my thanks to David Chan, Amanda Slaybaugh, and Judith L. Rothman. In benefiting from all of the above and acknowledging all of their support, in the final analysis, I alone remain responsible for all omissions and commissions.

Finally, this book is dedicated to the three faculty members who have most influenced my intellectual upbringing. While my shortcomings are in no way reflective of any of them or their influences, I am deeply indebted to each for helping me plant my own intellectual roots, then build confidence to explore

the unknown. Lyle McGeogh taught me how to convert wild and uncoordi-
nated writing into scholarly papers while directing my Master's thesis in West
European history in Ohio University. When he nudged me to his alma mater,
the University of Pennsylvania, Jack Nagel took charge of my graduate life,
including supervising my doctoral thesis, this time in political science. From
Alvin Rubinstein I learned not only how to teach, but also to survive under
pressure. In just one lifetime, I will in no way fulfill all their expectations or
even emulate even a fraction of their very high standards, but what I did learn
from them will keep me busy for at least the remainder of this lifetime. My
respect and regards for each.

A. Imtiaz Hussain
Mexico City
September 2005

Abbreviations

AFL-CIO:	American Federation of Labor-Council of Industrial Organization
APG:	American Policy Group
ASEAN:	Association of South-east Asian Nations
BICE:	See CABEI
BIP:	Border Industrialization Program
CA:	Central America
CABEI:	Central American Bank for Economic Integration (BICE)
CACM:	Central American Common Market
CAFTA:	Central American Free Trade Agreement
CA4FTA:	Central American Four Free Trade Agreement
CAIS:	Central American Integrated System (SICA in Spanish)
CBI:	Caribbean Basin Initiative
CBTPA:	Caribbean Basin Trade Partnership Act
CCRFTA:	Canada-Costa Rican Free Trade Agreement
CEC:	Council for Economic Cooperation
CEIP:	Carnegie Endowment for International Peace
CELA:	Canadian Environmental Law Association
CCIC:	Canadian Council for International Cooperation
CINDE:	Costa Rican Investment Board
CMM:	Cascading Modular Multilateralism
COG:	Congressional Oversight Group (US)
COPPAL:	Permanent Conference of Latin American Political Parties
CTN:	*Confederación de Trabajadores de Nicaragua*
CUFTA:	Canada-US Free Trade Agreement
CUPG:	*Comité de Unidad Patriótica de Guatemala*

DCs:	Developed countries
DFAIT:	Department of Foreign Affairs and International Trade (Canada)
DFD:	Diagnostic-formula-detail
EAI:	Enterprise for the Americas Initiative
EDA:	Export Development Agency (Canada)
EDC:	Export Development Council (Canada)
EU:	European Union
EZLN:	*Ejercito Zapatista de Liberación Nacional* (Mexican)
FICE:	Central American Import Financing Program (in Spanish)
FOCAL:	*Fondación Canadienne pour les Amériques*
FTA:	Free Trade Agreement
FTAA:	Free Trade Area of the Americas
GATT:	General Agreement on Tariffs and Trade
GSP:	Generalized System of Preferences
HD:	Hemispheric Diplomacy
IADB:	Inter-American Development Bank
IBRD:	International Bank for Reconstruction and Development
ILO:	International Labor Organization
IMF:	International Monetary Fund
INCAE:	Central American Institute of Business Administration (Costa Rica)
ISI:	Import Substitution Industrialization
ITA:	Information Technical Agreement
LDCs:	Less Developed Countries
LAFTA:	Latin American Free Trade Agreement
LEAP:	Labor Education in the Americas Program
MFA:	Multifibre Agreement
MFN:	Most Favored Nation
MOU:	Memorandum of Understanding
NAFI:	North American Forum of Integration
NAFTA:	North American Free Trade Agreement
NAP:	National Action Plan
NEC:	National Economic Council (USA)
NSC:	National Security Council (USA)
OAS:	Organization of American States
OCA:	Optimal Currency Area
PAN:	*Partido Accion Nacional* (Mexican)
PRONACOM:	National Competition Program
PPP:	Plan Puebla Panama
PPP:	Purchasing power parity

PRD:	*Partido de la Revolución Democrática* (Mexican)
PRI:	*Partido Revolucionario Institucional* (Mexican)
SACU:	South African Customs Union
SMEs:	Small & Medium-sized Enterprises
SOA:	Summit of the Americas
SPS:	Sanitary and phytosanitary (products/measures)
SPTF:	Social Progress Trust Fund
TAA:	Trade Adjustment Act (US)
TAN:	Transnational Advocacy Network
TBTs:	Technical barriers to trade
TCB:	Trade Capacity Building
TGIF:	Thank God its Friday
TPAs:	Tariff Preferential Arrangements
TPL:	Tariff Preference Level
TRIMs:	Trade-related Investment Measures
TRIPs:	Trade-related Intellectual Property Rights
TRQs:	Tariff Rate Quotas
UNAM:	*Universidad Nacional Autónoma de México*
URG:	*Unidad Revolucionaria Guatemalteca*
USTR:	United States Trade Representative
WTO:	World Trading Organization
YFP:	Yarn forward position

Chapter One

Introduction: Nothing But the Full *Enchilada*? Central America's FTA Rainbow & Goldpot

QUESTIONS

What led Canada, Mexico, and the United States to seek some sort of economic integration with Central American countries as the new century began? And why did the pertinent negotiations produce such different outcomes? Canada abruptly postponed negotiations in July 2004; Mexico relaunched its efforts in March 2004 after the initial drives from 2001 almost petered out during 2003; and only the United States actually signed a free trade agreement (FTA), on May 28, 2004, in fact. Since all three countries belong to the fairly successful North American Free Trade Agreement (NAFTA), and remain committed to the currently tottering Free Trade Area of the Americas (FTAA), how do we position their Central American engagements—as part of a NAFTA-Plus collective thrust with limited membership, a stepping stone towards coordinating and completing a broader FTAA collective, or simply independent pursuits promoting state interests? Inquiries into such questions benefit from at least three perspectives: the FTA surge across Central America (CA), the converging and diverging equation of forces, and a Central American overview itself, respectively.

FTA SPLURGE & CENTRAL AMERICAN CONVERGENCE

What explains the recent splurge of FTAs and convergence across Central America? The integration being sought is not alike, to be sure. Whereas Canada and the United States seek a free trade agreement, Mexico, with its selective FTAs across the region, is more interested in overlapping

1

infrastructural projects, connecting every country between its southern state of Puebla and the Panama Canal. Thus the Puebla-Panama Plan (PPP), involving Belize, Costa Rica, El Salvador, Guatemala, Honduras, Nicaragua, and Panama, is geographically wider than the two FTAs. It was first announced on September 5, 2000 by president-elect Vicente Fox Quesada, but formalized as a program from March 12, 2001. Mexico's earlier FTAs with Costa Rica in 1995, Nicaragua in 1998, and the Northern Triangle counterpart with El Salvador, Guatemala, and Honduras in 2001, paved the way for PPP. During the November 2004 Iberoamerican summit in earthquake-shaken San José, Costa Rica, Fox also invited Colombia into PPP, suggesting how the open-ended PPP southern border aligns so closely and mirrors so perfectly the purposes of FTAA.[1]

The US wrapped up a Central American Free Trade Agreement (CAFTA) with Costa Rica, El Salvador, Guatemala, Honduras, and Nicaragua, between December 2003 and January 2004, although the 2,400-paged document was signed in the Hall of the Americas at the Organization of American States (OAS) headquarters in Washington on May 28.[2] It became the first FTA concluded within the pre-announced time-frame, which, with 9 rounds over 12 months, also ranks as the fastest FTA negotiations known. Yet, as US Trade Representative (USTR), Robert B. Zoellick, observed at the signature ceremony, May 28 was "just the beginning of the most critical chapter for CAFTA," referring to the ratification required in Congress, which, in spite of a resounding Republican victory in the 2004 elections, just scraped through with a 217-215 margin in the last week of July 2005. Simultaneous Central American pressure for the "most rapid passage and implementation by the United States" thickened the plot.[3] As with Mexico's PPP, CAFTA negotiations more or less paralleled independent US FTA negotiations with the Dominican Republic and preceded those with Panama from April 2004. Similar US negotiations with Colombia, Ecuador, and Peru in the Americas, and Australia, Bahrain, Morocco, and Singapore, among others, elsewhere,[4] suggest more than coincidences at play, since all hemispheric FTAs are expected to converge into the FTAA, whose US-determined target date of January 2005 became questionable from the moment the Cancún WTO ministerial meeting collapsed in September 2003. Richard Feinberg argues an emerging competitive liberalization US trade policy approach hopes to revitalize the WTO through brick-by-brick reconstruction.[5] The Bush administration's references to a "little-by-little" rearrangement reflecting US interests augment this view.[6]

Irrespective of the piecemeal US approach, Brazil's increasingly reluctant FTAA participation may produce a watered-down FTAA-Lite version, acknowledging interests of less developed countries (LDCs), rather than the full-blown FTAA originally conceived in the Miami December 1994 Summit of the Americas (SOA) reflecting developed country (DC) interests. Feinberg's depiction of the Miami and subsequent FTAA summit negotiations through the cascading modular multilateralism (CMM) and hemispheric diplomacy (HD) models may likewise also change to reflect the shifting forces at work, creating an opportunity for this investigation to explore if that is happening with CAFTA, and if so, what the new emphases and directions may be.

Canada's Central American negotiations were with four countries—El Salvador, Guatemala, Honduras, and Nicaragua—thus christened the Central American Four Free Trade Agreement (CA4FTA).[7] Initiated in November 2001 and postponed by Canada in July 2004, these have been the longest of the three negotiations for countries with the shortest of a trading history, and have proved most unproductive at a time of a FTA flurry across both North and Central America. Canada's only other regional FTA claim is the one it signed with Costa Rica (CCRFTA) in April 2001, on the heels of the Québec FTAA summit. The ease and success of CCRFTA negotiations inspired other Central American states to propose similar arrangements to Jean Chrétien, Canada's prime minister. His departure did not stall the negotiations, but neither did Paul Martin's intention to realign with the United States following the deep post-9/11 policy differences between the two countries. Other explanations need to be explored.

Galvanized by Hurricane Mitch humanitarian support from November 1998, Canada's Central American engagements reflected a broader southern interest from as early as 1990, when the country belatedly joined the OAS. Mexico, too, developed a southern interest even as NAFTA was being negotiated, signing a FTA with Chile in 1992.[8] Meanwhile, the US, always looking south from as far back as the 1823 Monroe Doctrine, formulated a different rationale, embodied in President George H.W. Bush's 1990 Enterprise for the Americans Initiative (EAI) proposal. Initially Mexico emerged as the most attractive US economic partner.[9] In a June 1990 San Antonio hemispheric summit, Bush accepted Mexico's proposal for extending the Canadian-US Free Trade Agreement (CUFTA) south—made by Carlos Salinas de Gortari the previous February in the Davos World Economic Forum gettogether. US president-elect Bill Clinton was approached by Costa Rica, El Salvador, Guatemala, Honduras, and Nicaragua for a similar agreement as NAFTA, a gesture beckoning only an open-ended US commitment to a future FTA at the May 8, 1997 San Jose, Costa Rica, summit. George W. Bush expressed no interest at all until just two weeks after 9/11, when a September 25 joint declaration with Central American states opened dialogue.[10] As the US interest in Central America blossomed, though there is no direct relationship, Canada, Mexico and NAFTA received less priority: Chrétien was himself not too taken by a Bush presidency, and 9/11 distanced the US noticeably from its southern neighbor; having just failed to obtain a free-flow immigration deal from Bush the week before 9/11, Mexico's Fox felt left out to dry, and his commensurately declining interest in PPP also suggests any immigration deal would be in the same single basket as trade integration. NAFTA was progressing well enough for the US to look beyond NAFTA towards a fully functioning FTAA by January 2005, a date Bush set in his 2001 inauguration speech. Central America was not only the missing blank but also an increasingly significant stepping stone, thus breeding the notion of NAFTA-Plus.[11]

Canada's recent OAS membership and a vain historical tendency to diversify US relations, particularly in the south, made NAFTA-Plus an appealing option. Interestingly, Chrétien's predecessor, Brian Mulroney, who first proposed a FTA to the United States at the May 1985 Shamrock Summit and subsequently sought OAS membership, was not at all enthusiastic about Mexico extending CUFTA into NAFTA, in early 1990. Recognizing there was little, if anything, Canada could do to prevent this, he quickly changed his mind, yet even by the time of President Fox's October 2004 Canada visit, the United States continued to be the increasingly dominant North American trading partner of both Canada and Mexico. Mexico, with more legitimate historical reasons to be apprehensive about the US, continues to toss and turn about its bilateral US relations even after embracing neoliberalism in the 1980s. Fox, for example, became, as Laura Carlsen aptly observed, the most ardent advocate of a NAFTA-Plus.[12] Immediately after becoming president, he felt Mexico was "in the club" of privileged countries, and therefore, a "new phase of NAFTA" was needed, providing "more development, more trade, and more integration," something like a "European Union-style" of integration. An advocate of NAFTA-Minus, Carlsen claims Canada did not know what Fox meant by NAFTA-Plus, which is not consistent with the Canadian shift towards negotiating CA4FTA at that very moment. Fox's PPP was both consistent with NAFTA-Plus and the perfect vehicle to extend the liberalization message south from Mexico, that is, until 9/11. After 9/11, Central America remains part and parcel of any NAFTA-Plus conception, whether in Mexico City, Ottawa, or Washington, DC, only the United States continues in single-minded pursuit of this original goal.

CONNECTING THREADS AND DISSENTING TENDENCIES

With a free trade agreement being the Canadian and US target, and a project-based integration Mexican, are there any connecting strands, overarching platforms, or underlying thrusts to these pursuits? Since all three countries belong to NAFTA, FTAA, and WTO, even wider questions arise: Is the end-product regional integration, whether NAFTA-Plus or hemispheric, or multi-lateral? If indeed regional integrative efforts are as disparate as the previous section conveyed, could the three countries simply be connecting their different domestic interests with multilateral interests? And if this is the case, is Central America beckoning North American countries for humanitarian reason or compassion, or part of broader collective hemispheric interests, mobilized by competition from other parts of the world? With the US as not only the largest economic force among all of these countries, but also the only North American country to complete an encompassing Central American trade agreement, why did not Canada or Mexico simply hop on the US bandwagon and free-ride the result? And if US competitive liberalism continues as a policy approach, making both Central America a FTAA transit-point and FTAA a reconstituted WTO transit-point, how have the divisive Cancún issues been reconciled in the first place?

Multilateral commitments and agriculture are two of those thorny issues. Their relevance is intimately connected with Washington Consensus and US fast-track authority dynamics. All four issues prey upon the above questions.

Multilateral Institutionalism

Multilateral institutionalism exposes a North American dilemma: Each state prioritizes it differently, while established multilateral institutions increasingly seek greater independence from states. What do these cross-cutting patterns mean?

Although multilateral or international commitments provided the overarching insights into external economic engagements of countries from as far back as World War II, US influence, in spite of spawning discomfort in other countries, proved instrumental. Canada, for example, traditionally preferred United Nations (UN) over US efforts, particularly in the one area where it seeks global leadership: development. Its humanitarian responses to Hurricane Mitch followed the UN route as much as its developmental efforts seek multilateral channels. If it has to choose, Canada relegates White House decisions to those from the Washington-based multilateral troika of institutions: the International Monetary Fund (IMF), the International Bank for Reconstruction and Development (IBRD), also called the World Bank, and the Inter-American Development Bank (IADB). Mexico and the US have quite different relations with these institutions: They act independent of Mexican policy-making and, as will be seen, even set the pace for Mexico to follow, but remain dependent on US policy-making, following broad foreign policy targets set in the White House.

Unlike Canada, the Mexico of late prefers White House decisions, since these raise Mexico to a privileged position, over Washington-based multilateral counterparts. When import substitution was a holy policy strategy, Mexico remained aloof of both. Then, and in the post-9/11 era, however, Mexico elevated, and continues to prioritize, the UN over any Washington-based decisions, whether from the White House or multilateral institutions — identifying, in this sense, with Canada's bedrock foreign policy thrusts. But between the 1982 economic crisis and 9/11, Mexico increasingly made White House decision-making its own yardstick. From the White House perspective, both the UN and Washington-based multilateral institutions are independent actors when their policy pursuits streamline US preferences. If they don't, as the UN repeatedly finds out to its own consternation, the US can behave abrasively, even with hostility.

Even with WTO commitment as a common thread, all three countries differ in the degree of commitment, generating significant consequences: Canada, as the country to propose the WTO in the first place once the 1994 Marakkesh Agreement bringing the GATT Uruguay Round to an end was signed, remains fully committed to WTO purposes; Mexico, joining GATT only in 1986 prioritizes NAFTA over the WTO, for reasons of its increasing trade concentration; and the United States, which after alone establishing GATT may be finding too many cooks spoiling the WTO broth, thus earnestly seeking to reconstitute the world trading body in its own image at every opportunity, including most recently at the failed Cancún meeting.

The more the US seeks to reinvent the WTO according to its own framework of preferences, the more Canadian and Mexican policy-makers feel frustrated since there is no alternative for them but to follow the US lead, as was evident in Cancún, and eventually finding themselves more locked-in. The net-effect is greater Canadian and Mexican alienation from other parts of the world, be they developed, as across the European Union, or developing, as across Africa, Asia, but most particularly Latin America. In the final analysis, the more the rest of the world sees Canada and Mexico as US appendages, the less viable both Canada and Mexico become in those very multilateral institutions they revere: Mexico learned this as a non-permanent Security Council member when only Resolution 1441 stood before a US-led Iraqi invasion in March 2003; and Canada has, repeatedly learned it cannot remain the largest US trading partner without first interpreting its own hemispheric interests through a southern US prism.

However one interprets the role of multilateral institutions in Canadian, Mexican, or US policy-making, they are also beginning to breathe an independent life of their own, though not at the expense of either the symbiotic ties some of them have with the United States, such as the Washington-based troika, or the US support other such institutions, like the WTO, need. Yet, one can discern divergences between the US, on the one hand, and these institutions, on the other. These are more evident in the WTO than the Washington troika, but they are also there in Washington, not so much at the policy-making level, since there seems to be an underlying belief in the Washington Consensus within the troika and the White House (which I elaborate later), but at the project implementation level, where multilateral institutions find more leeway and prove more robust in policy pursuits. This is not to even suggest a hiatus between policy planning and implementation phases is routine, but dynamics in the trenches often necessitate on-the-spot decisions regardless of where the drawing board is and who is drawing at the board.

When Mexico-US bilateral relations cooled the week before 9/11, and chilled further immediately after 9/11, Mexico's slow, steady, but certain PPP retreat might just as well have nipped PPP in the bud and prepared it for burial—were it not for multilateral institutions resuscitating the program; and they did so without any US direction. PPP was simply premised upon too many projects necessitating multilateral funding, a significant proportion of which stems from the private sector. As Feinberg and others articulate, multilateral actors—his term is plurilateral—form an essential component of hemispheric diplomacy (HD) and CMM; while the private sector within this particular geographical context essentially refers to US corporations or investors.

Many PPP projects were considered ten or even twenty years earlier—indicating they serve developmental purposes without necessarily having to rely on such White House political decisions, as to when and where to begin and how much finance would be provided.[13] Indeed they made more economic sense in their own rights as to not even need political input. For instance, if a Mexican *maquila* plant along the Río Grande becomes uncompetitive, relocating it where wages are lower, such as Guatemala, is not a White House-based decision but may benefit if the White House also decides to pursue a free trade agreement with Guatemala. Decisions like these appeal to corporations seeking the competitive edge, as well as to Wall Street bankers, financiers, and investors, though the political circumstances permitting them to be implemented, such as security, could be, rather than would be, a political, or White House consideration.

Washington Consensus

Behind these nuances seems to be a bipartisan, multi-country embrace of the Washington Consensus: Whether the party in power is the Conservative or Liberal in Ottawa, PRI or PAN in Mexico City, or Democrat or Republican in

Washington, or whether the country is from North, Central, or South America, the underlying thrusts of the Washington Consensus remain ubiquitous. Proposed by top US economists in the early 1990s, five elements lay at its core: reduction of barriers to trade; across-the-board, as opposed to selective, tariff reduction policies; openness to foreign investment; market-mindedness; and opportunities for membership expansion.[14] Also called *open regionalism,* since its end-goal of global economic integration builds upon regional free trade agreements, the Washington Consensus is seen by Paul Krugman as a *speculative bubble* intertwining economic and political processes,[15] the former facilitating short-term market optimism, the latter involving a conducive, yet critical, reciprocal relationship between entrepreneurs and policy-makers.[16]

Sebastian Edwards modifies it for the hemisphere. Dubbed *Latin American Consensus,* it consists of macroeconomic stability through control of public sector deficits; opening external sectors to foreign competition; deregulation through widespread privatization; and poverty-reduction policies.[17] Originally criticized as an inadequate response to Latin America's *lost decade,*[18] the Washington Consensus appealed to a new breed of decision-makers across Central America,[19] a region, with the exception of Costa Rica, too traditional in economic structures, too impoverished, and filled with too many left-over tensions from long spells of institutionalized conflicts and pervasive impoverishment. For whatever they are worth, the Washington Consensus and the *Latin American Consensus*, were accepted hook, line, and sinker by the pockets of CA elites.

US Agriculture

Agriculture may be too specific—and sensitive—an issue to draw an overarching liberalizing theme from, but that is precisely why it is so relevant: Ever since the 1947 Geneva Trade Conference,[20] farming interests have held trade talks at bay, even after the 1992 US-European Union Blair House Agreement bailed the Uruguay Round out of its deadlock,[21] eventually producing the WTO. It has served as a US and EU *sine qua non* in trade talks. At stake is not necessarily the policy as a bargaining chip in international negotiations, but the power farming interests exert in tight domestic elections and how the pie is divided in legislatures. As the quintessential performer in all of these dimensions even before a European Community emerged, the US, amidst competition from the European Union today, even finds in protecting farmers the ace of spade to global market access: Not only linking FTAs to agriculture, but also liberalizing farm policies in the rest of the world while US farmers, echoing their European counterparts, reap the highest subsidies in the free market.

In spite of the US Uruguay Round insistence to liberalize farm trade and the EU refusal to do so, the March 2002 US farm legislation still authorized US$170b of farm subsidies. The legislation sustained (a) price supports for wheat and cotton; (b) subsidies for honey, mohair, and wool producers, while creating new subsidies for peanuts, lentils, and chickpea producers; and (c) conservation programs for livestock as well as fruits and vegetables. Among the states benefiting are Arkansas, Georgia, Iowa, Minnesota, Missouri, and South Dakota—some of them electorally sensitive states. Just as the farm bill fulfilled an electoral need within the domestic milieu, it also became not only the linchpin of US trade policy, but also the wrench reshaping trade policies elsewhere:[22] As the largest market in human history, the US would now, in the aftermath of perceived unfair Japanese or European trading practices, impose a market access *quid pro quo*—the more foreign farm markets would be opened to US exports, the more US markets would be opened to manufacture exporters in the rest of the world.

The ballgame was changed, not when US farm policies were first liberalized under Ronald Reagan, but in how the farm policies of other countries could be liberalized even without resorting to any FTA. With a FTA, especially any proposed by other countries, as for example, Central American, deeper farm market accesses are obtainable, in addition to other sectoral inroads. Central to this shift, and of the new trading order, is the fast-track authority. Although elaborated later, it now permitted the chief executive to usurp trade policy-making authority from Congress, liberalize farm policies elsewhere, boost US farm exports, and identify with upwardly-mobile LDC sections through the Washington Consensus magic—all with just one swipe of the pen. Infrastructural development and industrialization were no longer necessary LDC conditions to join any exclusive club—or for signing any free trade agreement, since paraphrasing a well-known cliché said it all: *Have farms, will travel!* The central trade-off to international trade became a purely domestic US exercise: subsidize farmers to get legislative fast-track support.

Of note is the huge LDC-DC mismatch. In several DCs, as the contribution of agriculture to economic growth steadily declined over the years, the political clout of farm interests over policy-making and electoral calculations continued to remain robust; whereas in several LDCs, agriculture not only continues to fuel economic growth, but the heavy political clout of farm interests is also muted by emerging urban sectors, such as those embracing the Washington Consensus, entrepreneurial groups, technocrats exposed to or having benefited from education abroad, and others of similar stripes.

Without recognizing foreign producer interests, US farm legislations breed misperceptions, deepen policy incompatibilities, and worsen economic conditions.[23] As the Cancún WTO breakdown illustrated, though the G21 coalition of advanced LDCs played an incisive role in torpedoing the ministerial meeting, a handful of impoverished African countries producing cotton—Benin, Burkina Faso, Chad, and Mali—provided the fatal shots. They mobilized African countries to protest the US farm bill cotton subsidies and found sympathy from Latin American countries with high agricultural ratios, such as Ecuador's 67%, Uruguay's 55%, Argentina's 52%, Bolivia's 39%, Colombia's 37%, Brazil's 33%, and Peru's 24%.[24] It is but a short step from there to understanding the Central American predicament. CA representatives at the G21 faced more disincentives than incentives from Robert B. Zoellick if they remained loyal to G21 interests, but the underlying issue of their own dependence on agriculture for exports and economic development, left them literally helpless.

US Fast-track Authority

The March 2002 US Farm Bill helped the passage of the August 2002 fast-track, or Trade Promotion Authority (TPA) legislation. First introduced in 1974, fast-track became a powerful presidential weapon, in relations both with US legislators and foreign countries: It prevents protectionist congressmen from obstructing trade policy options of the president; and it permits foreign countries greater access to the US market by precisely not having to go through congressional deliberations. Fast-track authority allowed CUFTA to be signed in 1988, and its extension in 1991 for two years allowed NAFTA to sneak in,[25] fortunately for Mexico. Once it had expired, Chile could not become a fourth NAFTA *amigo* in the 1990s, prompting it to mend fences with Argentine and Brazil, and join MERCOSUR in an associate capacity. However, it became the first FTA signatory when the 2002 TPA was adopted. Mexico, on the other hand, could feel more vindicated it had joined a very exclusive club, although the price it paid would only become visible and painful over the long-haul: As NAFTA's tenth-anniversary approached, Mexican corn producers faced the brunt of NAFTA shocks, as corn joined the free-trade list—forever changing the parochial peculiarity of Mexican *tacos, tamales,* and *tortillas*.[26] When it was revived in 2002, the TPA was approved by the narrowest of margins, 214–213, on July 28.[27] It cleared the Senate with a more handsome margin on August 1 only because of the insertion of a Trade Adjustment Act (TAA) to compensate displaced workers. President Bush signed it five days later, after reluctantly accepting the Democrat TAA initiative. US trade policy pursuits simply went beserk thereafter: FTA proposals from other countries were simply gobbled up, letting the US loose on a FTA binge.

Recapturing the trade authority, which President Clinton deliberately allowed to lapse in 1994 due to Democrat opposition of NAFTA, was critical to advancing competitive liberalism. In addition to Chile, Singapore's FTA extends US plans to other members of the Association of South-east Asian Nations (ASEAN), while negotiations with Australia, Morocco, and the South African Customs Union (SACU) convey the diffused nature of US trade policy.[28] FTAs seek far-flung arrangements, some on a bilateral basis, others with regions. Creating lock-ins for the would-be partner's negotiating capacities seems to be the key. Central America and CAFTA represent the heart of TPA currently, just as Chile was in 2002, but the real goal is FTAA.

Like the original fast-track authority, TPA requires Congress to vote up or down on the agreement only, not on any specific provisions, and prevents it from any amendments, while also providing only a short window of deliberation time. Among the differences: (a) By creating the Congressional Oversight Group (COG), with the most powerful members of the historically and trenchantly protectionist House Ways and Means Committee as well as their Senate Finance Committee counterparts, the executive branch's monopoly over trade negotiations, provided by the creation of the USTR in the Trade Legislation of 1964, is circumscribed, since the USTR must now keep COG informed of all elements under negotiations. (b) It redefines import sensitivity and tariff rate quotas (TRQs),[29] especially for farm products, requiring the USTR to keep both legislative chambers informed, through their specialized committees, of any liberalization of agricultural products. (c) It creates competitive opportunities for US farm exporters commensurate with those US farm importers enjoy. (d) It eliminates market-distorting subsidies. (e) It also eliminates practices adversely affecting perishable or cyclical products.[30] Agriculture not only finds a back-door trade-policy entrance, but overall trade policy pursuits are predictably dependent on the treatment of specific agricultural products.

CENTRAL AMERICA: FORBIDDEN FRUIT?

More remarkable than the approximate simultaneity of these initiatives is the sudden Central America attention. With the exception of Costa Rica, which boasts the longest stretch of democratic experiences south of the United States, El Salvador, Guatemala, Honduras, and Nicaragua were, until the 1990s, better known for protracted social conflicts,[31] low-intensity war,[32] civil war,[33] imperial control,[34] superpower rivalry,[35] plantation economies,[36] and/or genocidal outbursts.[37] Given their lack of infrastructures and impoverishment, how these latter four countries could transform a vicious into a progressive political climate, from "the sword and the cross" to ballot boxes and the *bolsa* in the historical wink of an eye,[38] is

both baffling and bothersome. Too many scars remain unsealed, the economy is too traditional and agricultural to sustain the demands of regionalism or piecemeal liberalism, and society was, is, and will continue to be
too polarized for any rewards to sink to the grassroots level, where a majority of the people still live, many of them cherishing indigenous claims.
The unfolding Central American plot thickens further with the inclusion of
Belize, hitherto British Honduras until 1973 and independent from 1981,
and therefore not sharing the central socio-cultural tendencies of the region;[39] Dominican Republic, whose next door neighbor, Haiti, has become
quite a thorn in regional development and especially US interests; and
Panama, whose canal, after almost a century of US control, seems to be
shifting towards too disparate foreign influences to provide regional
comfort—and indeed the search for an alternate inter-ocean passageway
explains, in part, the twenty-first century attention on developing Central
American infrastructure, since Mexico's Tehuantepec Isthmus and
Nicaragua also offer alternate inter-oceanic dry canal routes.[40]

From Table 1.1, we get a comparative overview of not only the huge country differences but also critical deficiencies—all consistent with the anomaly
observed earlier of the US disregarding infrastructures, development, and industrialization in favor of signing FTAs. Of the almost 34m people in the region, Guatemala accounts for slightly over one-third, yet ranks third in per
capita GDP and PPP across CA, fourth in Human Development Index (HDI)
ranking, and with the lowest urban population (40%). Except for Costa Rica,
which has the smallest population (3.9m), highest GDP and PPP per capita
(US$4,128; and $8,560), fewer people earning less than a dollar-a-day
(2.0%), and an illiteracy rate (5%) and HDI ranking (42) comparable to developed countries, all others would be lowly-positioned even among developing countries: El Salvador is ranked 105 on the HDI ladder, Honduras 115,
Guatemala 119, and Nicaragua 121, with 31.1%, 23.8, 16.0%, and 45.1% of
the respective population earning less than one dollar each day. All of them
are indebted countries, including Costa Rica, as the current account balance
figures show. Until the Washington Consensus influence emerged and FTA
thinking was prioritized in the early 1990s, they constituted banana or coffee
republics, with agriculture providing almost half of all employment in all except Costa Rica (17.2%) and El Salvador (21.4%), and accounting for a large
proportion of exports.

Free trade agreements involving CA are but a logical extension of the
Caribbean Basin Initiative (CBI), particularly the one engaging the United
States. Proposed by President Ronald Reagan to the OAS on February 24,
1982, the CBI is a developmental program for up to twenty-seven governments in the region, mostly islands, as well as the seven CA states included

Table 1.1. Central American Overview

Features	Belize	Costa Rica	Dominion Republic	El Salvador	Guatemala	Honduras	Nicaragua	Panama
Population (m)	.24	3.9	8.3	6.4	11.7	6.6	5.2	2.8
Population density (per sq. km)	10	74.6		302.9	105	57.4	41.8	
Urban population		60		61	40	53.6	56.5	
Illiteracy % (1997, m, f)		5, 5	17, 18	20, 26	26, 41	29, 30	37, 37	8, 10
GDP (2003 in US$b)	615m (1998GNP)	17.5	20.5	14.7	24.0	6.8	2.7	8.5b (1998, GNP)
GDP per capita (US$)		4,128	6,270	2,141	1,752	970	500	3080 (1998, GNP)
PPP per capita gross national income (2002)		8,560	6,270	4,190	4,030	2,540	2,350	
HDI Ranking		42	94	105	119	115	121	90
Current Account Balance (% of GDP)		−5.9	+4.5	−4.5	−4.3	−7.6	−17.6	
Population below $1 per day (%)		2.0	Less than 2.0	31.1	16.0	23.8	45.1	
Ag. As % of Emp.		17.2		21.4	52.5	43.9	43.2	
Ag as % of Exports					60			
Indigenous proportion (%)		.9			85		5	

PPP: purchasing power parity; HDI: human development index

Sources: Large proportion of figures from Office of the U.S. Trade Representative, *Interim Environmental Review: U.S.-Central American Free Trade Agreement* (Washington, DC: USTR, August 2003), 54–54; for figures on agriculture as % of GDP column and Salvadorean figure in agriculture as % of employment column, see Government of El Salvador, Tratado de Libre Comercio Centroamerica-Estados Unidos, *National Action Plan for Trade Capacity Building: Meeting the Challenge of Globalization*, 2 vols, vol. 1: *General Strategy* (San Salvador: Government of El Salvador, July 2003), 23; Government of Guatemala, Ministry of Economics and ECLAC, *National Action Plan for Trade Capacity Building in Guatemala: A Proposal by the Government of Guatemala in the Framework of the US-CAFTA* (Guatemala City, December 2002), 12; for Guatemalan, Honduran, and Nicaraguan figures in the agriculture as % of employment column, Vicki Glass, "CAFTA:the Latin American perspective," Washington Office of Latin America (WOLA), *Congressional Briefing*, Letter, January 22, 2004, from http://www.wola.org; J. F. Hornbeck, "The U.S.-Central America Free Trade Agreement (CAFTA):challenges for sub-regional integration," *Congressional Research Service*, Report, April 25, 2003, 32; indigenous figures from Alison Brysk, *From Tribal Village to Global Village: Indian Rights and International Relations in Latin America* (Stanford, CA: Stanford University Press, 200), 256; Jorge Nowalski, "Human security in Central America:building sustainable livelihoods," Latin American Studies Association, annual convention, slide presentation, October 2004; and Belize's figures from World Bank, *Entering the 21st Century: World Development Report 1999/2000* (Washington, DC: World Bank, by Oxford University Press, New York, 2000), 230–72.

in the integrative efforts being investigated here. Although erroneously dubbed a regional Marshall Plan,[41] since it is built upon bilateral assistance and not bilateral assistance as a precondition to forging a regional group like the European Community was, the CBI consists of three pillars:[42] (a) export-led development; (b) bilateral development assistance; and (c) private foreign investment. With key exports being agricultural, CBI is a straightforward plan: With US government and private sector support, diversify the economy utilizing export earnings.

Unlike the FTAs of today, CBI was characterized by "one-way free trade": the country could export duty-free to the US without reciprocating. Yet a large proportion of exports, 87%, already entered the US duty-free from the region. Among the exceptions were textiles, apparel, and sugar beyond the quota already allocated, thus leaving only beef as a CBI beneficiary. The thirty-year Multifiber Agreement (MFA) of 1975 was the maximum the US would concede in terms of textiles; and as it is dismantled over the next year or so, countries benefiting from it must either diversify, if they haven't already done so, or compete in the free market. This includes such CA countries as El Salvador and Honduras whose exports depend on textiles, as well as Mexico, projected by *The Economist* to be a big long-term loser.[43] Their silver lining may be the third CBI pillar, foreign investment. Conflicts during the 1980s discouraged foreign investment, but liberalization and peace during the 1990s invited them to relocate, and relocate at a time when in-bond plants in Mexico are becoming too expensive to sustain. Thus CAFTA/CA4FTA involve not just one-way traffic, but also stimulate economic diversification. Herein lies the twin problems: the diversification assumption opens up both CA agriculture markets to international competition when not enough farmers have left their farms and the fledgling service markets to US exporters even before local entrepreneurs can get their interests together, thereby being permanently stifled out of the competition.

ORGANIZATION

Exposing various dimensions of Central American liberalization or economic transformation is only the first step; how to compare and contrast them while drawing lessons for both policy-making and other similar cases are the obvious next tasks. Fulfilling them necessitates elaborating the relevant theoretical arguments to be drawn upon, the method of analysis to be adopted, and a preview of the remainder of the investigation. Three subsections filling in these missing blanks close the introductory chapter.

Negotiating Styles

How did such asymmetrical partners negotiate their ways to an agreement? If anything, NAFTA demonstrated how asymmetry could be managed successfully and productively. With Central American countries, on the other hand, dispensing the minimum developmental threshold seems to be the starting point of any ventures. As the first developing country to sign a FTA with developed countries, Mexico's landmark case unleashed both fears of a possible race to the developmental pit and hopes of pushing stagnant economies towards better futures. Be these as they may, the United States constantly spices any trade agreement, be it with a developed, developing, or underdeveloped partner, by offering limited market access, even if access involves idiosyncratic rules, self-defeating trade-offs, uneven playing fields, and political benefits overshadowing economic costs. The US sets the standards, not only of trade in our own era, but also of many icons of an integrative economy, such as McDonalds, Coca Cola, Sears, TGIFs, Fords and Chryslers, as well as Internet cafes. Somewhere in between is Canada, at once seeking to be different from the United States in its styles and goals, but also identical in consumer tastes, economic profile, and cultural propensities.

Priorities on the negotiation table, and the attitudes and behavior behind them, are bound to vary given these dissimilar orientations. They are also expected to be more unique than common for the different Central American countries, while for Canada and the US, restricted sectors should elicit more common than unique treatment in negotiations. Agriculture has been the privileged sector traditionally exempted in both Canada and the US, while market access is also likely to be strictly regulated given the wage differentials involved. In turn, both would like export market access for their own farm products, as well as in other competitive sectors they possess, such as services, in particular, telecommunications.

How can theoretical frameworks explain both commonalities and uniqueness in negotiations? If Central American pursuits are a step towards a coordinated and completed FTAA, must the negotiation patterns streamline those in the FTAA? If not, then why are Central American and hemispheric pursuits being approached differently? At least we get a preview of similarities and differences of three North American countries, two of them commercially exploring Central American for the first time. Since we face more question-marks than certainties or predictabilities at present, whichever way we look at Central America, we are able to fill at least some of these. Since Central America has rarely, if ever, been examined from comparative North American approaches, the study goes beyond just filling missing blanks: It carries the potential to provide new information, and thereby motivate different assumptions for hypotheses to explore different theoretical possibilities.

Examining negotiating styles, therefore, cracks open lingering substantive questions for whatever they are worth, while producing new substantive information too.

Among the various negotiations models, W. Mark Habeeb's depicting asymmetry and Fen Osler Hampson's offering explanations for both successful and unsuccessful multilateral negotiations are particularly relevant.[44] How Canada, Mexico, and the United States sought economic integration with Central American countries may be evaluated, from initiation to outcome, using the various benchmarks Habeeb prescribes. How these may be modified in the case of disagreements borrows from Hampson's blocking coalitions. Additional insights are thereby drawn from inter-connecting propositions. For example, phases and functions of negotiations, identified by Janice Gross Stein and Brian Tomlin,[45] among others, may be traced in the three cases, then compared. Whether the diagnostic-formula-detail approach of Maureen Berman and I. William Zartman,[46] or Daniel Druckman's turning points, produce similar or different observations for the three cases informs us of the momentum and future mileage of each.[47] Whether theoretical propositions are viable or not, the cases may themselves suggest theoretical modifications or refinements, and in the same spirit, just as theory helps interpret realities more cogently, actual developments place competing theories in relative value.

Before bringing in those postulations and paradigms, Central America is first thrown into Feinberg's CMM and HD frameworks for a simple reason: These models have been fruitfully applied to the FTAA, and since all the countries in the investigation are FTAA members, Central America can also be placed exclusively under Feinberg's microscopes—just to get a sense of what components will work, and what won't. By utilizing other negotiation theories, Feinberg's neglect of asymmetry is exposed as a possibly fatal flaw, necessitating paradigmatic rethinking.

The next chapter is devoted exclusively to elaborating these arguments, and fitting them into a framework suitable for this investigation. Beforehand, a word on the methodology and a manuscript overview.

Bringing Apples and Oranges Together: The Methodology

In executing both exercises for the three cases, comparisons demand more care. Alexander George's structured, focused comparative methodology helps distinguish between apples and oranges, thereby shedding more light than simply concluding both are fruits.[48] As the name itself indicates, structuring the cases along specific and neutral dimensions helps overcome case-specific biases; and the more in-depth the analysis, the less likely observations will be spurious.

To fulfill those tasks, the three cases are broken into the antecedental and actual components; and each is then disaggregated into various meaningful dimensions. Once the microanalysis is completed, the observations are then positioned at various macro-levels. For example, the Central American agreements, including the negotiations, are considered from broader NAFTA-Plus, FTAA, and multilateral levels. Ultimately, by conducting analysis along several levels, the study hopes to decipher and distinguish interests at the state, various regional and multilateral levels — making a comparative study of Central American trade pursuits from three North American angles different from other investigations.

Overview

Accordingly, the volume is divided into five chapters beginning with the most specific analysis, then broadening out as it proceeds. Once the negotiations models are presented in Chapter 2, Chapter 3 inquires what led the three North American countries to economically engage Central America, which paves the way for Chapter 4 to investigate the nature of negotiated agreements. As indicated earlier, both these chapters compare and contrast the three cases along a number of dimensions. Central American engagements are then placed in broader contexts — NAFTA-Plus, FTAA, and multilateralism, respectively, with the objective being to determine if they were pursued independently of, or in conjunction with, broader commitments. This is the task of Chapter 5. Chapter 6 draws empirical and theoretical conclusions before projecting implications for the immediate future, other engagements, and theory-building.

NOTES

1. From, Actividades de la presidencia, "Firma Presidente Vicente Fox la incorporación de Colombia al Plan Puebla-Panamá," November 19, 2004, from: http://www.presidencia.gob.mx/actividades/index.php?contenido=15893

2. This was precisely where President George W. Bush first announced the pursuit of such a goal in January 2002. See, United States Government, United States Trade Representative (USTR), "U.S.-Central American Free Trade Agreement signed:USTR says focus must now shift to winning approval of agreement," May 28, 2004, press release, from: http://usinfo.state.gov/ei/Archive/2004/Jun/01-149499.html

3. Eric Green, "Central American nations call for U.S. ratification of CAFTA: Central Americans vow to strengthen enforcement of labor laws," *Washington File*, July 14, 2004, from: http://usinfo.state.gov/xarchives/display.html?p=washfile-english?y =2004&m=July&x=. . .

4. A FTA was signed with Chile in December 2002, while other existing ones were with Israel (1984), Mexico (1985), Canada (1988), and Jordan.

5. Richard E. Feinberg, "The political economy of United States' free trade arrangements," Paper, Berkeley APEC Study Center (BASC), University of California, Berkeley, March 21–22, 2003.

6. From José Merino del Río, "CAFTA:a perspective from Costa Rica," *Americas Program* (Silver City, NM: Interhemispheric Resource Center, February 20, 2003).

7. See the official summary, within a broader, hemispheric context, in *Opening Doors to the World: Canada's International Market Access Priorities, 2004*, esp. ch. 4, from: http://www.dfait-maeci.gc.ca/tna

8. Since Mexico signed its first FTA in 1992 with Chile, it has become a world leader in this respect, bringing 32 countries and 870m consumers across 3 continents, yet ironically, increasingly concentrating its trade on the United States. According to Alejandro Ibarra-Yunez, Mexico's FTA seek "NAFTA parity," to signal the country's efforts at "being noticed," getting "cooperation," and effecting "policy lock-in[s]." Although he argues the evidence does not support a *spaghetti* regionalism pattern, the strategic foreign trade policy alternative he considers, and finds somewhat stronger an explanation, seems to be producing merely tentative, and not conclusive evidences: Mexico has not become either a regional or hemispheric leader, and multinational integration remains subordinated to North American integration. Ultimately, a strategic trade policy approach seeks diversification; with NAFTA the exact opposite is taking place. See "Mexico and its quest to sign multiple free trade agreements:spaghetti regionalism or strategic foreign trade?" April 2001, from: http://egade.sistema.itesm.mx/investigacion/documentos/documentos/2egade_aibarra.pdf

9. See Sebastian Edwards's anecdotal portrayal of the Mexican preference at the October 28, 1993 Wall Street Journal Conference on the Americas, in "Bad luck or bad policies? An economic analysis of the crisis," *Mexico 1994: Anatomy of an Emerging-Market Crash*, eds. Edwards and Moisés Naím (Washington, DC: Carnegie Endowment for International Peace, 1997), 95–96, but see 95–124. Shahid Burki summarizes in the same volume, "Mexico was consistently praised by the media, financial experts, academics, and the multilateral institutions as a major success." See "A fate foretold:the World Bank and the Mexican crisis," ibid., 248–49, but see 247–58.

10. From Association of Caribbean States, "Process of negotiations to establish the free trade agreement between Central American and the United States of America," mimeo, no author, no date, no Publisher. Henceforth, ACS, "Process."

11. Certainly a theme in Citizen's Trade Campaign, "With FTAA stalled, U.S. engages in NAFTA extension piece by piece," April 27, 2004, from: http://alcacmi.org/or/2004/04/4292.shtml Also seen as being equivalent to FTAA in "NAFTA Chapter 11 alarming," *The Charleston Gazette*, June 19, 2002, from: http://www.tradeobservatory.org/news/index.cfm?ID=3592

12. "NAFTA Minus," The Americas This Week, *The Americas Program* (Silver City, NM: Interhemispheric Resource Center, 2001).

13. For example, the World Bank invested $300m on the Chiapas Plan in the early 1980s to build a highway along the Guatemala-Mexico border.

14. Marío Esteban Carranza, *South American Free Trade Area or Free Trade Area of the Americas? Open Regionalism and the Future of Regional Economic Integration in South America*, The Political Economy of Latin America Series (Aldershot, Hants, UK: Ashgate Publishing, Co., 2000), 62–65.

15. From Jonathan Heath, *Mexico and the Sexenio Curse: Presidential Successions and Economic Crises in Modern Mexico* (Washington, DC: Center for Strategic and International Studies, 1999), 32–34.

16. Paul Krugman, "Dutch tulips and emerging markets," *Foreign Affairs* (July–August 1995):28–44.

17. *Crisis and Reform in Latin America: From Despair to Hope* (New York: Oxford University Press, for The World Bank, 1995), 58–59.

18. Jorge I. Domínguez, *Technopols: Freeing Politics and Markets in Latin America in the 1990s* (University Park, PA: Penn State University Press, 1997).

19. Feinberg, *Summitry in the Americas: A Progress Report* (Washington, DC: International Institute of Economics, 1997), 34–37.

20. See my *Politics of Compensation: Truman, The Wool Bill of 1947, and the Shaping of Postwar U.S. Trade Policy* (New York: Garland Publishing, Co., 1994), esp. chps. 4 and 8.

21. On this point, see Wayne Moyer, "The European Community and the GATT Uruguay Round:preserving the Common Agricultural Policy at all costs," *World Agriculture and the GATT*, ed. William P. Avery, International Political Economy Yearbook, vol. 7 (Boulder, CO: Lynne Rienner, 1993), 95–119.

22. Guy Poitras uses similar adjectives to explain US trade policy. See "Regional trade strategies:U.S. policy in North America and toward the Asia-Pacfic," Paper, International Studies Association, annual convention, Chicago, March 1995.

23. Raúl Pierri, "South America up in arms over US farm bill," *Inter Press Services* (May 10, 2002), from: http://www.globalpolicy.org/socecon/bwi-wto/wto/2002/0510safarm.htm

24. International Monetary Fund, *Direction of Trade Statistics, Yearbook, 2000* (Washington, DC: I.M.F., 2000), various pages.

25. Frederick Mayer, *Interpreting NAFTA: The Science and Art of Political Analysis* (New York: Columbia University Press, 1998), 67–69.

26. "Farming in Mexico:from corn wars to corn laws," *The Economist*, September 25–October 1, 2004, 50. This is a London-based weekly.

27. Figure from Dale Hathaway, "The impacts of US agriculture and trade policy on trade liberalization and integration via a US-Central American Free Trade Agreement," Paper, Special Initiative on Integration and Trade, Integration and Regional Programs Department, Inter-American Development Bank, Washington DC, October 1–2, 2002, 27. Henceforth, Hathaway, "Impacts of US agriculture and trade policy on . . . Central America." According to a US Labor Education in the Americas Program (LEAP) memo, the voting margin is 3. See US/LEAP, "Passage of fast track paves way for CAFTA, a step back for worker rights," from http://WWW.usleap.org/trade/FastTrackPass8-02.html. While LEAP is directly concerned with multinational company workers across Central America, such as in Starbucks, Hathaway is a veteran analyst of US agricultural trade policy patterns, in this article addressing Central America directly.

28. Treaty information from Feinberg, op. cit. (2003), 4.

29. The new TRQs are less generous than the long-established previous practices. Quotas for peanuts were abolished, and peanut support was streamlined through loan rates, marketing loans, loan deficiency payments, direct payments, and target price payments with other program crops, such as wheat, corn, cotton, rice, and soybeans. The TRQs themselves may be increased or eliminated without affecting producer income by resorting to generous compensations. Although the dairy support program was kept in place, the support level was not increased, as it was for pulses, wool, mohair, and honey. Sugar support programs saw an increase, and the US continued to utilize export subsidies, food aid, and market access as policy instruments to boost export competitiveness. See Hathaway, op cit., 11-20. All products with a TRQ and on which the Uruguay Round of GATT reduced tariffs by at least 15% are described as import sensitive products. Ibid., 29.

30. Hathaway, op cit., 27–30.

31. On the nature of these, see John Burton, "The procedures of conflict resolution," *International Conflict Resolution: Theory and Practice*, eds. Edward E. Azar and Burton (London: Longman, 1986), 92–116.

32. Term is used by Louis Proyecto's historical appraisal, "Class and indigenous roots of the Guatemalan revolution," April 13, 1998, from http://www.hartford-hwp .com/archives/47/172.html

33. See Billie R. De Walt's forceful appraisal as one source, "The agrarian bases of conflict in Central America," *The Central American Crisis: Sources of Conflict and Failure of U.S. Policy*, eds. Kenneth M. Coleman and George C. Herring (Wilmington, DE: Scholarly Resources, Inc., 1985), 43–54.

34. Mark T. Gilderhus, *The Second Century: US-Latin American Relations Since 1889* (Wilmington, DE: Scholarly Resources, Inc., 2000).

35. Among others reflecting on this rivalry, are Francisco Rojas Aravena and Luís Guillermo Solís Rivera, "Central America and the United States," *Latin American Nations in World Politics*, eds. Heraldo Muñoz and Joseph S. Tulchin (Boulder, CO: Westview Press, 1996), 105–128; and Augusto Varas points out how the original Soviet emphases on inter-governmental and inter-party correlationships shifted towards economic cooperation with the Brezhnev model of the 1960s, in "Soviet Union-Latin American relations:a historical perspective," ibid., 237–61.

36. Among others, see Steve Striffler and Mark Moberg, *Banana Wars: Power, Production, and History in the Americas*, American Encounters/Global Interaction Series, eds. Gilbert M. Joseph and Emily S. Rosenberg (Durham, NC: Duke University Press, 2003); and Jeffrey M. Paige, *Coffee and Power: Revolution and the Rise of Democracy in Central America* (Cambridge, MA: Harvard University Press, 1997).

37. How these memories still linger, and constrain developmental efforts, may be deduced from Sergio de Leon, "Guatemalans commemorate massacre victims," *Yahoo! News,* July 21, 2004, from: http://story.news.yahoo.com/news?tmpl=story&cid =589&ncid=734&e=2&u=/ap/200407. . .

38. *Bolsa* refers to the stock exchange. Quote first used in *Rockefeller Report on the Americas* (Chicago, 1969), 31; but borrowed from Luís Maira, "The U.S. debate on the Central American crisis," *The Future of Central America: Policy Choices for*

the U.S. and Mexico, eds. Richard R. Fagen and Olga Pellicer (Stanford, CA: Stanford University Press, 1983), 92, but see 66–97.

39. John H. Coatsworth raises this point, among others, in excluding Belize from his study of US regional influence. See *Central America and the United States: The Clients and the Colossus* (New York: Twayne Publishers, 1994), 1.

40. Even before Spanish rule ended in 1821, as Coatsworth elaborates, the US considered Nicaragua and the Colombian province of Panama for a canal, fighting off British challenge through the 1846 Mallarino-Bidlack Treaty with Colombia and the 1850 Clayton-Bulwer Treaty with Britain. See *Central America and the United States*, 26–27; and Charles L. Stansifer, "United States-Central American relations, 1824–1850," *United States-Latin American Relations, 1800–1850: The Formative Years*, ed. T. Ray Shurbutt (Tuscaloosa, AL: University of Alabama Press, 1991), 25–46; Edward H. Moseley, "The United States and Mexico, 1810–1850," ibid., 122–96; and Eugene R. Huck, "Early United States recognition of Colombian independence and subsequent relations to 1830," ibid., 197–227. The idea of dry canals has resurfaced, through Nicaragua under CAFTA and PPP, and through Tehuantepec in Mexico under PPP. On the former, see "Nicaragua's proposed dry canal:globalization and the Meso-American megaprojects," from http://www.nadir.org/nadir/initiativ/agp/colombia/puebla/drycanal.htm or http://environment.nicanet.org/dry_canal2.htm; and on the latter, see Wendy Call, "Roads, secondary projects catalyze PPP opposition," PPP Spotlight #3, Americas Program (Silver City, NM: Interhemispheric Resource Center, June 12, 2003), or check: http://www.americaspolicy.org/citizen-action/spotlight/2003/030602.html; Inter-American Development Bank, *Plan Puebla-Panama: Finance Commission Report on the Plan Puebla Panama* (Washington, DC: IADB, June 15, 2002); ——, Technical Commission for the Road Integration Initiative and Institutional Support Subgroup (SIECA, IDB, CABEI, CAF), *Report on Investments and Financing for the International Network of Mesoamerican Highways* (RICAM) (Washington, DC: IADB, December 18, 2002); and Vince McElhinny, "Update on PPP Mesoamerican transport integration initiative," March 11, 2004, from: http://www.interaction.org/idb or contact: vmcelhinny@interaction.org IDB=IADB here.

41. "A 'Basin' Marshall Plan," *New York Times*, March 3, 1982.

42. David F. Ross, "The Caribbean Basin Initiative:threat or promise,"*The Central American Crisis: Sources of Conflict and the Failure of U.S. Policy*, eds. Kenneth M. Coleman and George C. Herring (Wilmington, DE: Scholarly Resources, Inc., 1985), 140–48.

43. "The looming revolution," *The Economist*, November 13, 2004, 77, but see 75–77.

44. Habeeb, *Power and Tactics in International Negotiations: How Weak Nations Bargain With Strong Nations* (Baltimore, MD: The Johns Hopkins University Press, 1988): Hampson, *Multilateral Negotiations: Lessons from Arms Control, Trade, and the Environment* (Baltimore, MD: The Johns Hopkins University Press, 1995).

45. Stein, "Getting to the table:the triggers, stages, functions, and consequences of prenegotiation," in *Getting to the Table: The Process of International Prenegotiation*, ed. Gross Stein (Baltimore, MD: The Johns Hopkins University Press, 1989), 239–68;

and Tomlin, "The stages of prenegotiation:the decision to negotiate North American free trade," ibid., 18–43.

46. *The Practical Negotiator* (New Haven, CT: Yale University Press, 1982).

47. "Stages, turning points, and crises:negotiating military base rights, Spain and the United Status," unpublished manuscript.

48. "Case studies and theory development:the method of structured, focused comparison." *Diplomacy: New Approaches in History, Theory, and Policy*, Ed., Paul Gordon Lauren (New York, 1979) 43–68.

Chapter Two

Fitting the Cloth: Asymmetry, Undulations, & Postulations

INTRODUCTION

Negotiating trade agreements is daunting, increasingly so under globalization and democratization processes. Among other consequences, globalization whets consumer appetites, accelerating the revolution of rising expectations beyond the ability of negotiators to keep pace or capacity of agreements to remain valid. In addition, transportation improvements and just-in-time technologies bring desired products literally to one's doors in the fastest time possible, necessitating revolutionary trade policy adjustments, particularly for traditionally protected sectors. More rapid changes of these technologies outstripping the abilities of producers and consumers to structurally change the manufacturing processes, purchasing capacities, financing alternatives, and so forth, profoundly multiply complications. The assembly line invented just over a century ago commanded huge investments, but once established, could provide job security, production stability, and consumption incentives for a generation or so; on the other hand, neo-fordist production and information technologies today necessitate greater flexibility than investments in fixed plants, such as assembly lines, will permit,[1] thus making jobs as unpredictable as factories acquiring a floating propensity. Changing technologies is compounded by the rapidity of changes.

Another angle of this predicament is the spread of democratization. By liberating freedoms in many parts of the world, democratization invites instability as people strive to make up for missed opportunities of freedom: A survival-of-the-fittest surge among investors and financiers may produce not just the type of mafia markets China and Russia epitomize,[2] but also both push the limits of middle class patience and quash vested interest groups behind policy-making. The more the people in transition and the greater the missed opportunities, the deeper the instability expected. Critical to preventing anarchy are the trade-offs between the government and the suddenly enlightened public, and increasingly between elites and the masses in less developed countries (LDCs), with the former flaunting their purchasing power, the latter striving to make both ends meet. The relative strength of the two shows at the negotiation table, either in the compromises made or the constraints faced: FTA negotiations typically portray the interests of the elites, but they remain domestically unpopular. NAFTA, for example, barely scraped through the US Congress and remains unpopular to Mexico's middle classes, while the European Union (EU), in spite of adding members constantly, remains an ever unpopular pill for the common person to swallow. Even in spite of spreading democratization, there is little the public can do to reformulate these agreements, whether in North America or West Europe. It is unlikely to be any different in Central America, in fact, given the considerably lower thresholds of development, the gaps impose more stumbling blocks.

How did Central American states, one of whose commonalities is economic impoverishment, negotiate complex issues with affluent Canada and the US? While the substance negotiated and styles adopted are the subjects of the next two chapters, this chapter explores the negotiation ranges. It explains the possibilities these negotiations have under globalization and democratization inputs by drawing on theoretical propositions and frameworks suitable for parleys between developed countries (DCs) and LDCs: Stages and sequences, triggers and results, as well as agreements and disagreements are common to all negotiations; but paradigms emphasizing asymmetry, even better if they reflect actual Latin American exchanges with the United States, are particularly relevant to this Central American investigation. Accordingly, the discussions below begin with a familiar model to explaining the Free Trade Area of the Americas (FTAA) negotiations, then adjustments are progressively made to fit in the other components—processes, function, compromises and constraints, success or failure, and, most importantly, playing field unevenness.

FTAA IN THEORETICAL FRAMEWORK

Ever since the December 1994 Miami Summit of the Americas (SOA), attempts have been made to place the FTAA negotiating processes into some kind of a coherent theoretical framework. Among those efforts is one by an active participant in the negotiations leading up to the Miami Summit, Richard Feinberg.[3] His 1997 appraisal of hemispheric diplomacy (HD) among thirty-four countries utilized a cascading modular multilateralism (CMM) mechanism. How relevant are these in explaining the three integrative process under purview here? Two dimensions are extracted for examination: a CMM discussion, and an analytical HD appraisal.

Cascading Modular Multilateralism

Feinberg's CMM seeks to explain two crucial characteristics of the negotiations: (a) the multiple parties involved; and (b) the multiple issues prioritized by them.

Parties include both states and non-state actors. The states came in all sizes and shapes, from one superpower to tiny sovereign islands, from developed Canada to undeveloped Haiti and Nicaragua, from sprawling Brazil to much smaller El Salvador, from Mexico with shores lapping both oceans to land-locked Paraguay. The variations go on and on. Even among non-state actors, there was variety, from domestic interest groups to transnational organizations, from nationalized sectors to multinational corporations, from inter-governmental organizations focusing just on this hemisphere to intergovernmental agencies with a global agenda, and so forth. Even though so many disparities were brought under analytical purview, no attempts were made to grapple with the most obvious hemispheric feature: asymmetry in size, power, and influence.

Equally disparate issues complicate the network further. They too touch every nook and corner of interests, from tangible matters like capital markets and money laundering to intangible counterparts like biodiversity or mutual confidence, from controversial issues like corruption and terrorism to the more sedate alternatives of education and healthcare. Clearly, given the size of the participants, just as each actor, particularly each state, prioritized different issues, on the one hand, a huge comprehensive agenda emerged, on the other.

Putting these into a coherent framework led Feinberg to highlight three key components: issue-specific coalitions, bilateralism, and plurilateralism. To manage the multiple issues and spread responsibility among the thirty-four states, the SOA organizers developed issue-based coordination teams. Each team had a responsible coordinator and a routine co-ordinator, at the minimum; sometimes an actor, either a state or a plurilateral agency, was thrown in to play a support role. In this way, twenty-three different issues were assigned, making even small countries, for instance, Jamaica, the responsible coordinator of one issue, in this specific case, the issue of integrating society. Each country formulated its own preferences, but also had to respond to those of other states, necessitating a socializing function critical to easing the inherent asymmetries. As they went about these tasks, they relied upon supporting roles from largely non-state actors, such as the OAS or the Inter-American Development Bank (IADB), which are also multilateral agencies, thus legitimizing the third plurilateral component. Decision-making within each country, and how it connected externally, were accounted for by a conjoined model. Although his model utilized the US case, how relevant it is to some other Latin countries, or even to Canada, raises questions.

Hemispheric Diplomacy

Feinberg's hemispheric diplomacy (HD) model, disaggregates domestic negotiations and external negotiations into processes and components, before being brought together, as shown in Figure 2.1. It is based upon what he calls decentralized functionalism, which treats summits as photo opportunities, leaving the nitty-gritty work to specialists within bureaucracies. CMM, for example, plays a prominent part in the external setting, with its own three components both accessible to non-government actors and influence-exertion over consultative teams, which are responsible for the negotiations. Influence is actually exerted in every direction, for example, as the arrows show, NGOs influence all three CMM components and the consultative teams, but are in turn affected by each of these as well. These teams highlight a very decentralized form of functionalism, with the decentralization taking place within the executive branch inside the country. For the United States, as an example, before the president goes to the summit, all the "dirty work" is completed by deputy committees, such as the National Security Council (NSC) or National Economic Council (NEC), coordinated by an interagency working group, which itself is further disaggregated into economic, democracy, and social/environmental sub-groups, indicating the considerable diversification of post-Cold War priorities. These are precisely the agencies not always available across many Latin countries, and even if they are, the degree of autonomous, decentralized work assumed in Feinberg's models may not necessarily be there. Canada's parliamentary system may not also satisfy this second function. Nevertheless, consultative teams are expected by the Feinberg models to continue negotiating across national boundaries, just to keep discussions on track, and to prepare for the summits.

Central American Relevance

Both CMM and HD make a lot of sense when the negotiating groups are large, and each country has crossed an institutional stability threshold. Given the focus on Central America, with up to eight possible countries, what are strengths and weaknesses of applying Feinberg's model for an appraisal?

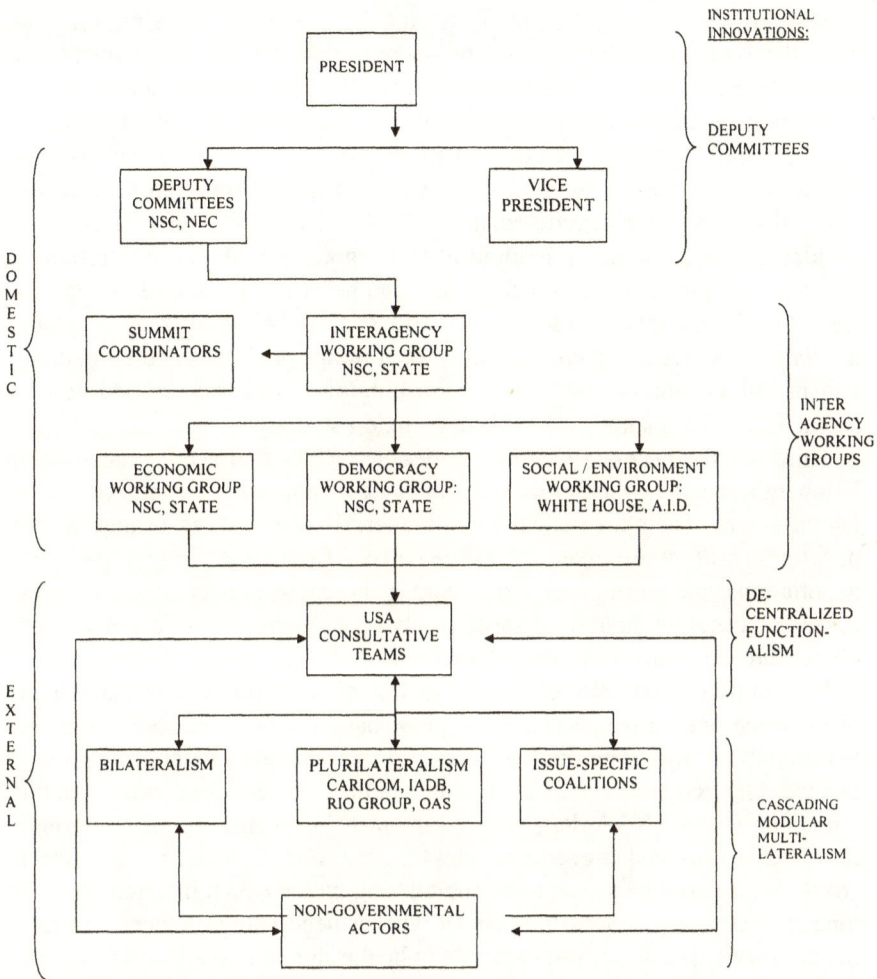

Figure 2.1. Richard Feinberg's Hemispheric Diplomacy Model

At least three sources of strengths may be identified. First, all of the three Central American integrative cases being examined carry prospects of expansion—in terms of either members or issues, or both. Therefore, under the best possible circumstances, Feinberg's models are of increasing relevance, especially if CAFTA, for instance, becomes the vehicle towards FTAA, or inducts the Dominican Republic or Panama as a new member, as it is poised to. Many Central American countries participated in FTAA, so will not be unfamiliar with the methods and procedures—opening a second source of strength.

Second, if not negotiators being identical across different bargaining tables, the issues invariably would be—whether with CA4FTA, CAFTA, or
PPP, on the one hand, or the FTAA, on the other. Converging styles and fa-
miliarity make agreement easier, as positions over the issues remain the same.
In other words, initial negotiating positions would more likely recur than not
subsequently. Besides, stooped as they are in the Washington Consensus,
many, if not all, of the negotiators in CA4FTA, CAFTA, PPP, and FTAA carry
an identity card not easily ignored at the negotiating table—and perhaps a
reason why agreement is inevitable at some point if the issues and negotiations remain confined to trade, as was true of CAFTA, and perhaps explaining why CA4FTA was meant to fail since it lumps principles and humanitarianism, which are not part of the Washington Consensus, in addition to
rational decision-making, into one negotiation strategy.

Third, all the necessary Central American actors find a potential spot in
Feinberg's models, whether they be the state or non-state, societal or multilateral actors. Their theoretical inclusiveness is a refreshing change in the
negotiations literature given the exclusiveness emphasized in regional trade
negotiations and during the Cold War. Feinberg's models fit the Central
American cases, without necessarily implying they are appropriate in the first
place, and acceptable to Central Americans in the second.

Several weaknesses also plague the model, at least four of them. First, none
of the three integrative cases deal with as many issues as Feinberg prepared
his framework for. Even the few issues on their agenda cannot hide the embedded hierarchy in North American countries negotiating with Central
American states: FTAA deliberately set out to dampen asymmetry through
the mechanisms and procedures adopted, but with Central America, each
North American state seems to be capitalizing on the extant hierarchy, unfortunately extracting concessions out of weaker negotiating partners, suggesting the survival-of-the-fittest principle to be the sign of our democratized, liberalized times. Sometimes getting an agreement or implementing a specific
project becomes the priority, thus narrowing or shifting attention even further
from the broader sustainable development picture FTAA originally emphasized so emphatically.

Second, the domestic milieu was not mobilized to make CMM and HD
meaningful models. All three North American countries practice democracy,
but characteristics describing those negotiations were far from being representative: negotiations were largely secretive, explained in such technical
terms as to remain incomprehensible to the lay public, and revolved around
an exclusive few. This was more so for Central American countries, which do
not have labor or environmental pre-requisites to satisfy in conducting free-
trade negotiations as Canada and the United States do. Yet Canada and the US

engaged in more clandestine exchanges than would be expected of any mature democracy, especially those chastizing the evils of privately concluded arrangements, and especially the US paid mere lip-service to environmental considerations.

Third, the issue-specific coalitions also does not constitute a necessary component. Since the total number of countries involved are so few, coalition creation is virtually impossible; and since every country is headed more or less in the same directions, at least in rhetoric, coalitions actually constrain more than facilitate progress. Lots of heads would be butting if they emerged—so in a sense, attempts were made to avoid confrontations, thereby minimizing the need for coalitions, thus resulting in superficial or partial rather than meaningful comprehensive agreements.

Perhaps the biggest weakness stems from its relevance to this study. Focusing as it does on negotiations, this study has to link the various rounds, find patterns, and account for both agreements and disagreements. Feinberg's model does not help at all in these respects. It represents a snapshot of a specific negotiation, and represents it very well. However, it does not create linkages between issues, or arguments whereby linkages can be admitted. There does not exist, by extending the previous argument, any scope to create stages, then link them into one framework. Above all, how and with what component do we explain a failure in the negotiations? The model does not explain how two entirely different outcomes—agreements and disagreements—can emerge. Even though it is one of the obvious explanatory model for hemispheric FTA negotiations, it must depend on components from other models to remain valid.

On balance, by adapting certain elements from Feinberg's model to other models, more explanatory mileage may be extracted. Many of these models, or components from models, have long been begging attention in significant theories. Three are useful for this study: the stages of negotiations, accounting for asymmetry, and models permitting multiple exit options.

STAGES

Over the past generation, negotiations have been disaggregated into phases, functions, triggers, and loops—enhancing our explanatory power. Some of the earlier works, by Fred Charles Ikle or Linda Brady, for example, clustered information into familiar but still encompassing packages, a necessary starting point to introduce directions, flows, and refinements. Just as Ikle distinguishes the various purposes of an agreement into extension, normalization, redistribution, innovation, or side effects,[4] Brady's disaggregation of a convenient information management scheme into a background (emphasizing the history, personal characteristics, culture, and so forth), context (focusing on prior relationship with the other side), substantive concerns, process considerations, and political factors (whether domestic, regional, foreign, or bureaucratic), also opens up the decision-making black-box.[5] Janice Gross Stein, Brian Tomlin, and others, however, spice up terms like phases, functions, triggers, and loops by specifying what kind of action goes into which category.

Stein introduced the term pre-negotiations,[6] Tomlin pre-pre-negotiations,[7] and both also specify functions for each stage. Before turning to them, it is useful to recognize a post-negotiations phase by extending Stein's and Tomlin's sequences. After all, negotiations are not the be-all and end-all of disputes, as Ikle noticed by discussing an *extension* agreement, but which more recent theorists, such as Robert Putnam with his two-level theory of ratification,[8] make greater, necessary, and more explicit use of. In showing Stein's and Tomlin's functions, Table 2.1 also creates and elaborates a fourth stage, while Figure 2.2 captures the flow of the relevant dynamics.

Ultimately, we still need to find out why we are at the table, where are we headed, how best to get there, and with whom. As observed, Feinberg's models make panglossian assumptions, with an implicit single exit leading to nirvana. It recognizes asymmetry, but assumes prescribed procedures will dampen this, which culminates in the more egregious neglect of alternate exit options once negotiations fail to deliver. Stein's and Tomlin's conceptualizations short shrift asymmetry, leaving us to wonder if all the functions will fall into their proper places, or even be relevant if asymmetrical influence enters the negotiations.

Compensating for some of these, William Mark Habeeb proposes an asymmetric model, built upon the Zartman-Berman diagnostic-formula-detail (DFD) argument and Daniel Druckman's turning point thresholds.[9] Figure 2.3 presents their combined contributions.

Very much like treating a patient, I. William Zartman and Maureen Berman interpret negotiations as seeking to diagnose a problem between states; once we have isolated the problem, like a doctor, we begin with a broad prescrip-

Table 2.1. Stages & Functions of Negotiations

Stages	Functions	Representative Theorists
Pre-pre-negotiations	Identify problem, Consider options	Tomlin
Pre-negotiations	Make commitment to negotiate, Communicate this to other side	Tomlin, Stein
Negotiations	Actual bargaining	Tomlin, Stein
Post-negotiations	Extension, Ratification, Modification	Ikle, Putnam

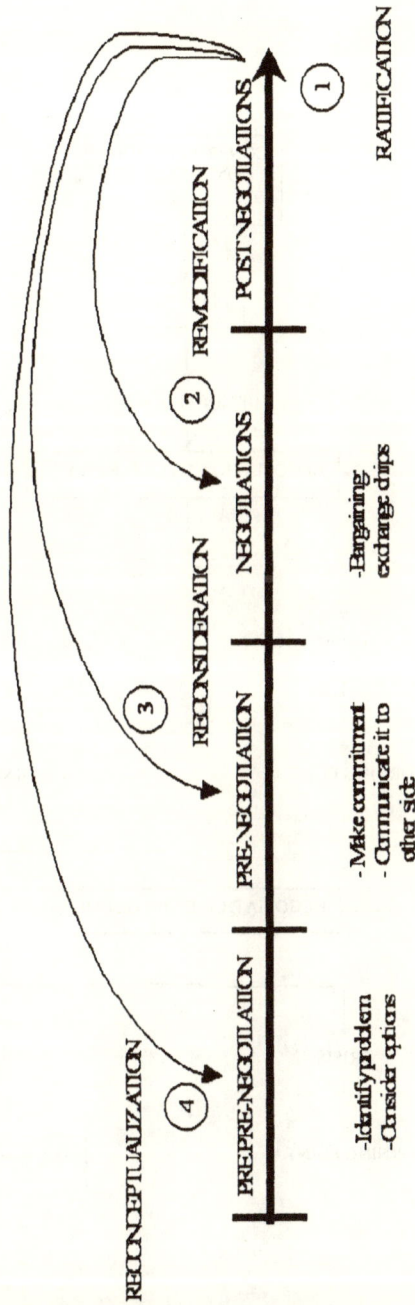

Figure 2.2. Stein-Tomlin Stages of Negotiations Extended

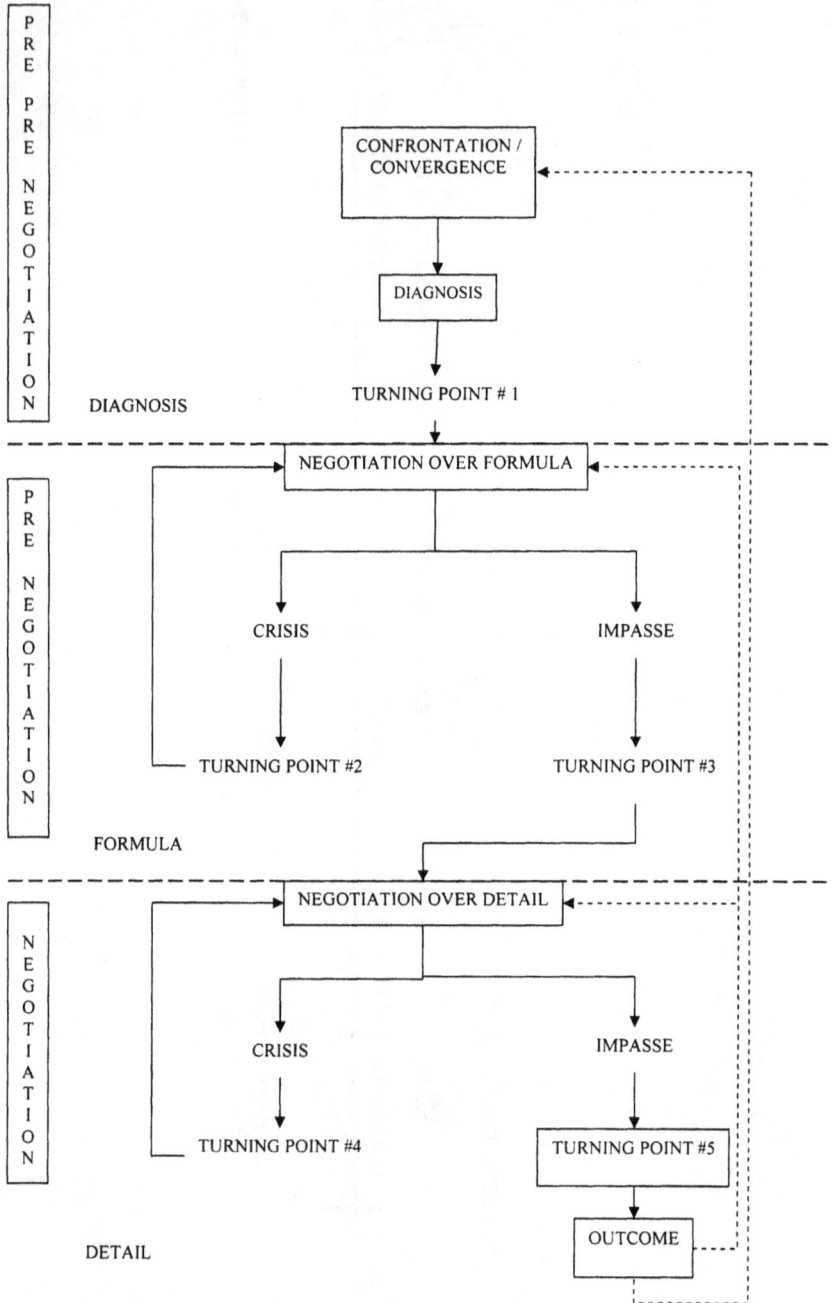

Figure 2.3. Packaging Mark Habeeb's Asymmetrical Model

tion until all the test results, such as blood, are in, and once they are in, we prescribe more precisely—much like initially proposing cancer to be the possible problem, then identifying it as a specific type of cancer.[10]

Once the diagnosis is made, negotiations can remain stuck at the formula or detail stage, running into either crises or impasses, as Figure 2.3 indicates. Crises are points of breakdowns, inviting new ideas to sustain the negotiations, while impasses are more hopeful occasions, directing the new idea towards eventual implementation. Crises and impasses recurring here help finesse the agreement. Once an agreement is reached—or cure seems visible—various post-negotiations functions, as outlined previously, demand attention. Nevertheless, it is important to bear in mind how any negotiations might just spiral around, or get bottlenecked, at either the formula or detail phase—much like CA4FTA did with the details and formulas by May 2004. This also is useful in any negotiations today—and certainly if we wish to coherently explain Costa Rica's decision to not sign in December 2003, before latching on in January 2004.

PLAYING-FIELD ASYMMETRY

One of Habeeb's salient contributions has been to address asymmetry in negotiations, an understudied theme in the literature. He points out not only how explanations of Cold War negotiations turned out to be a treatment of two symmetrically positioned powers, but also how superpower rivalry excessively dominated the initial negotiations literature. When asymmetry was brought under the microscope, whereas the DC approach reflected benign behavior, LDCs were either blinded by power or indulged in bandwagoning, and in some cases, exploited the privileged party's position. John Odell's analysis of Latin America exploiting the United States in negotiations elevates three noteworthy mechanisms: the possession of a critically traded commodity, such as oil; aligning with interest groups in Washington to boost policy-manipulation chances; or simply like-minded policy-makers converging in a tête-a-tête.[11] Although benevolence, compassion, convergence, or exploitation typifying these paradigms and cases can never be eliminated from either actual negotiations or the analytical framework within which actual negotiations are placed, rational behavior cannot also be exempted or ignored. Zartman, for example, shows, with African countries as his examples, how rational considerations undergird even LDC positions on a bargaining table. For example, they can influence agendas, play on morality, and refuse to agree when agreement is earnestly sought by others.[12] Utilizing the DFD proposition helps Habeeb bring the self-interest of asymmetrically oriented negotiating parties to the forefront.

MULTIPLE EXIT OPTIONS

His endpoint is an agreement. This, of course, need not always be the case: negotiations can end in disagreement. At least the analytical space should be there to accommodate and explain disagreement. Fen Osler Hampson's usage of bridging and blocking coalitions in multilateral negotiations fills this missing blank.[13] Figure 2.4 specifies how a disagreement may be traced to a particular category, either a group or belief, and so forth, which helps defuse the tension. One might argue none of the Central American negotiations have been truly multilateral, since the number of actors are but a handful. Yet, they satisfy his definition of multilateralism: three of more parties. More perti-

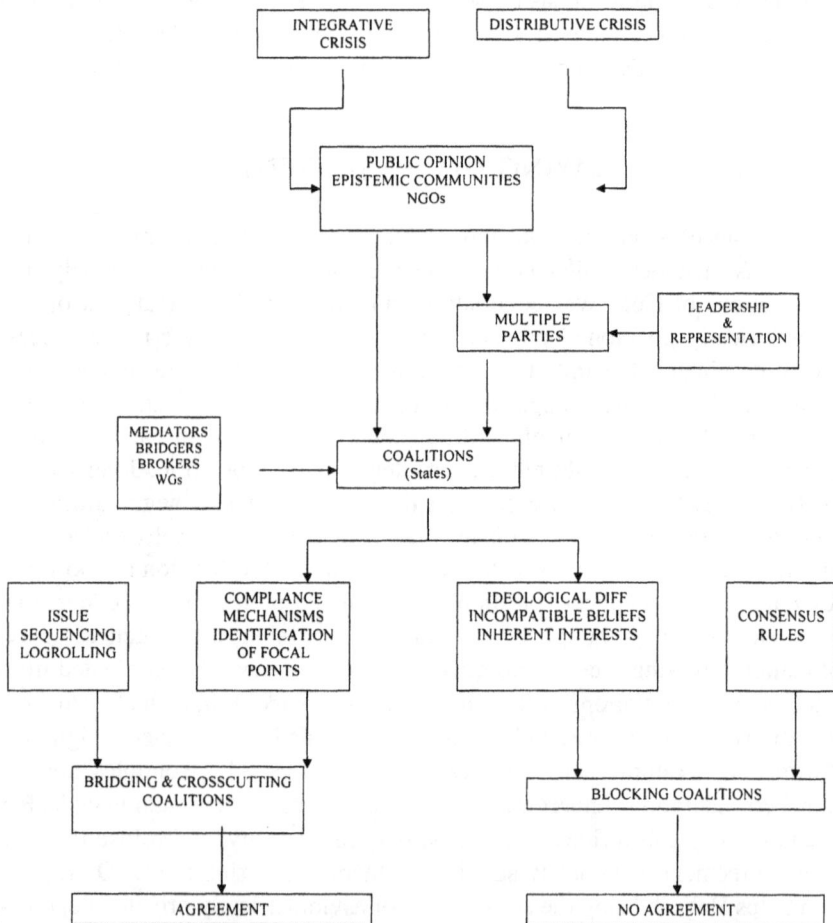

Figure 2.4.   Fen Osler Hampson's Model

nently, however, are (a) the limits to forging coalitions, especially against the US by historically such dependent countries as in Central America, in such a small setting; and (b) the prospects of Central American free trade agreements extending to the entire Latin America, to FTAA, when the setting would not only be large enough but also analytically competitive with other extant models, such as Feinberg's. Utilizing a modified Habeeb model helps under both circumstances—the former exposes constraints better owing to the fewer players available; the latter represents possibilities under best case scenarios. We can place both a disagreement, such as CA4FTA, and an agreement, such as CAFTA, in one theoretical framework.

CONCLUSIONS

Models, to be sure, are not road-maps to a negotiated outcome: The issues, individuals, and the interests reflected through them exert greater influence over the results. Nevertheless, they help enormously to comprehend the dynamics and position more precisely what is at stake. They add coherence to understanding the Central American negotiations in multiple ways.

First, given the various outcomes thus far, we can identify where negotiations have been stalled, and if they have been fulfilled, we can point to what is next in store with greater precision. We get a snapshot of the entire processes as well as the capacity to dwell on any singular instance. Descriptive analyses may offer more details, but cannot match the facility of a snapshot as conveniently.

Second, by mixing and matching models, in addition to capturing the dynamics and providing a sense of flow, we are also able to speak for asymmetry—an underlying concern in negotiating with Central American states. Although Habeeb's model is equally applicable to symmetrically inclined negotiations, we can at least trace asymmetrical stumbling blocks or breakdowns to specific instances or processes, and flush out idiosyncratic influences, such as any appeal to morality, from those processes. More importantly, we can distinguish the effects of asymmetry at the diagnostic, formula, or detail phase, and characterize them accordingly: Diagnostic phase asymmetry constrain negotiations, even if no outcomes substantially below optimally desired outcomes are available; yet the same symmetrically diagnosed negotiations may prove more burdensome on the table, though the outcome could be closer to the desired optimum.

Third, mixing and matching models also alert us to multiple possible outcomes between full agreement and full disagreement. As negotiations become more murky with expanding actors and issues, as well as proliferating technologies and gaps, our capacity to not just prepare for any outcome but also make adjustments between different outcomes is enhanced. We can specify turning points, distinguish between crises and impasses, explain various thresholds, and both create and connect loops as and when needed.

Fourth, we just learn a lot more of the dynamics by invoking model components and other categories—not just about processes and outcomes, but also how we color and characterize them. Newspaper reports bring us the information expeditiously, but when we interpret the information through stages, functions, and other relevant capsules, we begin contributing to the literature—squeezing more juice, triggering more debates, as well as comparing and contrasting.

Finally, we can place a select few LDCs more firmly within the framework of negotiations today. As Habeeb observed, previous negotiations theories not just emphasized symmetrical cases, but the US-Soviet Cold War symmetry particularly. Not only are LDCs being brought in through the treatment of asymmetrical cases, but Central American cases which usually get swallowed by broader hemispheric studies, such as Feinberg's on the FTAA, find a more robust and independent analytical presence in particular. Since they deal with three types of asymmetrically positioned neighbors to the north, we also get glimpses of not just one response, but multiple Central American responses to asymmetrical cases. What they convey is the subject of the next two chapters.

NOTES

1. Robert Kreklewich, "North American integration and industrial relations:neo-conservativism and neo-fordism?" *The Political Economy of North American Free Trade*, eds. Ricardo Grinspun & Maxwell A. Cameron (New York: St. Martin's Press, 1993), 261–70.

2. Russia's latest free enterprise takeover by Vladimir Putin's government offers a taste of the imbroglio in this relationship. See "Yukos could be sold to state firm," BBC News, September 24, 2004, from: http://news.bbc.co.uk/i/hi/business/3686110.stm

3. *Summitry in the Americas: A Progress Report* (Washington, DC: Institute of International Economics, 1997).

4. *How Nations Negotiate* (New York: Harper & Row, 1964).

5. *The Politics of Negotiations: America's Dealings with Allies, Adversaries, and Friends* (Chapel Hill, NC: University of North Carolina Press, 1991).

6. "Getting to the table:the triggers, stages, functions, and consequences of prenegotiation," in *Getting to the Table: The Process of International Prenegotiation*, ed. Gross Stein (Baltimore, MD: The Johns Hopkins University Press, 1989), 239–68.

7. "The stages of prenegotiation:the decision to negotiate North American free trade," *Getting to the Table: The Processes of International Negotiation,* ed. Janice Gross Stein (Baltimore, MD: Johns Hopkins University Press, 1989), 18–43.

8. "Diplomacy and domestic politics:the logic of two-level games," *International Bargaining and Domestic Politics*, eds., Peter Evans, Putnam, et al. (Berkeley, CA: University of California Press, 1993), appendix (431–68).

9. "Stages, turning points, and crises:negotiating base rights, Spain and the United States," *Journal of Conflict Resolution* 30 (June 1986):327–60.

10. They first reject the concession-convergence, or offer-counteroffer, thesis popularized by Howard Raiffa, *The Art & Science of Negotiations: How to Resolve Conflicts and Get the Best out of Bargaining* (Belknap Press, 1985); and Jeffrey Z. Barry and Bert Brown, *The Social Psychology of Bargaining & Psychology* (New York. Academic Press, 1975), ch. 1; among others. See *The Practical Negotiator* (New Haven, CT: Yale University Press, 1982).

11. This particular pragmatic possibility is also found by Harold Jacobson, Dusan Sidjanski, Jeffrey Rodamar, and Alice Hongassian-Rudovich, "Revolutionaries or bargainers:negotiators for a new economic order," *World Politics* 35, no. 3 (April 1983):335–67. Also see John Odell, "Latin American trade negotiations with the United States," *International Organization* 34, no. 2 (Spring 1980):207–28.

12. *The Politics of Trade Negotiations Between Africa and the European Economic Community* (Princeton, NJ: Princeton University Press, 1971).

13. *Multilateral Negotiations: Lessons from Arms Control, Trade, and the Environment* (Baltimore, MD: The Johns Hopkins University Press, 1995), 3–54.

Chapter Three

Pits-to-Pedestal Sojourn?
Central America in Northern Embrace

INTRODUCTION

What are some of the current Central American economic realities, seen particularly in historical perspectives? How do these translate into the various types of integration being sought with Canada, Mexico, and the United States? Through four sections, this chapter places trading relationships and stances in a historical context; traces the evolution of the three specific contemporary integrative efforts; fits observations into the theoretical framework constituted; and draws conclusions, lessons, and implications, respectively. Broad Chapter 1 observations are specified, which helps reinterpret empirical negotiations puzzles using theoretical propositions derived from various Chapter 2 models.

As a preview, integrative projects with North American states may conceivably bring Central American states out of their economic doldrums, but a longer list of constraints than reasons for hope temper these positive developments. Even though democratization is not brought under the microscope, its contribution to the outcome is acknowledged.

TRADING RELATIONSHIPS & STANCES
IN HISTORICAL PERSPECTIVE

Trading relationships and stances involve both economic and political considerations. Treated separately in the same order, both show the inescapable US domination: It is a common feature of trading relations, past and present, creating an uneven playing field from the very outset between (a) the United

States and Central American states, reinforcing past behavioral patterns; and (b) the United States, Canada, and Mexico in their separate integrative approaches to Central America, hinting the gravitational pull of US policy positions. While not a new observation, US asymmetry faces a different, more democratized Central American context for the first time. Whether it impacts Central American outcomes more positively or not remains the puzzle.

Economic Front

The economic front is disaggregated into Central American (CA) regionalism, structural changes, and development. They highlight the respective relationships of Canada, Mexico, and the United States; multilateral connections; and civil society pressures. No particular yardsticks were used to select these as criterion except relevance and capacity to illustrate historically different dimensions of the problems/questions. Before turning to each, an overview first.

Overview

Peanut-sized CA economies are unlikely to alter the economic/trading status quo with their three North American neighbors, but the United States is better positioned than Canada or Mexico to change CA structures. Although recent growth has been robust, only one-tenth of 1% of Canadian imports are from the four Central American states, while roughly one-twentieth of 1% of its exports find markets there.[1] As Canadian exports doubled, from $94m to $188m between 1995 and 2002, imports also climbed 89%, from $197.3m to about $372m.[2] The growth rate is noteworthy, needs to be sustained, yet still remains too paltry to have any forseeable impact. Even with geographical proximity, Mexico's picture is only slightly better: Significantly less than 1% of its exports reach each of Costa Rica, Guatemala, El Salvador, Honduras, and Nicaragua; and none of these CA countries account for even 1% of Mexico's imports.[3] By contrast, the US was not only their largest market, but also the biggest source of imports in 2000. As a market, it takes up a minimum of 57% (Guatemala's) and a maximum of 70% (Honduras), for an average of 52%, of CA exports; and as a source of CA imports, it accounts for anywhere between 24% (Nicaragua) and 58% (Honduras), for an average of 40% for the region. Canada exported $188m and the US $9.8b in 2002, for example, and Mexico $1.3b in 2000, with Canada and the US importing $372m and $11.87b in 2002, respectively, and Mexico $331m in 2000. While Canada and the US had trade deficits of $184m and $2b in 2002, Mexico actually had a $1.03b surplus in 2000.[4] Whereas Canada's exports doubled and imports climbed 89% between 1995 and 2002, by expanding only 17% and 28.3%

between 1998 and 2002,[5] US exports and imports, respectively, still under-scored the critical US position relative to CA: May be one explanation why CAFTA negotiations ended so quickly and bargaining remained so restricted, and possibly why CA countries were increasingly bolder in negotiating with Canada, stems from the patterns of trade behavior just described. Mexico's moderate-size Central American trade reflects the advantages of contiguity and necessity for the latter, but also the disadvantage of still playing second fiddle to the US counterpart. Latching on to the larger Canadian and Mexican economies may not necessarily boost short-term CA trade values and vol-umes, let alone threaten US linkages.

Table 3.1 confirms exports as the engine of growth. Except in Costa Rica, GDP growth was negligible for all, or negative, as in Nicaragua, during the 1980s; but in the 1990s, particularly after peace had been restored, in spite of natural calamities, and even before the FTA took off, every country, even Costa Rica, registered impressive GDP growth. With exports playing a dom-inant role for all, though to a lesser extent for Guatemala, two features pre-dict Central American's trading future: greater integration in the global econ-omy than one might expect from their miniscule economic size and impoverished status; and as Table 1.1 indicated, with agriculture occupying such a prominent position in Central American exports, diversifying an agri-cultural base is not just a contemporary imperative but also crucial to diluting

Table 3.1.   Central American States: An Economic Profile

Countries	GDP growth (%) 1980–1990	GDP growth, (%) 1990–2002	Exports as % of GDP	Ag. As % of GDP	Ag. As % of exports	Ag. As % of emp.
Belize						
Costa Rica	3.0	4.9	42.7			17.2
El Salvador	.2	4.3	28.9	12		21.4
Guatemala	.8	4.0	18.6	23	60	52.5
Honduras	2.7	3.1	38.3			43.9
Nicaragua	−1.9	4.3	32.5			43.2

Sources: Large proportion of figures from Office of the U.S. Trade Representative, *Interim Environmental Review: U.S.-Central American Free Trade Agreement* (Washing, DC: USTR, August 2003), 54–54; for figures on agriculture as % of GDP column and Salvadorean figure in agriculture as % of employment column, see Government of El Salvador, Tratado de Libre Comercío Centroamerica-Estados Unídos, *National Action Plan for Trade Capacity Building: Meeting the Challenge of Globalization*, 2 vols, vol. 1: *General Strategy* (San Salvador: Government of El Salvador, July 2003), 23; Government of Guatemala, Ministry of Economics and ECLAC, *National Action Plan for Trade Capacity Building in Guatemala: A Proposal by the Government of Guatemala in the Framework of the US–CAFTA* (Guatemala City, December 2002), 12; for Guatemalan, Honduran, and Nicaraguan figures in the agriculture as % of employment column, Vicki Glass, "CAFTA:the Latin American perspective," Washington Office of Latin America (WOLA), *Congressional Briefing*, Letter, January 22, 2004, from http://www.wola.org; and other scattered figures from J. F. Hornbeck, "The U.S.–Central America Free Trade Agreement (CAFTA):challenges for sub-regional integration," *Congressional Research Service*, Report, April 25, 2003, 32.

Table 3.2.   Central American Economic Dependence on US Foreign Trade (in %)

Country	Exports				Imports			
	1948	*1960*	*1970*	*1980*	*1948*	*1960*	*1970*	*1980*
Costa Rica	78.6	52.3	42.5	34.9	77.7	45.5	34.8	34.5
El Salvador	77.4	35.1	21.4	29.7	73.5	42.9	29.6	25.2
Guatemala	89.0	55.6	28.3	28.7	76.2	46.0	35.3	33.7
Honduras	72.9	57.9	54.6	53.1	78.7	55.9	41.5	42.2
Nicaragua	74.5	40.4	33.2	38.7	83.8	52.7	36.5	27.5
Panama	91.5	96.1	63.4	49.9	75.5	51.5	39.8	33.8

Source: John H. Coatsworth, *Central America and the United States: The Clients and the Colossus* (New York: Twayne Publishers, 1994), 19.

future dependencies. Regional integration, with all its promises of boosting intra-regional exchanges while also strengthening inter-regional capacities, could be one important and relevant strategy whose time has finally come. Central American states are a leader in this respect, and past experiences may prove more useful for them than for other compacts in the hemisphere.

Comparatively, US linkages are neither new nor purely economic, and considerably stronger than Canadian or Mexican counterparts. Just as Table 3.2 shows, economic dependence on the US was historically greater than at present, Table 3.3 suggests how undulations in post-World War II economic assistance reflected political considerations, with the Cuban and Nicaraguan revolutions of 1958 and after 1978, respectively, spiking the amounts disbursed. Interestingly, in response to both revolutions, the US emphasized economic integration, more rapidly yet less successfully after 1958, but more glacially and with greater long-term meaning after the 1980s. Canada, on the other hand, did not enter the Central American picture until 1997, seven years after joining the Organization of American States (OAS). Its economic and political presence remains too negligible to this day to make any tangible Canadian or Central American difference; Mexico's lesser role than the US nevertheless

Table 3.3.   US Economic Assistance (in 1982 $)

Periods	Costa Rica	El Salvador	Guatemala	Honduras	Nicaragua	Panama	Totals
1953–57	25.6	3.1	41.9	10.3	9.2	27.2	117.3
1958–61	24.0	6.9	52.9	16.8	23.1	19.0	142.7
1962–64	40.9	58.7	36.0	25.6	27.9	58.9	248.0
1965–69	42.4	30.7	33.4	25.9	47.5	62.5	242.4
1970–77	21.8	14.7	29.4	29.3	31.1	43.6	169.9
1978–81	16.9	56.3	26.6	40.0	27.3	18.4	185.5
1982–88	154.5	343.6	82.6	137.7	0	21.2	739.5

Source: John H. Coatsworth, *Central America and the United States: The Clients and the Colossus* (New York: Twayne Publishers, 1994), 107.

parallels many US patterns with one conspicuous exception: Whereas the US *determines* directions of bilateral Central American relations, Mexico both *takes initiatives,* as it did until the 1990s and under President Vicente Fox Quesada, and *follows* Central American leads, as in the 1990s.[6] Although economic Central American dependence on Mexico, especially over trade, may not be as huge as with the US, it is deep enough to matter.

Regionalism

One of the pioneering hemispheric integrative efforts, the 1959 Central American Common Market (CACM) depended on US initiative, although twenty years later, the US was instrumental in also keeping Central American states apart. As those conflicts decimated intra-regional trade to the extent of 58%,[7] interestingly, Mexico's efforts to revive CACM were more pivotal than US attempts. During 1958–59, however, several Central American countries signed agreements to eliminate tariffs amongst each others, integrate regional industries, and work towards a customs union under the Committee of Economic Cooperation (CEC) of the Economic Commission for Latin America (ECLA). In 1957, they adopted quotas on coffee exports to Brazil, Colombia, and Mexico, culminating in the Latin American Coffee Agreement the next year—an early attempt at sectoral integration often overlooked amidst the more fanciful cases of regional integration between countries today,[8] yet still defying contemporary Central American efforts to integrate.

Inspired by the US, four CA countries signed the General Treaty of Central American Economic Integration in December 1960, with Costa Rica following suit in 1963; and very much like Mexico's PPP seeks today, the US established the Social Progress Trust Fund (SPTF) under the Inter-American Development Bank (IADB) on July 11, 1960 to build infrastructures. This was a time when Mexico did not see eye-to-eye with the US, deciding not to support the US-pressured 1954 OAS resolution against Guatemala's Jacobo Arbenz, sustaining cordial relations with Fidel Castro's Cuba against US wishes, and condemning the 1965 US invasion of the Dominican Republic. During the 1980s, however, it became more active than the US on the economic front: Through the San José Accords of 1980 with Venezuela, Central American states were provided petroleum supplies at preferential rates; preferential trade was conducted with Central American states through a 1980 Latin American Free Trade Agreement (LAFTA) exemption; with the World Bank providing $300m, the Chiapas Plan sought to strengthen infrastructures over six years, and produced the Southern Frontier Highway along the Guatemalan border, although other projects fizzled out; Mexico offered over $100m developmental loans through the Central American Bank for Economic Integration (BICE, in Spanish);[9] and it established the Central American Import Financing Program (FICE, in Spanish) in February 1989. In spite of accounting disproportionately for CA trade, the US could only muster the Caribbean Basin Initiative (CBI), whose one-way free-trade orientation did not open any new economic areas immediately, but by consolidating CA bilateral economic ties to the US, cast a longer shadow of dependence, than Mexico's disparate and more regionalistic efforts. Ironically, when regionalism was to return as a priority towards the end of the century, attention would shift more to the US than to Mexico, demonstrating that gravitational effect alluded to earlier.

Steps to revive and expand intra-Central American trade since the 1980s commenced with a Salvadorean and Guatemalan initiative, the Framework Agreement for the Establishment of a Customs Union, on January 13, 2000. Later in August, Honduras and Nicaragua also sought membership, with Costa Rica joining the pack in June 2002. The road towards these integrative steps began with the September 13, 1991 Protocol of Tegucigalpa establishing the overarching Central American Integrated System (SICA in Spanish), consisting of economic, political, social, and environmental subsystems,[10] and the 1993 Protocol of Guatemala adopting a flexible common external tariff, with rates ranging between zero and 15%, left at each member's discretion.[11] All members agreed to complete the customs union obligations prior to fulfilling economic union obligations when they acceded to the January 2000 Framework Agreement.[12] On October 15, 2001, they signed a FTA with Dominican Republic, while another was signed, in principle, with Panama on May 16, 2001.

Revived CACM trade during the 1990s, evident in Table 3.4, produced the FTA proposals to the US and Canada, and provided Mexico greater confidence in creating its own FTAs with Central American states and proposing PPP later. Not surprisingly, the proportions of Central American trade openness by the end of the century were among the highest in the world: 100% for Costa Rica, Honduras, and Nicaragua, and 70% for El Salvador and Panama, with Guatemala's 50% as the only laggard case.[13] Table 3.5 shows the steep

Table 3.4. Central American Exports (% of GDP)

Countries	1991 Exports/GDP	2001 Export/GDP
Costa Rica	22.8	31.0
El Salvador	11.3	20.8
Guatemala	12.8	14.2
Honduras	26.7	31.7
Nicaragua	21.4	52.6

Source: J. F. Hornbeck, "The U.S.-Central America Free Trade Agreement (CAFTA):challenges for sub-regional integration," *Congressional Research Service*, Report, April 25, 2003, 8.

Table 3.5.   Average Central American Tariffs

Countries	1985	1989	1994	1999
Costa Rica	53.0	16.4	11.2	3.3
El Salvador	23.0 (1986)	16.0	10.1	5.7
Guatemala	50.0	16.0	10.8	7.6
Honduras	n.a.	41.9	n.a.	8.1
Nicaragua	54.0	n.a.	17.4	10.9

Source: Daniel Lederman, Guillermo Perry, Rodrígo Suescún, "Trade structure, trade policy and economic policy options in Central America," Paper (Washington, DC: World Bank, November 2002), 13.

declines in average tariffs. Daniel Lederman, Guillermo Perry, and Rodrígo Suescún argue high capital market mobility and labor flows also reduce hindrances to establishing an optimum currency area (OCA): Although emigration is not as much to other CA countries as to the US,[14] net remittances accounted for 63% of Nicaraguan, 21% of Honduran, and 19% of Guatemalan export earnings. In turn, CA states fulfill three of the OCA criteria: trade openness, high trade interdependence criteria, and high capital and labor mobility. The only one not fulfilled is the absence of asymmetric shocks: Central to measuring this criterion are the consequences of changes in the US economy on CA economies; and although more time is needed to correctly appraise these correlationships, thus far positive US economic developments have benefited CA, while US downturns have also slowed CA economies.[15] With trade, labor, and capital flows interlinking CA and US economies, the obvious question of dollarizing Central American currencies is likely to surface should CAFTA be ratified and prove productive. Canada and Mexico cannot make comparable claims: Even though both receive Central American immigrants, remittance levels are considerably less, and therefore impacting the capital market negligibly at present. The other three OCA criteria barely warrant serious considerations for Canada and Mexico.

Conflicts alone did not retard development across CA during the 1980s. Economic structures also had to be adapted to new circumstances, culminating in what is known as the *lost decade* in just about every country south of the United States,[16] including across Central America. As previously observed, led by Costa Rica, some of the Central American countries sought FTAs and other commercial arrangements, oftentimes through proposals they themselves made, as for example, to Canada and the US. Proposals, in turn, need to be buttressed by domestic policy and institutional changes. At least on this front, Central American countries were not found wanting. Nudged by the US government through its trade capacity-building (TCB) machineries,[17] almost all CA countries prepared national actions plans (NAPs), synchronizing them with the CAFTA timetable, that is, either during 2002 or in the early months of 2003.[18] Interestingly, Canada's FTA negotiations and Mexico's PPP played neither a causal role in formulating these plans, nor were affected by them, at least not in the initial stages by virtue of their earlier starting points. By the same token, CA countries not engaged in CAFTA—Belize and Panama—did not have counterpart plans or documents publicly available, or at least accessible for this particularly research. In short, the US not only became the only NAFTA country to complete an agreement, but also provide all the technical and institutional details—all in record FTA time.[19]

National Action Plans: Engine of Structural Changes?

Table 3.6 highlights these plans for five countries, specifying the inherited problems, transformational challenges, structural reforms undertaken, and specified developmental priorities for each. In identifying the problems and proposing plans, each plan mirrors the US TCB format, as expected—a sharp shift from the endogenously oriented approaches hitherto adopted towards not just the exogenous counterpart, but also an exogenous counterpart anchored in Washington. In keeping with the TCB tradition, for example, all plans identify priorities in terms of preparing for trade negotiations (including such horizontal needs as promoting free trade to civil society), implementing the agreement (specifying rules of origins and customs procedures, sanitary and phytosanitary measures, technical barriers to trade, subsidies, anti-dumping and countervailing measures, competition policy and consumer protection, intellectual property, and others), and the transition to free trade, during which many country-specific priorities are broadly institutionalized. For some of the most impoverished and conflict-ridden states in the western hemisphere, these sweeping changes substitute secretive policy-making with greater transparency, policy-making priorities from political and security considerations toward economic, and idiosyncratic institutions for rationality-reflecting mechanisms more readily recognizable abroad. But they also erode domestic controls over developmental policies: Not only are NAPs instrumentalized by US TCB measures, but also TCBs create opportunities for the Washington-based troika of institutions to furnish project financial support.

Although the adoption of similar national action formats produces more convergences than divergences, the country-specific tone cannot be ignored; and similarly, although many items are prescribed, only four dimensions serve illustration. As previously observed, all plans are expected to address three stages of institutionalized detail: preparing for the negotiations, implementing the agreement, and transition to free trade. Not only did the US National Action Plan guidelines of October 3, 2002 necessitate these, but by following through, CA states permit the United States to also influence

Table 3.6. National Action Plans for Selected CA Countries

Countries	Inherited Problems	Transformational Challenges	Structural Reforms	Areas Prioritized for Improvement
Costa Rica	• Import Substitution • Primary product exports	• Small-sized market • Dependence on primary imports • External debt • Insertion in global economy • US integration	• Liberalize trade, capital flows, foreign exchange market, finance • Develop non-traditional exports • Denationalization	• Rural development • Business environment & investment climate • Benefit SMEs • Science & tech
El Salvador	• Conflict zone • High protection • Agro concentration • 1992 Peace Accord ends 12-yr war	• Denationalization of banks and industries • Decentralizing government	• Monetary Integration Act • Liberalize pension & financial sectors	• New Alliance • Rural development • Business environment & investment climate • Benefit SMEs • Science & tech
Guatemala	• Civil war (December 1996 peace accord • Nationalization • Weak per capita tax base	• Building civil society linkages • Lack of information • Education • Weak trade-related disciplines • Intra-government coordination	• Joined GATT 1991 • Law on Free Trade Zones (1989) • National Competitiveness Program (PRONACOM) • Law on Foreign Investment (1998) • Fiscal Covenant • Modernization Program • CBI until 2008 • CBTPA Act (2000)	• Strengthen human resources • Rural development • Business environment & investment climate • Benefit SMEs • Science & tech

Honduras	• Farm depression • Rural poverty • Dependence on remittances ($700m) • 1969 Soccer war disruptive • Nicaraguan refugees	• Low pay for government staff • Weak staff training • Lack of info • Intra-government coordination • Lack of hi-tech group	• Joined GATT 1994 • Industrial • Convert Modernization Program into regional program	• Strengthen governmental institutions • Rural development • Business environment & investment climate • Benefit SMEs • Science & tech
Nicaragua	• Civil war • Starting from scratch, even creating government institutions, staff, training staff, learning English	• Fiscal reforms		• Business environment & investment climate • Benefit SMEs • Science & tech • Rural development (lowest priority)

domestic institution-building, streamlining emerging structures along familiar US styles. Neither Canada nor Mexico can make any comparable contemporary claims: Canada still remains too new and too distant to make any waves presently; and, unlike the 1980s, Mexico is mostly riding the US crest than offering alternatives.

As with all other dimensions, inherited problems show several commonalities among the five countries, in addition to unique features. Except for Costa Rica, all faced civil war directly, or the immediate impacts of these, such as refugee overflows. In turn, these retarded growth during the 1980s, a decade of transformations elsewhere in the hemisphere but only conflict across Central America; and they imposed unnecessary constraints in the 1990s, especially in the early half. All, even Costa Rica, faced the economic structuration problems as the rest of Latin America did. Key problems stemmed from the collapse of both import substitution industrialization (ISI) and entrenched nationalization programs.[20] As the most advanced of the five, Costa Rica faced the ISI crunch most,[21] but this enabled a more rapid shift to service sector industries, placing the country in the leading ranks, and also helping displace coffee and bananas as the export staples. In fact, all other countries in the region are not only more dependent on agricultural exports than Costa Rica, but also remain hostages to coffee and banana price fluctuations in the international market.[22]

Guatemala's bloody civil war,[23] directed largely against indigenous rural residents, was brought to an end by the December 1996 Accord for a Firm and Lasting Peace, while Honduras finally found respite from the devastating consequences of the 1969 soccer war, CACM derailment, and the Nicaraguan revolution spilling over. Nicaragua itself had to start from scratch, a development all too embarrassingly evident in its own national action plan: This was the only plan with actual costs of every minute detail of the necessary institutional changes, down to such items as learning English, WTO modalities, labor and environmental laws, and, in short, Nicaragua's own assets and liabilities. It is painstaking reading, evidently the work of neophytes, and the least comprehensively revealing plan of the lot, in spite of the attention to detail.

One advantage of starting from scratch is to not face the pressures of vested interest groups. As the most developed and stable CA state, Costa Rica faces too many of them, thus becomes most vulnerable in fulfilling some CAFTA disciplines. For example, many sectors are constitutionally required to remain under state control, including seaports, airports, railroads, sewage, water distribution, and energy. The most controversial among them is telecommunications, whose expected liberalization under CAFTA, led to vociferous Costa Rican protests, even Costa Rica's refusal to sign CAFTA in December 2003 with the other members.[24] Nevertheless, as the CA leader in literacy (95%), it has attracted several information-based industries, such as Intel, and other pharmaceutical industries, like Abbott Laboratories, and Procter & Gamble, to locate in the country.

Turning to the second dimension, transformational changes, we again see numerous parallels. Among these are the small-sized market of each country, the dependence on primary products, insertion into the global economy, which often necessitates integration into the US economy first, as well as denationalizing industries and decentralizing government. For the most backward countries, like Guatemala, Honduras, and Nicaragua, there are additional burdens: They have neither sufficient information, nor information infrastructures and technologies; educated personnel are far and few in between; intra-governmental coordination is both new and difficult; civil society linkages under the new priorities are virtually non-existent; official remunerations are often so low as to pose formidable barriers to staff retention, and thereby continuity in policy implementation; and the tax-base is very, very weak, with Guatemala having the second smallest per capita tax-rate in Latin America, after Haiti.[25]

These, in turn, influence structural reforms, the third dimension. Obviously, the country parallels continue: liberalizing trade, capital flows, foreign exchange markets, and the financial sector are also among the priorities of institutional development, since institutional functions stem from such liberalization; joining GATT/WTO became a necessity, for example, Guatemala joining in 1991, Honduras in 1994, and so forth; and denationalizing several industries and sectors, such as banks and insurance, also became foremost tasks. Several programs were adopted by each country to facilitate these, for example, Guatemala's National Competitiveness Program (PRONACOM), the Fiscal Covenant for a Future with Peace and Development (2002), Law on Foreign Investment (1998), and the Modernization Program for the National Financial System (1998); El Salvador had its own New Alliance Program, disaggregated into specific alliances for macroeconomic stability, employment, solidarity, the future, and security; Honduras similarly adopted the National Competitiveness Initiative composed of seven subgroups, on strengthening trade negotiations capacity and promoting exports, creating technological centers, improving investment, enhancing infrastructure, improving national quality system, boosting national training system, and increasing the competitiveness fund.

Finally, the last dimension addresses areas prioritized for improvement. Here the choices are few, and four dimensions appear as mandatory under CAFTA negotiations, though their ranking differs for each country. These dimensions are rural development, business environmental and investment climate, benefit small and medium-sized enterprises (SMEs), and boosting science and technology, particularly in the information industry. Guatemala, for example, places rural development at the top, while Nicaragua positions it at the bottom; Honduras interprets rural development broadly to include health, education, security, and infrastructure, while Costa Rica sees all four of them with equal priority.

Development

Although the three North American countries emphasize different types of development, each version depends on the counterparts. Just as CA4FTA emphasizes humanitarian development and PPP infrastructural development, CAFTA gives institutional development the pride of place. Humanitarian development becomes meaningless without the simultaneous promotion of the other two types, just as infrastructural development both necessitates and enhances institutional development, and similarly for institutional development, which assumes both human and infrastructural developments. Institutional development is clearly the critical type for regional integrative efforts: These efforts rally around policies, which assume infrastructural development and are as coherent, legitimate, and potentially effective as the institutions they are formulated within.

Some common patterns are evident: one leading institution serves as a gatekeeper of the trade-based transformation; it is disaggregated into a number of competencies; it is horizontally connected with other governmental agencies; and it has vertical linkages with societal groups, at one end, and multilateral institutions, at the other. Table 3.7 captures this network in comparative CA format. Once again, Nicaragua stands out from a lack of clear information and sequence.

One notices how the economic ministry or the foreign trade ministry becomes the leading Central American agency of liberalizing/regionalizing trade. This is significant for several reasons. First, it affixes an external orientation for a developing country whose democratic obligation should be domestic development, thus necessitating an internal orientation. Second, by extension this creates a top-down order within democratizing countries, and with it developmental inconsistencies: An external orientation necessitates more education, exposure, and external engagements which are usually found in urban residents than in rural, and appeals more to an upwardly mobile group of citizens, than the typically ascriptive, conservative rural LDC citizen. Third, the external orientation becomes implicitly affixed to the United States, thus opening up arguments of dependency, particularly of the original version Albert O. Hirschman formulated about Germany's clients in East Europe before World War II.[26] Fourth, on the other hand, this US-based external orientation may still be the catalyst to bringing at least four of the five coun-

Table 3.7. Central American Institutional Development

Countries	Gatekeeping Institution (with disaggregated agencies):	Institutions Facilitating Horizontal and Vertical Linkages
Costa Rica	COMEX (Ministry of Foreign Trade): Established mid-1980s	Customs Service (Ministry of Finance) Ministry of Economy, Industry, and Commerce (MEIC) Ministry of Agriculture (MAG) Costa Rican Foreign Trade Corporation (PROCOMER) Costa Rican Investment Board (CINDE) Ministry of Health Ministry of Justice General Auditor office of the Republic (CGR) Costa Rican Industrial Chamber (CRIC)
El Salvador	Ministry of Economy (MINEC): • Vice Ministry of Economics • Vice Ministry of Trade & Industry	*Vice Ministry of Economics* • Trade Policy Office (*Dirección de Política Comercial* = DPC); MINEC coordinates: Ministries of Agriculture, Public Heath & Social Assistance, Labor, Finance, and Environment & Natural Resources) • Trade Agreements Administrative Office (Dirección de Administración de Tratados = DATCO) • National Council for Science & Technology *Vice Ministry of Trade & Industry:* • Competitive Development Exports Office (Competitive Intelligence Unit; Center for Export Services) • Trade & Investment Office (National Investment Office; Support to Business Development) • Office of the Fund for Export Development (FOEX) • National Commission for Investment Promotion (PROCESA) • National Commission for Micro & Small Enterprise (CONAMYRE)

(continued)

Table 3.7. (Continued)

Countries	Gatekeeping Institution (with disaggregated agencies):	Institutions Facilitating Horizontal and Vertical Linkages
Guatemala	Ministry of Economics (from 1997): • Vice Ministry of Integration & External Trade (from 2002) • Vice Ministry of Investment & Competition (from 2002) • Vice Ministry of Micro, Small, & Medium Enterprises (from 2002)	*Vice Ministry of Integration & External Trade:* • Exterior Trade Policy • Administration (implementation) • Economic Analysis CONAPEX (National Council for Promotion of Exports, from 1986): • Private Sector (appointed by Cámara Empresarial de Guatemala from agricultural, industry, retail, finance, tourism, cooperative sectors) • Public Sector (Ministry of Economics heads ministries of Finance; Agriculture, Livestock, & Food; Communications, Transport, & Public Infrastructure; and Central Bank)
Honduras	Secretary of Industry & Commerce: • Vice Secretary of Business Development & Internal Commerce (General Directorates of Intellectual Property; Consumer Protection; and Micro, Small, & Medium Growth) • Vice Secretary of Economic Integration & External Trade (General Directorates of Economic Integration & Commercial Policy; and Foreign Trade Promotion & Investment)	*Coordinates:* • Secretaries of Finance & Executive Directorate of Revenue (DEI); Agriculture & Livestock; Natural Resources & Environment; Foreign Relations; Health; and Tourism • Central bank of Honduras (BCH) Legislative branch (unicameral) *Private Sector:* Honduran National Business Council (COHEP) Foundation for Investment & Development of Exports (FIDE) National Manufacturers Association (ANDI) Cortés Chamber of Commerce & Industry (CCIC) American Chamber of Commerce in Honduras (AMCHAM) Tegucipalga Chamber of Commerce & Industry (CCIT)
Nicaragua	MIFIC	

tries from their pitiful economic conditions in the fastest time available; and even though the various institutions needed for CAFTA predict long-term planning, the emphasis on upwardly mobile sectors rather than traditional agriculture, which so many people engage in, imposes a short-term game plan which cannot be viable unless it speaks for a more representative proportion of the population. Finally, as with trade policy, Central American foreign policies also accent the US disproportionately, certainly to a degree conspicuous enough as to make Canada and Mexico appear too trivial a partner.

Political Front

Turning to the political/military front, instead of issues, each country is treated separately in terms of its own experiences. Instead of the alphabetic pattern of treating the three North American countries in the manuscript, this sub-section begins with the historically most concerted player to have the most sustained experiences, the US, moving next to Mexico and Canada, before making some comparative observations.

US Experiences

US military intervention or *coup d'etat* connections throughout the twentieth century echo the economic patterns just described. Table 3.8 highlights the frequent pre-World War II cases corresponding to US dependence, and the post-World War II spurts, with heavy increases following the Cuban and Sandinista revolutions, paralleling economic assistance undulations. These historical patterns are useful to keep in mind in the wake of CAFTA after 9/11. Nevertheless, differences should not be ignored: Both Central American states and the United States are economically active in more parts of the world today than before World War II, thus reducing Central American dependence on the United States; and although US political/military intervention may never disappear, it is less important today when Central American farm exports, particularly bananas and coffee, belong to one or another stable global trading network when one century ago they did not, and both democratization and transparency offer more widespread watchguards today than ever before.

Mexican Experiences

Mexico is particularly sensitive to US political/military engagements along its southern border, and has been so historically. Even as late as the 1980s, it promoted the *Contadora* peace process, much to US chagrin, but this ultimately failed for being too unilateral. It also revived the Permanent Conference of

Table 3.8.   US Military Intervention in and Around Central America

Year	Place
1901	Panama
1902	Panama
1903	Honduras
1903–14	Panama
1907	Honduras
1910	Nicaragua
1911	Honduras
1912	Honduras
1912–15	Nicaragua
1918–20	Panama
1919	Honduras
1920	Guatemala
1921	Costa Rica, Panama
1924	Honduras
1925	Honduras
1925	Panama
1926–33	Nicaragua
1954	Guatemala
1961	El Salvador
1961	Bay of Pigs support from Central American states (except El Salvador)
1963	Guatemala coup
1963	Honduras coup
1964	Central American Defense Council (CONDECA) established
1965	Dominican Republic
1983	Grenada
1989	Panama (seize Noriega)
1994	Haiti
2004	Haiti

Latin American Political Parties (COPPAL) in 1989 under PRI gatekeeping, although this was done to prevent growing PRD influence within COPPAL since its 1979 establishment; and balance immigration controls against Central American states by absorbing refugees. Behind these contemporary concerns lies a history of thorny relations, particularly between Guatemala and Mexico.

Mexico's general Central American policy approach differs for Guatemala, or so Adolfo Aguilar Zinser argues.[27] Writing in the early 1980s, slightly before Mexico began its enormously painful neoliberal shift, he casts Mexico's CA policy approach as rejecting (a) the socio-political order of domination and US hegemonic influence; (b) repression, authoritarianism, and human rights violation, and (c) US intervention. Although Guatemala epitomized all of these, Mexico still treated it differently, in part owing to a rancorous historical relationship. Table 3.9 profiles this relationship.

Among the reasons why Mexico behaved differently with Guatemala, according to Zinser, were (a) uncertainty of how to respond to the military; (b) taking any position would complicate relations with both Guatemala and the US; (c) lack of consensus in government; and (d) Mexico's ministries and provinces having different stakes, creating structural impediments to a clear decision. Interestingly, Mexico's shifting US views between then and today parallels similar shifts toward Guatemala—synchronizing Mexico's southern orientations toward Guatemala and Central America. Yet again the gravitational US presence is so stark.

Table 3.9. Guatemala-Mexico Historical Spars

Year	Feuds
1821	• State of Chiapas declares independence from Spain; opts for Mexico in 1824
1821	• Captaincy General (Costa Rica, El Salvador, Guatemala, Honduras, Nicaragua) declares independence from Spain, September 15; Mexican invasion follows, but resisted only by El Salvador
1824–38	• United Province federation created; independence from Mexico sought
1841	• Soconusco region of Chiapas taken by Mexican General Juan Pablo Anaya from Guatemala's Colonel José Pierson; leaves Guatemala aggrieved until 1882 border treaty (implemented from April 1985): Guatemala's grief smoulders and extends to Belize
1944	• Guatemala's revolution drew favorable parallels with Mexico's
1954	• US-Backed Colonel Carlos Castillo Armas evicts Jacobo Arbenz, June 19; restores oligarchy
1959	• Adolfo López Mateos broke relations January 1 following killing of 3 Mexican fishermen on December 31, 1958; Guatemala apologized, relations restored
1980	• Guatemala's peasants take and burn Spanish embassy; López Portillo cancels Guatemalan visit (meant to reciprocate Romeo Lucas García's 1979 visit to Tapachula, Chiapas, with US officials as mediators)
1981	• Guatemala's *tierra arrasada* (scorched earth policy) creates refugees for Mexico
1981	• Belize independence recognized by Mexico; Guatemala affronted
1981	• September López Portillo visit to Guatemala cancelled owing to anti-Mexican feelings
1981	• Mexico and France recognize Salvadorean FDR and FMLN, which angers Guatemala, creating threats to assassinate López Portillo should he visit Guatemala by *Liga de Protección al Guatemalteco, Liga Guatemalteca Antimexicana and Comando Guatemalteca Pro Recuperación de Belice*
March 1982	• Efráin Ríos Montt overthrows Lucas García; and 3 Mexican diplomats go missing from Malacatán consulate
May 1982	• Mexican Malacatán consulate closed

López Portillo distinguished El Salvador from Guatemala: A political solution to lawlessness was needed in the former, but no alternative to a political solution existed in Guatemala, in spite of the presence of the *Unidad Revolucionaria Guatemalteca* (URG) and the establishment of *Comité de Unidad Patriótica de Guatemala* (CUPG) in Mexico under Luís Cardoza y Aragón. With so many refugees and emigrants from Guatemala, Mexico's ambiguity towards Guatemala is unlikely to simply evaporate, even though Guatemala has shifted from military rule to democracy, and economic agreements have been signed: Attitudinal changes are not as quick as policy changes, and just as Guatemalans see Mexico as an arrogant colossus of the north, much as Mexico sees the US, Mexicans themselves see Guatemalans as belonging to a lower socio-cultural or political-economic order.

Canada's Experiences

According to a May 2003 EKOS Survey, in 2001, when Canadians were asked if trade promotion meant jobs and economic benefits for their own province, 61% agreed, up from 57% the year before; and pushing the point, when asked which part of the world should the government emphasize in boosting trade, Latin America got 23% of the vote, behind the US and Asia, each with 25%, and ahead of Europe's 20%.[28] If anything, these statistics reaffirm the need to prioritize one element of a Canadian strategic trade policy: diversify beyond the United States, and particularly south of it where paltry trade flows leave a huge gap to fill, at least if public desires are to be quenched. The hemisphere south of the United States commands greater popular fascination among Canadians: Compared to the negligible proportion of trade with Canada, Latin America scored a resoundingly high public preference in the survey.

Before Canada signed the March 1998 Memorandum of Understanding (MOU) with Central American countries, barely $100m worth of exports left Canada and only twice that amount of imports entered; and only $209m were invested across Central America by Canada. After the MOU, exports doubled and imports went up 25% immediately, signaling greater opportunities awaiting.[29] Even as trade expanded, in 2002 El Salvador accounted for .02% of Canadian imports and absorbed .01% of Canadian exports, Guatemala .04% and .03%, respectively, Honduras .04% and .004%, and Nicaragua .01% and .003%.[30] If minuscule-sized economies of these countries are themselves a barrier, even the larger South American economies did not do any better with Canada. For example, in 1999, Mexico, a NAFTA partner, accounted for only .46% of Canadian exports and 2.98% of its imports, while Brazil recorded .29% and .42%, respectively.[31] Canadian trade reflected its interests, and these were minimal on the eve of the FTA negotiations. Compared to Mexico and the United States, Canada has been on the slow FTA track, concluding only two south of Mexico since entering NAFTA: those with Chile in 1997 and Costa Rica in 2001.[32] Although Canada and Mexico forged a FTA with Costa Rica with greater ease than the US, this proved to be a function of size and development: With greater US trade, Costa Rica will inevitably find more hurdles and disagreements; but equally gripping, the more developed a country, the more interest groups are likely to resist policy changes.

North American Experiences in Comparative Perspectives

Exogenous reasons may prevent Canadian-Central American hiatuses from narrowing, especially since Canada, unlike the recent Mexico and the United States, makes democratic governance, human rights respect, and development preconditions to conducting foreign relations. Central American states present other developmental hurdles. In terms of 1998 GNP per capita ranking, Costa Rica stood 93rd, El Salvador 107th, Guatemala 115th, and Honduras 151st.33 Ranked 76th in the same year, Mexico shows exits are possible, but other constraints compound the CA picture: at least half the population still live in the countryside; with some of the highest hemispheric indigenous proportions of the overall population, the resistance potential remains high; quality of life standards are marginal; and physical and policy-making institutional infrastructures are simply absent.

Trade relations with CA states expose Canada's diversification tendency, Mexico's stubborn US concentration, and a reinvigorated US trade policy approach based on competitive liberalization. Each is anomalous: Canada's belated Central American motivation, triggered by humanitarian needs and the US crusade towards one hemispheric market, is hard to explain given its post-World War II foreign policy tradition of seeking alternate partners to the US; Mexico's commercial neglect of its southern neighbors is equally baffling, given the drug trafficking and illegal immigration problems it faces; and the US hastening a FTA agreement in record time with so inconsequential trading partners. Canada's global view is evident in Paul Martin's desire to match the US record of forging free trade agreements,[34] and in Jean Chrétien's trinity of well-being (emphasizing prosperity, security, and *canadianness*).[35] It came across most forcefully in Pierre Trudeau's Third Option and institutionalized multiculturalism, even though they failed to cultivate hemispheric roots. Mexico refuses to learn from similar US experiences with Mexico, of inviting temporary CA workers or creating CA jobs, to combat fairly identical problems; and the US may be overplaying its hand when previous regional pursuits were subordinated to fighting unnecessary regional wars.

EVOLUTION OF INTEGRATIVE PROPOSALS

In evaluating the specific proposals, their antecedents and triggers, it is helpful to be reminded of the theoretical parameters and thresholds yet again. After all, analyzing developments and data for their own sake does not help comparisons or to draw future lessons. To recall, the negotiating framework was divided into a diagnostic-formula-detail sequence, which more or less corresponds to pre-pre-negotiations, pre-negotiations, negotiations, and post-negotiations phases. At the same time, Feinberg's CMM and HD models also provide specific parameters stemming from FTAA experiences, which are adapted to Osler Hampson's multilateral negotiations framework providing dual exit options. How these relate to the evolution of integrative efforts is specified throughout this section, so that the next section can treat them in summarized form.

The emerging picture of Canada and Mexico not fulfilling their own initiatives and efforts owing to a lurking and ubiquitous US presence also stems from their own lack of a comprehensive long-term plan and insufficient momentum. In profiling both pre-pre-negotiations and pre-negotiations, Table 3.10 creates a number of informative dimensions, some derived from the actual aforementioned functions of the stages, others addressing relevant themes or providing a negotiation overview.

What problem necessitated negotiations or project implementation? The first pre-pre-negotiation function revolves around this question, and it obviously varies for the three countries. For Mexico, PPP represents a single attempt to tackling multiple problems: Beginning with the most immediate, it would keep *maquilas* from migrating away from Mexico; the impoverished south would be uplifted, thus nipping political problems; and in the process, thorny Guatemalan relations would also improve, clearing the way for Mexican regional leadership. Canada was not driven by such mundane considerations. It did, however, seek to avail of the opportunity to boost its image across Latin America: Hurricane Mitch provided the occasion to accent its humanitarian concern, while the subsequent FTA proposals carried economic spin-offs too. The United States, on the other hand, also found opportunities knocking, and in its own inventive ways, manufactured some of its own. A deeper Central American engagement would continue its long association, extend CBI feelers in a different age, boost US exports in a competitive international economy, and strengthen its own competitive claims by securing more markets in the emerging competitive era. There was clearly a lot to be gained by all three North American countries, not to mention Central American counterparts, whose transition from *depression dictatorships* would be accelerated.[36]

Table 3.10. Before the Negotiations: Comparative Central American Observations

Dimensions	PPP	CA4FTA	CAFTA
1. Problems	• Exert leadership • Facilitate economic dev.	• Uplift human condition • Expand economic relations • Improve Canadian profile	• Continue economic dev. • Facilitate democratic transition • Connect with FTAA • Make us more competitive globally
2. Options considered	• Maquilas relocating elsewhere	• Lost Latin opportunity at leadership	• Lost opportunity to boost competitiveness
3. Background	• Chiapas Plan of 1980s: infrastructural development, creates border highway • February 1992: PRI proposes infrastructural development of Mexico's southern states for security reasons; connected with Mexico's free trade • President Zedillo considers a Tehuantepec highway in 1998 • During the 2000 elections, Treasury Under Secretary Santiago Levy circulated a pamphlet, "The south also exists"	• Memorandum of Understanding 1998, with CA4 on trade and investment • Help with debt burden and development since Hurricane Mitch (1998) through World Bank CA Emergency Trust Fund • CCRFTA: From June 30, 2000 to April 23, 2001 in 7 rounds, implemented January 2002	• 1992: Five countries propose FTA to Clinton 1997: US proposes only reciprocal treaties, not FTAs • January 22, 2001: Bush prioritizes FTAA over all other FTAs, save Chile's • Bush's *third border*, April 17, 2001 • September 24, 2001: Both sides agree to explore prospects of deeper relations • November 27, 2001: All 6 countries hold workshop on technical cooperation (followed by 6 in 2002): prelude to FTAs • Bilateral free trade talks • March 24, 2002: Bush meets his 5 • October 16, 2002: US and Costa Rica sign Increased Commercial Statement *(continued)*

Table 3.10. (*Continued*)

Dimensions	PPP	CA4FTA	CAFTA
4. Commitment communicated	• President-elect Fox's September 5, 2000 proposal	• CA4 proposal, September 28, 2000 in Guatemala to Canadian Jean Chrétien	• Bush's January 2002 speech to Organization of American States
5. When initiated	• March 12, 2001: implementation made public	• November 21, 2001, by Pierre Pettigrew • FOCAL roundtable, May 30-31, 2002, Ottawa	• January 8, 2003 ministerial meet
6. Targeted end	• No fixed date, but multilateral agencies have 20-year plan	• Open-ended; not pre-determined	• December 2003; pre-determined at the outset in January 2003
7. Rounds of talks	• No formal *a priori* negotiations, talks only to coordinate	• Not pre-announced, but ten rounds so far	• Nine full rounds for all countries, except Costa Rica, which went through ten
8. Preconditions	• Nothing explicit	• Environmental safeguards	• Environmental & laboral pre-conditions play only nominal role
9. On FTAA	• Not a priority, and PPP not consciously aiming for FTAA adoption	• Canada seeks FTAA leadership, but CA4FTA not being pursued as FTAA-stepping stone	• Explicit goal, would like CAFTA to serve as stepping stone
10. Nature of development	• Mundane considerations: *maquiladora* relocation	• Humanitarian considerations	• Strategic considerations: market access
11. Nature of multilateralism	• Part of political agenda	• Part of diplomatic agenda	• Part of political agenda
12. Approach	• Nationalistic/North American	• Multilateral/Hemispheric	• Nationalistic/Regional/Multilateral
13. National Plans	• Not needed	• No	• Required

Equally clearly, all three integrative efforts were well-thought out, not just by the three North American countries, but also the Central Americans. For the latter, each integrative effort was a long time coming, given their expressed interests from as early as 1992. As recipients of Central American proposals, Canada and US had plenty of time to evaluate their options: Canada decided to extend the Canada-Costa Rica Free Trade Agreement (CCRFTA) arrangements to Central America; US to simultaneously engage other Latin countries as would-be FTAA partners; and both to avail of the many embedded opportunities, discussed previously. Mexico was the only North American proponent, but clearly the proposal was neither new, nor unimportant since *maquilas* escaping the country would impose huge costs.

Various developments paved the way for the actual CA4FTA and CAFTA negotiations and PPP implementation. Some of them, in the background box of Table 3.10, go as far back as to the early 1990s, others to the early 1980s. Mexico's President Miguel de la Madrid, who began the break with an import substitution culture, confronted the Central American civil wars by overtly seeking peace through the *Contadora* processes, hosting refugees selectively, and sustaining the traditional distance from the United States. Less noticed was a 6-year Chiapas Plan not only anticipating PPP by almost two decades, but also invoking multilateral initiatives and engagements, ultimately to the tune of $300m from the World Bank. Among other ramifications, in spite of the White House and *Los Piños* differing over concurrent Central American policies, Washington, DC, and Mexico City were not at all far apart over future economic directions. Another echo of this identity was in 1998, when President Ernesto Zedillo de Ponce considered a highway across the Tehuantepec isthmus in Oaxaca, rekindling the railway the British had contemplated in the late nineteenth century and similar passageways crossing the minds of Spanish *conquistadores*, and which eventually necessitated multilateral funding. It didn't come to pass then, and faces problems under PPP even now, but the gist of Mexican attention was summarized by Santiago Levy's pamphlet, "The south also exists," making the case underdeveloped southern states could breed Mexican turmoil if not adequately addressed—a theme equally applicable to Central American states. Mexico's active role contrasts with Canada's *noblesse oblige*-based first appearance and a rather withdrawn US following unobtrusive intervention during the 1980s. As observed earlier, CA4FTA did not have much of a background, while CAFTA's was elaborated in Chapter 1.

Mexico proposed to CA states in the same month as Canada received the CA proposal, but how each proposal originated created different trajectories. As PAN's presidential candidate, Fox's September 5, 2000 PPP proposal to Mexico's seven southern neighbors reflected a personal choice, which coincidentally streamlined business interests and the Washington Consensus; but the combined September 28 Salvadorean, Guatemalan, Honduran, and Nicaraguan proposal to Canadian prime minister, Jean Chrétien, during a Canada-Central America Summit in Guatemala, was more of a *me-too* call instead: It was inspired by the CCRFTA talks from June 30, 2000, and not reflective of either the very little extant bilateral trade with Canada or the very little scope of such trade expanding rapidly. Mexico's domestic considerations contrasted with Canada's external image-building triggers. For the US, President Bush's description of CA as the *third US border* reflected both domestic and external interests.[37] CCRFTA was concluded on April 23, 2001, and Bush's January 16, 2002 FTA proposal was formally presented to Congress on August 22 by US Trade Representative, Robert B. Zoellick. Canada accepted the CA proposal, not just because Mexico and the US were moving in similar directions, but also to remain consistent with a long-standing Canadian policy approach of providing non-military global leadership.

Fox's proposal was not new, but Canada's Central American entrance was. Although the early 1980s, Mexico proposed, along with World Bank plans and financial support, the Chiapas Plan of the 1980s left only one completed highway behind, along the frontier with Guatemala, PRI's Florencio Salazar Adame proposed another infrastructural development of Mexico's south in 1992, this time to curb narcotrafficking and illegal emigration through CA. His idea meshed with President Carlos Salinas de Gortari's February 1990 Davos proposal to create a North American free trade agreement to his US counterpart, George H.W. Bush, in particular with the constitutional amendment this entailed of privatizing *ejidos* (lands collectively owned by indigenous inhabitants). Zedillo's 1998 Tehuantepec highway consideration emerged from this same background. By circulating a pamphlet, "The south also exists," Zedillo's Treasury Under Secretary, Santiago Levy, even competed with Fox's PPP campaign during 2000. What appeared as bipartisan identity actually reflected a graver and growing national concern: *Maquiladoras* represented one of Mexico's top sources of foreign exchange and domestic employment, and their flight reaffirmed how international economic restructuration imposed greater Mexican costs than Canadian, generating quite different Central American intensities.

PPP seeks to shift the *maquiladora* fulcrum from the Mexico-US border. Created by the Border Industrialization Program (BIP) of 1965 to stem Mexican emigration, these plants also provided over a million jobs by the 1990s, facilitated the inflow of new skills, thus upgrading the country's technological base, and created a secure pre-NAFTA cross-border Mexico-US integration.[38] Significant though *maquilas* were to Mexican development, they inevitably became uncompetitive. Mexico's average *maquila* hourly wage is $2.4, but in its southern states only 96c and in Guatemala $1.4. It is six times higher than China's 40c.[39] PPP dampens North American industrial out-migration by making CA rather than Asia the industrial destination; and it extends the ripple effects of commercial undertakings, establishing forward linkages across Central America to retain North American fruits in North America. International restructuring affects Canada less, but Canada upholds safeguards against *maquiladora* disadvantages, such as environmental degradation, gender exploitation, and human rights violations, more robustly than Mexico.

Once Canada, Mexico, and the US had considered the options, each would commit to some form of integrative efforts, then communicate this to the other side. PPP was publicly announced on March 12, 2001, one day after *Zapatistas* marched into Mexico City, Pierre Pettigrew initiated the first CA4FTA round in November that year, and Bush through his January 2002 OAS address. CAFTA's first ministerial meeting, on January 8, 2003, was followed within days by the first round of talks. Only the US had a fixed target closure in mind: end of 2003, after 9 rounds. What these rounds would cover were not specifically indicated at the outset, but neither were PPP implementation plans nor any part of the CA4FTA agenda.

Not surprisingly, PPP did not involve specified rounds of talks, although several ministerial meetings did bring all the countries together, and CA4FTA also did not announce, as the US did with CAFTA, how many rounds there would be. Mexico did not impose any preconditions on PPP, but by law, Canada was required to prepare an environmental report, which the US was also obligated to prepare for both labor and environment. These reports eventually played a very nominal role in the actual negotiations, suggesting, even though they are legislatively required, their presence in integrative negotiations might actually be superficial.

Whether FTAA was an influential consideration or not produced varied results. Mexico was the least enthusiastic about FTAA, from as far back as the 1994 Summit of the Americas, since FTAA was seen as eroding Mexico's NAFTA-based special place with US decision-makers. On the other hand, Canada increasingly elevated FTAA, seeing it as an opportunity to constrain excessive US engagements in the hemisphere. Besides, Canada's recent OAS membership also carried a tone of making up for lost time by going the extra distance and seeking some leadership role.[40] The FTAA was the ultimate US objective, so became an all-important part of the Central American pursuits of all three countries, with Mexico being the only reluctant partner.

A developmentalist Central American approach, though common to all three countries, is interpreted differently by each. Canada sees it as reflecting every uplifting human goal, Mexico's in terms of such mundane priorities as industrial competitiveness, and the US through strategic eyes. These conveyed Canada's humanitarian perspective, Mexico's competitiveness, concern as recipient of foreign investment, and US competitiveness concerns both against other countries and in sustaining domestic jobs. Canada's engagement began with a 1998 Memorandum of Understanding (MOU) with Central American states on trade and investment, and the humanitarian assistance needed next year led to contributions to the World Bank's Central American Emergency Trust Fund to alleviate debt burdens and implement necessary disaster safeguards.[41] Mexico commenced with a lot of enthusiasm, only to find this ebbing after 9/11; and the US proved to be the most determined to set and attain goals. Mexico's adjustments to international economic restructuring was not only caused by but also deepened its US economic attachments. One might argue, as the US prioritizes FTAA over NAFTA in its Central American pursuits, Mexico's PPP interests not only become redundant, but also leave the country more exposed to international competition than before. Canada, the largest US trading partner, thus also deeply dependent economically on the US, still claims more diversified partners than Mexico, thus capable of standing slightly more aloof of the US than Mexico.

Timing produced an unwitting 9/11 casualty. Whereas Fox formally presented PPP to his Central American colleagues on November 30, 2000, Pierre Pettigrew, the Canadian Minister for International Trade, announced CA4FTA negotiations on November 21, 2001. It was not 9/11 *per se* which cooled Mexico-US relations, since the failure to reach an immigration agreement the previous week started the breach, but by shifting US priorities, 9/11 challenged the PPP assumption of unflinching US partnership; while CA4FTA, by commencing after Canada and the Central American states had already adjusted to the 9/11 shocks, produced a more stable negotiating atmosphere. As PPP lost its steam, multilateral organizations, rather than Mexico, resurrected it; but since CA4FTA was more focused on adjusting domestic issues, at least for Canada, multilateral institutions were seen as helpful, but only for project implementation, not in the negotiations. Similarly for the US: the only role for multilateral institutions is in policy implementation, not in policy formulation. Besides, CAFTA, emerging as it did after 9/11, carries fewer adjustment problems than PPP or CA4FTA, at least for the US, although Central American countries must now go the extra mile to insulate trade flows from security bugs.

A closer scrutiny shows even the nature of multilateralism differed. For CA4FTA, it belongs to a diplomatic agenda, for PPP and CAFTA a political agenda. Yet, CAFTA and CA4FTA negotiations are conducted by established governmental agencies, such as departments/secretariats; while a specifically created agency responsible to the president dealt with PPP until the External Affairs Secretariat absorbed it after 9/11.

Reliance on multilateral organizations is common to all three, and indeed an essential component of FTAA. This strategic similarity conceals differences in modalities and tactics. Emphasis for the PPP is on the physical infrastructure, for CA4FTA the policy-making infrastructure, and for CAFTA a lop-sided market access opportunity as part of a global competitiveness strategy. Therefore, while the PPP spells out projects, CA4FTA seeks an appropriate trade/investment playing field first, and CAFTA single-mindedly seeks a simple agreement, as a pre-requisite to a possible FTAA. Through negotiations, CA4FTA has descended from the high-road seeking human betterment to the realistic route of balancing costs and benefits, and adjusting distinctive policy-making traditions and imperatives; PPP shows less dynamism than before in its implementation stage; while CAFTA's liberalizing effects on Central American states serve as a façade towards forging a single hemispheric market. As with the US, Canada is upbeat about FTAA; while Mexico prefers an exclusive NAFTA-based US relationship over an inclusive FTAA.

Finally, were any of these forms of integration premised upon national plans? Canada's was not, Mexico had at best a sporadic one fluctuating not only to the different party in power but also to whimsical directions of Washington-based policies, while only the US made it a necessity for all countries. Eventually, these would further consolidate the US place on the Central American saddle, as the plans would specify the institutions around which future economic policies, debates, and developments would cluster.

VIEW FROM THE IVORY TOWER

How do these developments align with the theoretical propositions outlined earlier? What do they predict for forthcoming developments? Some of the functions of the pre-pre-negotiations and the pre-negotiations stages were identified, as Table 3.11 highlights. In Berman's/Zartman's conceptualization, all three forms of integration fulfilled the diagnostic phase: the problem was identified and a diagnosis made. It now remained for a broad formula and nitty-gritty details to be worked out. In turn, these predicted a future of exchanges and negotiations. Even though these were some of the most stable outcomes one could predict in a region blasted by war, hatred, and natural calamities, they still remain exposed to unpredictabilities, as the onset of 9/11 would prove, especially for Mexico.

Table 3.11. Integrative Background and Negotiations Theory

Stages	PPP	CA4FTA	CAFTA
Pre-pre-negotiations			
a. *Identify problems*	a. identifying less development in the south	a. humanitarian/ development needs	a. hemispheric market
b. *Consider options*	b. go solo, use multilateral institutions	b. go solo, use multilateral institutions	b. induce Central American states
Pre-negotiations			
a. *Communicate*	a. Propose bilateral & multilateral projects	a. Through MOU; then Pettigrew's initiation of rounds	a. Bush's OAS speech in January 2002
b. *Make commitments*	b. Specify especially funding	b. Through MOU and Pettigrew's initiation	b. Ministerial meeting in January 2003

CONCLUSIONS

Even though they converged upon economic integration, no matter what type, Canada, Mexico, and the US came from quite different directions, with dissimilar motivations, and with unique intensities. Whether they converged on the negotiation table or over project implementation or not, several observations may be made and lessons drawn.

Observations

At least four observations vie for attention. First, whether they were identifying problems or exploiting opportunities made a difference in their approaches: If they were exploiting opportunities more than identifying problems, as Canada and US were, they still have to face those problems at some future point, simply because an uneven playing field left them better off at the start, but did not soften the inherent asymmetry. If they were identifying problems more than exploiting opportunities, such as Mexico was, their willingness to bury any past hatchets augurs well for future cooperation, not necessarily for this particular integrative effort, but any other.

Second, size matters, not just in implementing policies, but also in formulating them. Only the United States could see the end-point at the start, but more than that, even as a latecomer, it skewed Canadian engagement and Mexican initiatives just by joining the pack, thus casting a shadow over the fate and future viability of both CA4FTA and PPP.

Third, at least in the preliminary stages, exclusiveness more than inclusiveness characterized negotiations. This is consistent with regional integration theory in which elitism occupies a salient place.[42] Yet, it is not in harmony with the FTAA's inclusion of civil society in the negotiations. There is a fine line between keeping negotiations clandestine until the details are agreed upon and opening the entire process to public scrutiny. No attempt was made to define a legitimate line, and the preponderant tendency of pulling shutters over the public view left much to be desired.

Fourth, no prior or conscious attempt was made to iron out the tussle between coordination and competitiveness, not only within each set of negotiations but also between the three sets, with the result of force closing more than facilitating negotiations: CA4FTA got off to a perfunctory rather than pragmatic start since Canada's developmentalist approach was humanitarian and CA states saw more illusions than nitty-gritties; CAFTA was too single-minded to even be ready to face the multiple intricacies of negotiations of this sort produce; and PPP had a whimsical pillar resulting in its post- 9/11 waywardness.

Better agenda coordination may have produced more effective negotiations. Even between the three sets, there was the glaring neglect of the FTAA impulse. All three countries were conscious of Central America being a part of broader FTAA targets, yet with the exception of the US, no other explicit attempts were made to coordinate individual country efforts with the two other countries. Mexico came close to doing so with PPP, relying as it did on multilateral institutions and seeking a bridge into the heartland of US policy-making networks. Neither attempts were realistic enough to work; and indeed a greater dosage of realism may have pushed each of the three dominating negotiating partners more decisively on to the negotiating table. As Chapter 5 elaborates, both Feinberg's CMM and HD did not function as purely as he intended them, or as he witnessed them perform in Miami during December 1994; but neither were they abjectly rejected.

Both the pre-pre-negotiations and pre-negotiations stages also alert us to how crises and turning points are interpreted differently over Central America in Ottawa, Mexico City, and Washington, DC. For Canada, Hurricane Mitch constituted a crisis, albeit a humanitarian one consistent with Canadian foreign policy principles; for Mexico the crisis was as much global industrial restructuring producing negative domestic results as the absence of sufficient southern cooperation producing developmental obstacles; and for the US the crisis was simply the need to lock-in hemispheric markets in the increasingly cut-throat global competitiveness.

Not surprisingly, the turning points were also interpreted differently. Canada's routine FTA with Costa Rica spawned other Central American countries to propose one of their own, which Canada took up earnestly, and especially as at the Québec FTAA summit, it promoted its leadership credentials. This gesture clearly led to the formulation of trade relations and agreements.

Fox's presidential elections constituted Mexico's turning point, although Central American infrastructural development was also a previous PRI priority. By the same token, 9/11 proved to be another turning point, preventing the formula from proceeding to the detail phase. The lack of a single precise turning point also indicates the lack of a single-minded goal, and obviously prelude to slippages in the negotiation processes. Whereas Canadian and Mexican turning points were triggered from within the bilateral relations, that is endogenously, the US turning point emerged from exogenously driven opportunities to utilize Central America to safeguard US security interests; and to acquire greater market accesses to remain globally competitive. Neither of these were discrete events like Canada's or Mexico's, or translated into specific policy pursuits or projects. Instead, they produced a broad FTA policy objective consummated in the fastest possible time, indicating the presence of that single-mindedness absent in Canadian and Mexican approaches.

Lessons

At least four lessons may be drawn. First, a distinction is helpful between negotiations which are results-oriented, such as Mexico's and the US's, and those which are exploratory, much as Canada's tended to be. For effective conclusion, the first type needs to begin by placing all cards up-front on the table: The US fulfilled this more convincingly than Mexico. The second necessitates greater motivational and mundane factors to sustain expectations: Canada continues to be bedeviled on this front.

Second, models permit not just a sum of the various segments, but also sketch *a posteriori* space, that is, interpreted practically, they create forward momentum. For example, we get insights on motivations, while anticipation is encouraged, ultimately breeding that awfully important predictive function. That rocky roads lie ahead in each of the three instances may already be deduced, and how these may be ironed out captures our attention far ahead of time, possibly before policy-makers take them into reckoning.

Third, in turn, models help us interpret negotiations with greater length, breadth, and depth. By creating new dimensions of analysis, we not only add more information and knowledge to our stock, but we also introduce greater order. That these are applied to relative newcomers to FTAs across Central America also speaks of the elasticity in model application.

Finally, asymmetry speaks louder than words. Central American states typify less developed countries generally, negotiating a free trade agreement:

There is too much optimism, too little, if any, resort to kinky behavior,[43] and thereby rather superficial bargaining. More emphasis is placed on reputation-enhancement through great power association than modality-adjustments negotiations of this type ultimately need. If that is an early signal of either a failed or suboptimal outcome, then we must factor such responses into the model. Thus strategies could be distinguished from each other based on how abstract or pragmatic the targeted goals are. We could then measure the impact of asymmetry more accurately, comparing with negotiations on a more symmetrically oriented table, hypothesizing, for example, abstractions to be more a part of asymmetrical negotiations than symmetrical, and pragmatism the other way around. Which moves more effectively would be the next measurement.

NOTES

1. Government of Canada, Department of Foreign Affairs and International Trade, "Initial strategic environmental assessment report of the Canada-Central American Four Free Trade Negotiations (El Salvador, Guatemala, Honduras, and Nicaragua)," June 18, 2003, from: http://www.dfait-maeci.gc.ca/tna-nac(IYT/ea0423-en.asp

2. John Newcomb, "Comment on Canada-Central America free trade proposal," January 9, 2001, from: http://www.csf.colorado.edu/forums/elan/2001/msg00022.htm

3. International Monetary Fund, *Direction of Trade Statistics Yearbook 2000* (Washington, DC: International Monetary Fund, 2001), various pages.

4. Mexico's figures from International Monetary Fund, *Direction of Trade Statistics Yearbook, September 2001* (Washington, DC: International Monetary Fund, 2001), 180. Even with lesser volumes traded, a similar Mexican surplus pattern prevailed in at least the five previous years, with a low of about $600m in 1995 and a high of $1b in 1998. See I.M.F., *Direction of Trade Statistics Yearbook*, 2000, 326.

5. J. F. Hornbeck, "The U.S.-Central America Free Trade Agreement (CAFTA): challenges for sub-regional integration," *Congressional Research Service*, Report, April 25, 2003, 20.

6. On this point, see Cheryl L. Eschbach, "Mexico's relations with Central America:changing priorities, persisting interest," *Mexico's External Relations in the 1990s*, ed. Riordan Roett (Boulder, CO: Lynne Rienner, 1991), 172–77.

7. Eschbach, op. cit., 184. Exports of Guatemala fell by 23%, Nicaragua's by 42%, and El Salvador's by 54% during the 1980s.

8. The 1965 Canada-US Auto Pact often symbolizes the prospects of sectoral integration. See Charles Pentland, *International Theory and European Integration: Studies in International Politics* (London: Macmillan, 1973).

9. The Spanish acronym of CABEI, BICE, is more commonly used in the literature.

10. The Protocol is supported by over 222 treaties, and SICA is chaired by the presidents of the various countries. See Luis G. Solis and Patricia Solano, "Central

America:the difficult road towards integration and the role of Canada," *FOCAL Policy Paper*, May 2001.

11. Hornbeck, op. cit.

12. From Government of Guatemala, *National Action Plan*, 12–13.

13. Daniel Lederman, Guillermo Perry, Rodrígo Suescún, "Trade structure, trade policy and economic policy options in Central America," Paper (Washington, DC: World Bank, November 2002), 1–2, 7.

14. This is not to say it is insignificant or inconsequential. As Coatsworth contends, at the time of the El Salvador-Honduras July 1969 soccer war, of the 300,000 Salvadoreans living in Honduras in abusive conditions, almost one-third were literally kicked back to El Salvador, in fact to even worse refugee camp living. Another casualty of the war was CACM, which was just about ready to shift from the import substitution phase to developing integrated intermediate and heavy industries. See *Clients and the Colossus*, 126–28.

15. Lederman, Perry, & Suescún, op. cit., 25–26.

16. Sebastian Edwards details this period in *Crisis and Reform in Latin America: From Despair to Hope* (New York: Oxford University Press, for IBRD, 1995).

17. Although the US is the world's largest provider of TCB funds, TCB is not an exclusive US instrument (or even initiative). It stemmed from the relationship between trade and development made at the World Trading Organization's (WTO's) November 2001 Doha ministerial meeting in Qatar. As part and parcel of the Doha Development Agenda, TCB is spelled out by paragraphs 41–43 of the Doha Ministerial Declaration—providing specific technical assistance and capacity building commitments to a wide variety of policies, from trade to competition to intellectual property rights; and the creation of an Integrated Framework for Trade-Related Technical Assistance to Least Developed Countries. By 2003, the US provided $752m TCB funds, up from $369m in 1999; and although they strengthen the supply-side approach to development, at least they are mobilizing some very undeveloped countries, as across Central America, to make some much-needed structural and institutional changes. Several civil society groups oppose CA4FTA, CAFTA, and PPP for precisely this supply-side flavor: It hurts rural communities, the impoverished, and women. Across Central America, they argue, 60% of the people live in the countryside, and two-thirds of them live in poverty, or even as high as Nicaragua's three-quarters; one-third of the poor, that is, about 13% of the overall population, are indigenous; and 8–10m rural households are headed by women. Emigration provides one escape, availed of by almost one-quarter of a million people each year; while other groups engage in the endemic growth of gang-related activities. CA4FTA, CAFTA, and PPP, they further argue, not only divert resources from the countryside, but also reduces local producer prices for grains, dairy, and pork, which hurt CA farmers as much as they help US counterparts. All figures from Glass, op. cit. See Office of US Trade Representative, Office of Trade Capacity Building, *U.S. Contributions to Trade Capacity Building: Improving Lives Through Trade & Aid* (Washington, DC: USTR, September 2003).

18. Government of Costa Rica, Tratado de Libre Comercio entre Centroamerica y Estados Unídos y Agencía Integral de Cooperación, *U.S.-Central America Free Trade Agreement Integral Cooperation Agenda: Conceptual Proposal for a National Action*

Plan (San José, CR: Government of Costa Rica, December 2002); Government of El Salvador, *National Action Plan for Trade Capacity Building*; Government of Guatemala, *National Action Plan for Trade Capacity Building in Guatemala*; Government of Honduras, *U.S.-Central Free Trade Agreement (US-CAFTA): National Action Plan for Trade Capacity Building: Honduras* (Tegucipalga: Government of Honduras, June 2003); and Government of Nicaragua, *Operational Program for the National Action Plan for Institutional Strengthening: Republic of Nicaragua* (Managua: Government of Nicaragua, December 2002).

19. In fact, all CA countries negotiating a FTA with the United States were required by a National Action Plan guidance paper of October 3, 2002 to submit their plans along three dimensions: (a) trade negotiation preparation and participation, (b) trade agreement implementation, and (c) transition to free trade. Not only that, but the US provided $47m to prepare these plans (figure is from Hornbeck, op. cit., 12), in addition to support from the private sector, IADB, BICE, ECLAC, IBRD, and OAS — a network of such importance in bringing state and society together with multilateral institutions, I analyze their impact in greater detail in Chapter 5.

20. Marc Edelman and Rodolfo Monge Oviedo, "Costa Rica:non-market roots of market-access," *Free Trade and Economic Restructuring in Latin America*, eds. Fred Rosen and Deidre McFadyen (New York: Monthly Review Press for North American Congress on Latin America, 1995), ch. 5.

21. Government of Costa Rica, *National Action Plan*, 10–11.

22. John D. Abell, "Coffee production and sustainable development: San Lucas Tolimán, Guatemala," *LASA Forum* 35, no. 2 (Summer 2004):5–7.

23. See Pierro Gleíjesos, "Guatemala crises and response," *The Future of Central America: Policy Choices for the U.S. and Mexico*, eds. Richard R. Fagen and Olga Pellicer (Stanford, CA: Stanford University Press, 1983), 187–212; and Adolfo Aguilar Zinser, "Mexico and the Guatemalan crisis," ibid., 161–86.

24. Government of Costa Rica, *National Action Plan*, 12, footnote.

25. Government of Guatemala, *National Action Plan*, 31.

26. *National Power and the Structure of Trade* (Berkeley, CA: University of California Press, 1981).

27. Zinser, op. cit., 162–63, but see 161–86.

28. EKOS, "Canadian attitudes toward international trade:survey findings," May 6, 2003, pages not numbered from: http://www.ekos.com

29. All figures from Canadian Gazette, "Canada-Central American Four free trade agreement negotiations:consultations on trade negotiations with the Central American countries of El Salvador, Guatemala, Honduras and Nicaragua," January 6, 2001, from: http://www.dfait-maeci.gc.ca/tna-nac/ca-gazette-notice-6jan01.en.asp

30. Government of Canada, Department of Foreign Affairs and International Trade, Trade Negotiations and Agreements, "Initial strategic environmental assessment report on the Canada-Central American Four free trade negotiations (El Salvador, Guatemala, Honduras and Nicaragua)," June 18, 2003, from: http://www.dfait-maeci.gc.ca/tna-nac/IYT/ecn0423-en.asp

31. Greg Anderson, "Hemispheric integration in the post-Seattle era:the promise of and problems for the FTAA," *International Journal* LVI, no. 2 (Spring 2001):205–33.

32. Another was with Israel in 1997, while similar terms were included in a 1999 economic cooperation framework agreement with the Palestine Authority. See World Trade Organization, Secretariat, Trade Policy Review Body, "Trade policy review: Canada," Report, February 12, 2003, #WT/TPR/S/112, from: http://www.sice.oas .org/ctyindex/wto/canada/tprs112c_e.asp

33. International Bank for Reconstruction and Development, *Entering the 21st Century: World Development Report, 1999/2000* (Washington, DC: IBRD; 2000), various pages.

34. "Canada's Martin plans to keep up with the U.S.'s trade agreements," January 13, 2004, from: http://quote.bloomberg.com/apps/news?pid=10000082&sid=au3 .DIqR1ys4&refer=canada

35. Government of Canada, "Government response to the report of the standing committee on foreign affairs and international trade:strengthening Canada's economic links with the Americas," Catalogue # E2-474/2002. From: http://www.dfait-maeci .gc/tna-nac/Consult3-e.asp

36. Term embedded in Lawrence Whitehead, "The imposition of democracy," *Exporting Democracy: The United States and Latin America*, ed. Abraham F. Lowenthal (Baltimore, MD: The Johns Hopkins University Press, 1991), ch. 13, in particular his distinction of "democracy by imposition" into incorporation (Puerto Rico), invasion (Panama), and intimidation (Nicaragua). Historian Stephen D. Rabe's mention of "communists not dictators" being the enemies of the United States in the early 1950s, when 14 Latin states were under dictatorial regimes, is observed by Mark T. Gilderhus in *The Second Century: U.S.-Latin American Relations Since 1889* (Wilmington, DE: Scholarly Resources, Inc., 2000), 139–57. John D. Martz, in turn, sees democracy representing hypocrisy, fluctuating between wilsonian moral righteouness and "overtones of external control and economic integration" in " Democracy and the imposition of values:definitions and diplomacy," *Latin America, the United States, and the Inter-American System*, eds. Martz and Lars Schoultz (Boulder, CO: Westview Press, 1980), 155, but see ch. 6.

37. From Caribbean Latin American Action, "Strengthening the third border:2003 trade & investment forum overview," CAFTA and foreign investment—a public/ private sector partnership, CLAA trade & investment forum, Guatemala, July 22–23, 2003, from: http://www.claa.org/caftaforum_over.html

38. For a thorough discussion, Leslie Sklair, *Assembling for Development: The Maquila Industry in Mexico and the United States* (San Diego, CA: Center for US-Mexican Studies, University of California, San Diego, 1993, 2nd ed., originally 1989, by Unwin Hyman, Inc., London).

39. David Zuñiga, "Availability of cheap labor in the south does not compensate for the absence of proximity with the USA," *La Journada*, November 19, 2001, tr. Adele Olivieri, from: http://www.globalexchange.org/campaigns/mexico/ppp/journade111901 .html

40. Thesis is consistent with middle power theorists. See Louis Bélanger and Gordon Mace, "Building role and region:middle states and regionalism in the Americas," *The Americas in Transition: The Contours of Regionalism*, eds. Mace, Bélanger (Boulder, CO: Lynne Rienner, 1999), 153–74.

41. "Canada and Costa Rica . . . ," 2001

42. Joseph S. Nye, *Peace in Parts: Integration and Conflict in Regional Organization* (Boston, MA: Little & Brown, 1971), various pages.

43. Robert Putnam's term. See "Diplomacy and domestic politics:the logic of two-level games," *Double-Edged Diplomacy: International Bargaining and Domestic Politics*, eds. Peter Evans, Putnam, *et al* (Berkeley, CA: University of California Press, 1993), appendix.

Chapter Four

Sticky Feet, Tied Hands, & Cold Showers: Old Wine in New Bottle?

INTRODUCTION:
POLICY FORMULATION VERSUS IMPLEMENTATION

Since CA4FTA and CAFTA formed a series of trade policy-adjustment negotiations, and PPP focused on infrastructural project implementation, the comparative analysis comes in two parts: bilateral CA4FTA-CAFTA analysis, followed by a PPP-included trilateral. As will become evident, PPP faced fewer
endogenous problems—that is, obstacles stemming from the actual negotiation processes—but raised enormous exogenous concerns. On the other hand,
CA4FTA and CAFTA faced both endogenous and exogenous hurdles. Yet,
whereas CA4FTA regressed rapidly from high enthusiasm to inevitable deadlock, CAFTA not only survived, but was also completed in the stipulated
time, crossing those hurdles, and emerging as the pacesetter of Central American integration. Simply pointing to the wider gap between US relations with
Central American states than Canada's does not inform us why there were so
many similarities in both negotiations, and ultimately how to even explain the
relationship both had with PPP. Even though PPP emerged chronologically
earlier, by addressing CA4FTA-CAFTA first, PPP is actually understood
more comprehensively, which facilitates the trilateral comparison.

Theoretical discussions follow a similar sequence: CA4FTA-CAFTA negotiations, PPP project implementation, then a trilateral thematic evaluation.
Turning to CA4FTA-CAFTA first, having reached Brian Tomlin's negotiations phase, distinctions are made by invoking the formula-detail components
of the broader Maureen Berman-William Zartman conceptualization. Based
both on hindsight and foresight, the formula phase addresses such broad
agreements as tariff reduction, market access, treatment of agriculture, dereg-

ulating nationalized sectors, and how new industries, such as telecommunications, are dealt with. How these are interpreted for specific products, in turn, creates the detail-phase agenda.

Not all of these parameters are relevant for PPP for a number of reasons. First, many PPP goals are/were parts of Mexico's own domestic plans, so implementation does not necessitate any essential Central American input. Second, many are also projects of multilateral institutions, again dispensing the need for negotiations thresholds set by Tomlin, Berman-Zartman, and others. Third, PPP was simply overshadowed by CAFTA, that is, Central American states prioritized CAFTA imperatives over PPP counterparts. Theoretical relevance is reduced when urgency itself is minimized on the playing field. Finally, negotiations generally become more extensive and intensive with policy formulation than with project implementation. Because *a posteriori* dynamics do not involve the same range of discussions and exchanges as *a priori* dynamics, theoretical considerations also subside in relevance, although often the results of implementation provide the final theoretical word. At least in this study, above assertions hold.

Policy implementation and policy formulation are nonetheless related in more than sequential terms. Comparing and contrasting them adds perspectives, but necessitates stepping outside the negotiations domain without actually abandoning it. How Costa Rica bedeviled one set of negotiations, albeit briefly, while becoming the beauty queen of another points to a number of relevant comparative themes: wages and industrial migration; developed versus less developed country engagements in trade liberalization; and the nature of the entire societal-state-supranational nexus of inter-relationships. While these are utilized in the PPP context, CA4FTA-CAFTA-PPP comparisons address the negotiations structure; development gap; cultural styles; levels of policy-making; and exogenous affiliations.

CA4FTA-CAFTA: OF FRUITS AND FRUITFUL COMPARISONS

Apples and oranges are fruits but quite different fruits. Although CA4FTA-CAFTA negotiations began enthusiastically and purposefully, they produced quite different results, in part because the nature of negotiations varied, and in part owing to the unique treatment of Costa Rica. An amalgamation of CA state interests, influences exerted from within, and external impacts on decision-making provide useful comparative yardsticks.

Two weeks before the October 2002 San José parley, the United States began circulating the National Action Plan guidelines, which the eager CA states were required to follow: It marked the beginning of the fulfillment of their decade-long dream of deeper economic integration, while the US retracted from Bush's inaugural speech pledge of not signing any FTAs other than with Chile before a FTAA deal. Even as Chile's came through in December 2002 and CAFTA in December 2003, FTAA itself slid toward a deadlock, hastened by the failure of the WTO Cancún ministerial in September 2003;[1] and while Canada's FTAA enthusiasm spilled over into CA4FTA talks during 2002,[2] only to smoulder during 2003, before completely evaporating by July 2004. What transpired? A capstone illustration of these may be gleaned from Costa Rica's experiences.

Costa Rica: Ugly Duckling or Darling?

Costa Rica's symbolic role is evident in at least two ways: Canada's FTA negotiations with Costa Rica inspired leaders of four other CA states to propose a FTA of their own to Canada; and, according to Rigoberto Stewart, the 15-year agricultural tariff moratorium in a San José, October 16, 2002 meeting with US officials,[3] representing a Druckman turning point, inspired CAFTA negotiations themselves. Yet, Costa Rica refrained from accepting CAFTA in December 2003—and would wait a full month, without obtaining any concession, before signing, raising questions about some of the endogenous obstacles deliberately sidelined just to get an agreement within the US time-frame. On the other hand, as the most developed CA state, Costa Rica automatically appealed to Canada, but the agreement, signed just after the FTAA Québec summit in April 2001, raised questions about DC-LDC trade agreements, particularly slowing ratification in Costa Rica.[4] By the same token, however, Costa Rican interest groups threatened both CA4FTA and CAFTA, demonstrating a veto power as formidable as Costa Rica is more developed than other Central American countries.[5] Costa Rican responses encapsulate societal, statist, and external interests.

Comparative Negotiations: Down to the Wire

In providing the backbone of discussions, Table 4.1 lists the various rounds of negotiations for both CA4FTA and CAFTA. Table 4.2 similarly profiles the coordination meetings of CAFTA. We learn how CAFTA negotiations were more open, at least in that more press conferences were rallied, than CA4FTA, and considerably greater volumes of pertinent information were made available to the public than for CA4FTA. Nevertheless, and this is fundamental, even CAFTA was shrouded with secrecy, public engagements littered with evasive responses,[6] and too many documents were shifted "for foreign policy and security reasons" to an untouchable category.[7] The Table 4.1

snapshot of the full picture of each set of negotiations is comparable, though round-by-round negotiations obviously are not. A quick rundown of each set of negotiations highlights the central features: agriculture, textiles, labor, and telecommunications concerns were common to both; but whereas CAFTA overcame these, CA4FTA could not. Following an overview of CA4FTA and CAFTA, this chapter turns specifically to how each of these four economic sectors were treated, followed by comments on the impacts of the environment and the power-policy relationship, before concluding with the end-products of the negotiations.

Table 4.1. Comparative Observations from Two Sets of Talks

Round	CA4FTA	CAFTA
First	• San Salvador, El Salvador, from December 9, 2001: Issues brought to the table here were business facilitation, safeguards, rules of origins, and customs procedures; Costa Rica's INCAE's Danilo Lacayo optimistic of FTA by mid-2002, implemented by 2003	• San José, Costa Rica, January 27, 2003: Time-table and agenda set, wide-ranging discussion held, negotiation groups meet, and third party agreements (with Mexico and Chile) discussed
Second	• Managua, Nicaragua, February 11–15, 2002: market access, governmental procurements, institutional dispositions, and dispute settlement	• Cincinnati, OH, February 24–28, 2003: Disagreements raised, but not resolved; detailed negotiation group discussions; no US agreements on agriculture, labor rights, and telecommunications
Third	• Ottawa, April 8–12, 2002: Issues considered include competitiveness, market access, rules of origins, customs procedures, governmental procurement, investment and services, sanitary and phytosanitary measures	• San Salvador, El Salvador, March 31–April 4, 2003: Convergences and divergences specified; US proposes Dominican Republic and Panama as docking stations with CAFTA, and export subsidies; discussions on textiles and rules of origins; and agriculture
Fourth	• Guatemala City, July 15–19: Lacayo estimates 70% of the agreement already completed; issues discussed market access, investment and services, settling disputes, institutional dispositions	• Antigua, Guatemala, May 12–16, 2003: Decision taken to enforce labor laws even if they violate human rights, and lift farm tariffs over 5–12 years; market access introduced: Guatemala opens up 78–81%, as opposed to 72% by others; Central America's tariff preference level (TPL) on textiles; all proposals on table

(continued)

Table 4.1.   *(Continued)*

Round	CA4FTA	CAFTA
Fifth	• Tegucipalga, Honduras, October 7–11: Optimism leads El Salvador's Eduardo Ayala Grimaldi to predict conclusion by March 2003	• Tegucigalpa, Honduras, June 16–20: US proposes market access; 70% agreement, 30% without consensus (textiles, agriculture)
Sixth	• San Salvador, El Salvador, December 4–6, 2002: continued discussions of 4th Round issues	• New Orleans, LA, July 28–Aug. 1: More discussion on market access, intellectual property rights and government procurements; and labor & environment
Seventh	• Ottawa, Canada, January 20–24, 2003: issues discussed include market access, government procurement, and 2 parallel accords; Lacayo contends 70% of FTA complete, 80% on market access	• Managua, Nicaragua, September 15–19: US refuses call to eliminate subsidies, but agrees to 15–year protection of sensitive products, creating 5 baskets; textiles ignored, to Nicaragua's chagrin
Eighth	• Managua, Nicaragua, March 3–8, 2003: Discussions on private sector, civil society; *Confederación de Trabajadores de Nicaragua* (CTN) participation; governmental procurement, dispute settlement, rules of origins, financial servcies, telecommunications, and investment also discussed	• Houston, October 20–24:Central Americans unsuccessfully seek inclusion of immigration and workers rights
Ninth	• Ottawa: July 2–5, 2003: Not the expected final round; textiles, agriculture, and labor remain unsettled	• Washington, DC, December 8–12: Agreement reached by all but Costa Rica on CAFTA
Tenth	• Ottawa, February 16–20, 2004: Services & investment discussed; progress on labor; agreements still pending on textiles, sugar, meats, and exemptions	• Agreement with Costa Rica, January 27, 2004
Eleventh	• Guatemala, June 2004: Expected to be the final round before negotiations were postponed indefinitely	• Signature, May 28, 2004

Overview

Since CA4FTA talks began in San Salvador on December 9, 2001, almost one dozen rounds were held in the different capitals until the Canadian government decided to indefinitely postpone further negotiations in June 2004. Scanning through the issues discussed, one is struck by how identical they are with CAFTA. They are also prescribed by the FTAA. Yet, as the Honduran

Table 4.2.   CAFTA Coordination Meetings

Rounds	Dates	Venues
1st	January 15–16, 2003	El Salvador
2nd	February 18–19	Costa Rica
3rd	March 18–19	Guatemala
4th	April 19–30	Honduras
5th	June 3–4	Nicaragua
6th	July 15–16	Costa Rica
7th	August 26–27	El Salvador
8th	October 7–8	Guatemala
9th	November 25–26	Honduras

ambassador to Canada, Ana Carolina Galeano, observed, the differences can be both subtle and stark. She called the negotiations not only "our rehearsal for the trade agreement with the United States," but also predicted a draft agreement by March 2003.[8] She was not alone in her optimism. Nicaraguan Professor of Business at Costa Rica's prestigious Central American Institute for Business Administration (INCAE),[9] Danilo Lacayo, and El Salvador's Director of Trade Policy, later Vice Minister of Economics, Eduardo Ayala Grímaldi, also publicly pointed to an early 2003 completion, the latter during the first round, then again during the seventh, the former during the fifth. CA4FTA negotiations took a left-turn by the seventh round. The causes were the same mundane endogenous hurdles CAFTA would sideline, but which Canada wanted to face head-on: agricultural, textiles imports, labor concerns, among others.

Empirically, Galeana's comment encapsulates a general Central American attitude: Canada was too remote for immediate economic gratification, there was just too little of trade to extract economic mileage, whatever was traded with Canada could by and large be obtained from or provided to the United States, and the most important Canadian contribution would be to spur US into greater than expected concessions. The interesting theoretical implication is the notion of leverage across entirely different negotiation tables: Could negotiating with Canadians, as Central Americans hoped for in a panglossian world, enhance the value of Central American bargaining chips on the CAFTA table? Of course, the answer turned out to be negative, but at least a theoretical possibility not sufficiently addressed in the literature was raised.[10] Yet, the flip-side argument is equally plausible: Instead of extracting advantages by leveraging one conference with another, a participating country, especially if it is relatively weaker, can also free-ride the results of another conference it has participated in. As becomes obvious, Central American states could not profit from leveraging and did not have sustained interest in CA4FTA to free-ride CAFTA negotiations to the fullest extent possible.

Similarly, Canada had the clearest opportunity to free-ride CAFTA, since CA4FTA rested upon the same FTAA disciplines, but settled instead behind some unwavering domestic interests.

Blemishes were not a part of CAFTA. Negotiations were predetermined from the outset: there would be nine rounds, to conclude in December 2003. The agenda for each round thus became meaningless, in fact, no specific issue would be pushed unless Central American countries persisted on it, even if the issues were sensitive, such as textiles or agriculture.[11] Whereas CA4FTA negotiators focused on specific issues in such detail, they could not predict the next step; this was regardless whether they were optimistic, as at the beginning, or pessimistic, as towards the end. By contrast, even when specific issues came up in CAFTA, the responses were evasive, not just by one negotiator, but by them all. As previously noted, CAFTA negotiators engaged in press conferences, CA4FTA negotiators did not. Yet, the outcome was more similar than not: rhetoric and evasion in the former kept journalists still guessing at the end, which is hardly an improvement from not having any press conferences in the first place.

Table 4.1 shows the critical issues of agriculture, textiles, and labor entered CA4FTA negotiations later than CAFTA's. It was not until the 9th Round in Ottawa, during early July 2003, that they dominated the CA4FTA agenda, but with CAFTA, agriculture and labor were on the table in the 2nd Round in Cincinnati, from February 24 to 28, 2003; and textiles entered the picture in the very next round, held in San Salvador between March 31 and April 4. Thereafter, labor and agriculture were always on the CAFTA agenda, but discussions over textiles were delayed or deferred by the United States, particularly in the 7th Round in Managua, Nicaragua, during mid-September. Castigating CAFTA "a shot-gun wedding," Katherine Stecher of the Nicaragua Network, one of the many participants of the opposition CAFTA Coalition, argues how benefits would accrue, not for US family farms, but only US agribusiness. Similar provisions in NAFTA, she argues, lowered average farm incomes 43% in the US between 1993 and 2001, 19% in Canada between 1989 and 1998, and 15m Mexican small farms were actually shut down under NAFTA during a similar duration—all predicting even worse conditions for Central America, especially for Nicaragua where over 40% of the people still live in farms, three-quarters of them in abject poverty.[12]

How these issues were treated confirms contrasting orientations: Canada did not escape the issues, but neither did it budge from its positions; while the US deferred or de-emphasized discussion over the issues in favor of other issues, yet still managed an agreement. The US was to adopt a similar stance over CA desires to include immigration and workers rights on the agenda in the 8th Round at Houston during late October:[13] Each was raised, each was heard, and each was ignored in the final analysis.

What about the specific issues not rejected from discussions? As with the United States, Canada shelters its farmers behind a wide array of defensive mechanisms, such as price supports, from cheaper imports. These were on the line in any trade agreement with agriculture exporting LDCs. With textiles, however, Canada's angle of concern was different from the US. US interest groups sought to protect fibers from cheaper imports, whereas Canada depended on fibers from many other parts of the world, such as India, streamlining its domestic multicultural and diversified international leadership policy outlooks—thus faces possible CA4FTA threats.

Telecommunications proved to be another sticky issue in both negotiations, but like labor, would be subordinated to other issues in CA4FTA, whereas CAFTA was almost derailed by Costa Rica over telecommunications. As a competitive US sector, it threatened Costa Rica's sheltered industry, but more critically, invoked vested interests whose growth was possible by Costa Rica remaining more stable and developed than counterpart Central American states.

Labor negotiations create problems, particularly when wage differentials persist, and while suspicion is to be found on all sides, both Canada and the US, as well as Central American states, Canada proved more respectful of labor principles than any of the others, but US papering over labor rights probably elicited more Central American approval than would otherwise have been the case. A similar set of stances was evident over the environment, with Canada stuck on the principles, US relegating it as far from the table as was possible, in spite of producing more reams of required studies on it, and Central American states aligning more with the US than Canada. Finally, in terms of the influence of power over policy results, the US took more credit than Canada. The results sections connects some of these observations and draws comparative conclusions.

Agriculture

Agricultural discussions revolve around tables 4.3 and 4.4, the former listing how the US treats farm imports from five Central American countries, the latter identifying the agreements made. In addition, domestic legislative implications represent the third issue addressed in this subsection. In terms of farm import treatment, several types are identified: (a) tariff rate quotas, (b) existing US support programs, (c) export subsidies, if any; (d) products listed by the US as being sensitive; (e) tariffs; (f) affected Central American country products; (g) Nicaraguan tariffs; and (h) US imports. Not all of these types of US treatment are relevant for each Central American country.

The tariff rate quotas (TRQs) were adopted after the Uruguay Round to convert non-tariff barriers (like quotas) into tariffs, with a provision to establish a market access threshold for those products at 3% of domestic

Table 4.3.   US Treatment of Central American Farm Products

Country	US Treatment
Costa Rica	• TRQs on pork, poultry, dairy, beef, rice, corn, beans, sugar, tobacco • US support program for dairy, rice, corn, sugar, and tobacco • Receives US export subsidies: dairy, sugar, and tobacco • Costa Rican rice producers heavily threatened, as too beans producers • US tariffs possible on sugar related products, melons
El Salvador	• TRQs threaten beef, dairy products, yellow corn, vegetable oils, sugar, tobacco • Sensitive products for US: rice, wheat, corn, poultry, beans • Problems for El Salvador over maize, rice, and beans • US imports: coffee, sugar
Guatemala	• TRQs threaten maize, rice, sugar, tobacco, dairy, fruits (apples, pears, grapes), sorghum, soya • Tariffs on melons • Big problems for Guatemala over maize and rice
Honduras	• No US TRQ threats • US Tariffs on rice • Problems for Honduras over maize • US imports: coffee and bananas
Nicaragua	• TRQs on maize, rice, sorghum, vegetable oil, beans, beef, poultry, milk, sugar • Nicaragua places tariffs on maize, sorghum, rice • Nicaragua not in top-thirty of US export market, and is least dependent on US farm market

Source: Dale Hathaway, "The impacts of US agricultural and trade policy on trade liberalization and integration via a US-Central American free trade agreement," Background paper, Seminar on "Agricultural liberalization and integration," by Inter-American Development Bank, October 2002.

consumption. Except for Honduras, every country has a list of products, some of them, as shown under Costa Rica's case, listed on the US support program. These become sensitive if imports cross the agreed-upon limit, invoking tariffs; and some US exports, like dairy, sugar, and tobacco, receive subsidies. Of these, sugar poses a huge problem, which is why its subsidy levels were not cut under CAFTA. In fact, increased sugar market access for Central America in the first year would only tantamount to one day's production of the US sugar industry,[14] that is about 1.2% of US sugar production and 1.1% of sugar consumption— growing over fifteen years to only 1.7% of production and 1.6% of consumption. The US would establish TRQs at 99,000 metric tons (MT) in the first year, growing to 140,000 in fifteen years. In spite of these safeguards, sugar producers were willing to shift party allegiances during the 2004 presidential campaign if protections were not preserved. Sugar was not the decisive reason for the way two swing states voted in the 2004 US presidential elections, Florida went to the Republicans and Minnesota's delegates went to Kerry while congressmen were divided equally by the two parties. Nevertheless, sugar generated political heat.

Table 4.4. CAFTA'S Agricultural Tariff Elimination

Product	Tariff Elimination Timeframe (yrs)	Immediate Action	Tariff Rate Quotas (TRQs)	WTO Binding Range	USA Action
Beef	15	Prime and choice cuts	Only if WTO TRQ fits	35–79% (15–30%)	26% to be eliminated in 15 years
Pork	15	Bacon	Base: 9,450 metric tons (MT), grow 5–15% yearly	35–60% (15–47%)	Zero tariffs
Poultry	18 for chicken legs (CR)		21,810 MT (or 5% of regional poultry production), CR: 300MT	35–250% (1641%)	Zero tariffs exist
Dairy	20		(10% a year)6,000 MT reciprocally	35–100% (up to 60%	(60% reduction over 20-yr
Vegetables	All eliminated (except CR fresh onions); various phase-outs	Selective products		3–60% (15%)	
Fruits	Up to 10 years (mixed concentrates; oranges)	Selective products (majority of them by far)		20–60% (15%)	
Peas & Beans	5–15	Selective		25–110% (5–20%)	Zero tariffs exist
Potatoes	15	Selective types		25–60% (15%)	
Wheat & Barley	15 on wheat flour	US lock-ins		35–60%	

Table 4.4. (*Continued*)

Product	Tariff Elimination Timeframe (yrs)	Immediate Action	Tariff Rate Quotas (TRQs)	WTO Binding Range	USA Action
Corn & corn products	15	Immediate for CR	TRQs to be established, with base from 65,000 for Nicaragua to 500,000 for Guatemala	15–75%	Zero tariffs exist
Rice	18 (20 for CR)		TRQs to be established, range: 50,000 CR	35–90 (15–60)	Zero tariffs exist
Sugar	15		97,000 MT growing to 140,000 in 15th year, thereafter 2% annually		100% out-of- quota will not be cut
Tobacco					US export subsidies to be eliminated in 15 years; US tariffs: 15-yr phase-out
Cotton	Duty-free lock-ins				15-yr phase-out of tariffs

Source: US Trade Representative, "CAFTA agriculture-specific fact sheet," from USTR homepage.

"They can't be producing sugar," Minnesotan farmer Terry Vipond contended about Central American states, "with no environmental laws and labor laws and expect us to compete with that." Charlie Melancon, a Louisiana sugar farmer, was more succinct in this belief: "Every candidate is running away from CAFTA because of the sugar vote. . . ."[15]

CAFTA's treatment of selected products is elaborated in Table 4.4, indicating the WTO binding range and US-specific action. Many products will enter duty-free regimes after fifteen years, some, such as Costa Rican rice over 18–20 years and dairy over 20 years. A number of products will immediately have duty-free status, as shown in the third column, for example, bacon in the pork row, and selective fruits and vegetables. The fourth column indicates the present TRQ thresholds, and the expected future changes, while the fifth column gives the WTO ranges on these TRQs, both in terms of prescription (top line) and practiced (second line). Finally, the last column indicates how, for the US, a number of products are already at zero tariff levels (pork, poultry, peas and beans, corn and corn products, and rice), while others receiving protection will not change significantly (sugar), be slowly marketized (dairy, beef), or be completely eliminated (tobacco, cotton).

CAFTA is clearer than CA4FTA on how agriculture negotiations moved from the formula phase to the detail phase. By the end of the 4th Round, the areas without consensus remained largely in agriculture, textiles, and selectively distributed market access privileges across Central America.[16] Since agriculture poses both problems of market access for US exports and US protection from imports, it exposes how the uniform agricultural approach the US seeks in trade negotiations rarely, if ever, addresses the specific concerns of each negotiating partner. Table 4.3 lists the US TRQs valid for each of the five Central American countries, as well as sensitive products, that is products threatened by significant imports, and US exports likely to threaten Central American countries. Also listed are US imports subjected to sanitary and phytosanitary (SPS) and technical barriers to trade (TBT) restrictions, imposed mostly on CA poultry and beef products. In addition to exposing the country-wide variations, a common CA problem is also evident: detrimental consequences from liberalizing these products. Trade negotiations resemble a time-bomb. On the one hand are US demands for market access and defenses against imports, on the other are the considerably weaker Central American capacities to sustain their own market access demands of the US and defenses against US exports. The result, while small CA producers "could be wiped out," and large farms "could go bankrupt," US dumping would have the same effect as NAFTA on Mexico, pushing it "from a large agricultural producer," to the "largest importer of US basic grains in Latin America"—a fate imperiling the lives of 2.5m Mexican corn producers, for example.[17]

During the WTO Cancún ministerial breakdown in September 2003, two members from the US Senate Finance Committee, its chairman Charles Grassley and ranking member Max Baucus, unambiguously stated they would take a "dim view" of countries not playing a "constructive role" in those negotiations —a direct threat to Costa Rica and Guatemala, both members of the G-21 resisting US demands in Cancún, and to other Latin members in that coalition. Grassley and Baucus had their own CAFTA concern and expectation. "Central American negotiators are making unrealistic demands regarding market access," they proposed, "barriers imposed on U.S. farm products—including beef, pork corn, wheat, and soybeans—should be eliminated as soon as possible, and preferable immediately." At the same time, cautioning CA against greater sugar exports to the US, they noted "Central American countries indicate to us an unwillingness to engage in a fully constructive manner. . ."[18] Although the US refused to concede on subdizing agriculture at the 7th Round in Managua, it agreed to place sensitive products in a 15-year time-frame. Nevertheless, US sugar producers were not happy then,[19] as their bipartisan elected representatives, Neil Abercombie (D, HI), Allen Boyd (D, FL), Ben Cardin (D, MD), Ed Case (D, HI), Eliot Engel (D, NY), Mark Foley (R, FL), Alcee L. Hastings (D, FL), Adam Putnam (R, FL), indicated. Shrimp producers were also not happy at the 8th Round in New Orleans, one of the US headquarters of the shrimp industry.[20] Their clout is not shrimp-sized. After CAFTA had been signed, the US imposed stiff tariffs on imports from China and Vietnam (112%), Brazil (67%), India (27%), Thailand (10.2%), and Ecuador (9%), even though 87% of all the shrimps it consumes are imported.[21]

As previously observed (a) Central American states are likely to face greater impacts over CAFTA's farm treatment than their US counterparts, simply owing to the huge economic asymmetries and wide disparities in living and other social conditions; and (b) with more products at the duty-free level, especially with wheat, corn, and rice, the US leverage to open markets in other countries over other products increases. This second observation clearly makes US agriculture a broader trade policy instrument. Canada's agricultural orientation is similar, but the external power it wields is considerably less than in the United States.

Textiles

Two problems emerged from negotiating textiles, one generic to the negotiations, the other textile-specific: the former was evasiveness in reporting progress about the negotiations to reporters, the latter over cumulation. Whereas evasiveness created, by and large, a sense of identity among the negotiators, cumulation revealed how divided the US textiles industry was over CAFTA.

Over textiles, we learned nothing more than the bland statements of purpose. Chief US negotiator, Regina Vargo, hoped "the entire region will operate under one textile regime in terms of the rules of origins . . . . This will be a subject of negotiation, frankly, not only here in the region, but back in the United States as well between our very many different interests along the production and distribution and retail spectrum . . . ." When asked for specifics, Vargo continued to skillfully evade them. Over a purported Central American division over duty-free access, one reporter asked Vargo how the US interpreted the absence of a 100% consensus. "That's again the type of question that involves a large amount of hypothetical . . . . So I guess my answer at this point is just 'We'll keep talking and working on it'." Talked and worked they did to produce the agreement, yet translating the details into practice proved quite different from converting formulas into details: Market access was generally agreed upon, but each country, including the US, sought selective sectoral or industrial exemptions. Costa Rica got its agro exemptions in the October 2002 San José parley; but whether the same was true for other Central American states in the negotiations or not, and if it was, to what extent for the quite disparate countries and over which specific products, were not elaborated, at least during most of the negotiations. If these represent formula-phase discussion and terminology, the detail-phase textile concern invokes, among other issues, the notion of rules-of-origin.

In the talks, rules-of-origin boiled down to a controversy over *cumulation*: fibers, yarns, fabrics imported from any country with a free trade or preferential agreement with the US should qualify as Central American manufacturing inputs for duty-free exports to the US under CAFTA. This was the unanimous Central American view, but stringently opposed by US textile groups. They wanted only US fabrics, fibers, and yarns to qualify as Central American textile inputs. The narrow US view of the rules-of-origin versus the broader Central American view raised at least two profound sources of conflict: (a) Countries with US trade agreements, such as Mexico, are high-cost producers of fibers, fabrics, and yarns compared to African and Caribbean producers who do not have US agreements, and would automatically benefit from Central American cumulation, and thereby favor integrating Central American and North American economies against the rest of the world; and (b) US textile producers find vociferous opposition from US retailers and wholesalers who want cheaper imports in a fiercely competitive world.[22] Whereas the US defended its yarn forward position (YFP), that is, regional apparel to be made from regional yarn and fabric, Central America sought textiles tariff preference levels (TPLs) from as early as the 4th Round on the basis of cumulation.

Telecommunications

As a booming service sector industry, telecommunications is critical to 21st Century trade, therefore its treatment in the negotiations addresses two issues: gaps between DCs and LDCs, as well as vested and competitive interest groups. Both proved contentious, and probably not fully settled as yet. Costa Rica refused to sign in December 2003 partly owing to this second factor, while other Central American countries were uncomfortably positioned with the agreement because of the first factor.

Costa Rica was not alone in compromising telecommunications, insurance, and other such sectors. Irving Guerro, Honduras's Vice Minister of External Commerce, also indicated even before CAFTA talks began, his country would go slow with this sector.[23] The disagreement showed in the 4th Round press conference. "Telecommunications," began Vargo, "and other key infrastructure sectors are going to be the backbone that everybody else utilizes in terms of being competitive . . . So we think that this is an entirely appropriate discussion to have at the table." Her Costa Rican counterpart, Anabel González, quickly retorted: "I thought that after three rounds of repeating the same thing I would be able to save myself from doing so in this opportunity, but I think that for the record I must again state that the President of Costa Rica has stated that our country's position in this area is that it will not open telecommunications in the context of the agreement because our country considers this an internal decision or discussion within our country."

Clearly not every issue could be evaded; and Costa Rica eventually had to relent on this particular position. Getting the agreement might have uplifted Central American negotiators, but that some of them had to swallow hard also points to the particularly privileged position of the US—and possibly of problems to follow.

To be sure, telecommunications is on the list of quick WTO liberalization. Yet, liberalization snatches away from LDCs the opportunity to build their own telecommunications industries, an opportunity unlikely to come knocking again. Offsetting missed opportunities of this kind are *maquila* plants shifting low-cost telecommunication production to LDCs, much like Mexico moving into semiconductor chip production by the 1990s. Yet, on the flip side of the same slippery coin is the protection the emerging telecommunications industry receives from LDC countries, not to mention DCs too. Both became costly circumstances, with Costa Rica depicting the latter, and other Central American states the former.

Labor

Labor laws impinge trade negotiations, but although a source of contention in CA4FTA, they were essentially subordinated in CAFTA negotiations. Canada is not alone in being sensitive over labor rights, but the US has the capability to brush them under the negotiations carpet in a way Canada has not been able to, nor may be willing to, repeat. If disagreements over textiles and sugar had not pushed CA4FTA into a deadlock, labor laws would not be far behind in doing likewise. Unlike Canada, the US simply ignored these—an attitude warmly embraced by many Central American negotiators since their own treatment of labor is itself spotty. Nevertheless, labor laws touch several other issues, as a discussion of principles and labor relations with trade capacity building measures shows.

The Bush administration was reluctant to push more than the enforcement of local labor laws. Canada and US labor groups, however, demanded more, a minimum of applying the International Labor Organization's (ILO's) five cardinal principles:[24] freedom of association, right to organize, collective bargaining, abolition of forced labor, and equality of opportunity and treatment.[25] Fulfilling these, quite rightly, entails enormous sociological transformations across historically stratified, subjugated Central American societies. Yet, Montana's Democrat Senator Max Baucus frequently insisted the US Congress would accept nothing less before any ratification.

Canada's adoption of the ILO principles led to "considerable advances" in CA4FTA's 10th Round during February 16 and 20, 2004, in Ottawa, yet, not enough to prevent the June 2004 11th Round breakdown in Guatemala. Sharon O'Regan of FUNPADEM argues, FTAs "are a sign of good political will between nations," and indeed Central America "has more at stake and has more to fear than Canada does," since it is a "marginal market" for Canada. Yet, the deadlock was a Canadian imposition, not Central American.[26]

As with textiles, US chief negotiator proved to be equally vague and evasive over labor rights in press conferences. When asked, after the 4th Round in Guatemala City, if CAFTA would deprive Central American exporters of CBI and GSP preferences,[27] she refrained from "get[ting] into the particulars of the offer . . ." When another reporter asked her to "concretely" spell out US labor proposals, her response was more specific but remained equally evasive: "I think our labor approach to this negotiation has three different tracks . . . . The first is the negotiations of obligations in this agreement . . . that each of the parties . . . is responsible for effectively enforcing their [sic] own labor laws . . . . we have a second track, I think, of a very active bilateral dialogue . . . to talk about ways that the labor regimes can be improved and enforcement strengthened . . . . And then on yet another level, we have a very active discussion going on about trade capacity assistance . . . ."[28]

We are left to speculate how labor regime obligations would be improved and enforced, and what their relationship with the nature of TCB measures. TCB addresses (a) resource mobilization for micro, small and medium enterprises; (b) collecting, manipulating, and disseminating statistical data; (c) disseminating knowledge of US market requirements; (d) strengthening relevant institutions; and (e) coordinating consultations between the private sector and civil society.[29]

Agency TCB reports are more informative, but how TCB measures connected with negotiations on agriculture, textiles, market access, or telecommunications are left open-ended. "New trade agreements accept local labor laws as they are," Stephen Coats of the US Labor Education in the Americas Project contends, "and local labor law in Latin America is often far below international norms."[30] Whether they remained open-ended in the actual negotiations or not only time will tell, since societal groups are not convinced they have been redressed and only policy implementation will subsequently reveal their status. Nevertheless, any DC-LDC identity over subordinating labor laws in trade negotiations goes a long way in preventing stalemates. Since Canada is more reluctant to ignore labor laws than the US, Canada faces a steeper trade negotiations slope to climb.

For countries with overwhelming agricultural populations, significant indigenous segments, deep impoverishment, and recent memories of civil war or persecution, TCB programs and expectations are far too ambitious—reflecting again the top-down Washington Consensus undertone being imposed upon a society untutored in its essence. It drastically differs from what may be called the traditional bottom-up developmental approach emphasizing social inclusion and sustainability, such as Canada partly seeks. The results are likely to be quite different: TCB benefits and is the weapon of the very limited modernizing segments of the population residing in urban areas, thus potentially strengthening traditional wielders of corporatist decision-makers, such as the business elites and military leaders, and in the process deepening societal divisions and repressive tendencies. In the final analysis, TCB could simply squeeze sustainable developmentalist projects out of existence.

After CAFTA was agreed upon, AFL-CIO's Thea Lee, Assistant Director of Public Policy,[31] rejected Zoellick's comment of providing unprecedented labor protections as a "flat-out lie."[32] Across Central America, corporations thrive under lax labor laws, especially in the agricultural sector, imposing all sorts of discriminatory practices. Taking the case of bananas, of which Central America provides more than 40% of the world supply, Kate Mendenhall and Margaret Reeves point out in addition to egregiously persecuting union banana workers, corporations routinely resort to utilizing pesticides harming the workers. Among the pesticides are paraquat, a toxic producing itch, burns, dermatitis, and in extreme cases death; propiconozole, which destroys the soil, and through run-offs, kill fish in streams; and dibromochloropropane, which leads to sterility; among others.[33] In Guatemala, 900 workers of Del Monte's Bobos plants were illegally fired, but pressure from *Sindicato de Trabajadores Bananeros de Izabal* (SITRABI) led to the corporation getting off with fines; and in Ecuador, the world's fourth largest banana producer, Noboa, fired all workers in its Los Alamos plantations for seeking union rights, leading the National Federation of Free Peasants and Indigenous People of Ecuador (FENACLE) to boycott Bonita bananas from 2002. Similarly, Jim Lobe reports of 5,000–30,000 Salvadorean children working in sugar cane plantations,[34] helping Coca-Cola, among other US corporations. Clearly, labor rights are far from being as congenial as Zoellick believed.

But resolving them necessitates crossing first the domestic divide between business and labor, sometimes masked along state-society contours, then reconciling domestic positions with international standards or rules—in turn, requiring all partners to any trade negotiations engage in a level playing field. Anything less is a recipe for future disaster in an age of an increasing me-first attitude.

Environment

Another neglected issues was the environment, but it also shows the Canada-US divergence over agenda positioning. "Trade and environment issues," John Audley of the Carnegie Endowment of International Peace (CEIP) correctly observed, "have virtually disappeared from negotiations" under the pressure of trickle-down arguments of trade proponents.[35] From the "once-pivotal" role it played, environmental concerns lost their "leverage," in his view,[36] a predicament Eric Green from the US State Department, even senses for women, children, and indigenous people unless fully addressed in the negotiations—which clearly did not happen.[37]

Canada was mandated by the (a) 1999 Cabinet Directive on the Environmental Assessment of Policy, Plan and Program Proposals, (b) February 2001 Framework for Conducting Environmental Assessments of Trade Negotiations, and (c) Export Development Act (EDA) of December 21, 2001, which requires Export Development Canada (EDC) to monitor if corporations seek social leadership. Although the United States produced more reams of environmental studies of Central America than did Canada,[38] it did not factor these into the negotiations as Canada did. Paradoxically, the Canadian environmental report's conclusion of CA4FTA having minimal impact on Canadian trade, investment, and environment contrasts with CAFTA's intentions to minimize any environmental, or even labor, considerations in implementing the agreement regardless of the report recommendations.[39]

Power and Policy: Means and Ends Relationship

How the United States overcame the same constraints Canada could not raises the issue of power asymmetry. An overview of the CAFTA agenda informs us it might easily be passed off as a CA4FTA agenda, the similarities are so striking. A closer look conveys, although no US concessions were made, CAFTA still crossed the finishing line in December 2003, after twelve months of negotiations with the same four countries Canada was loggerheading with for thirty full months. A support for or against principles could partly explain this differential, as discussions of labor just indicated. Another could be the relative power or the reputation to resort to power by any negotiating partner.

The United States could bring power to bear on CAFTA negotiations in a way Canada could not on CA4FTA: This was explicit market power derived from existing traded volumes, but also the implicit political power derived from its unassailable military position worldwide—a position far different from the 1980s when it had to fend off so many rivalries across the entire Central America. With claims to neither forms of power, Canada was content to let the means determine the ends, while for the US the ends of an agreement by December 2003 not only determined the means, but also without any concessions.

The take-it-or-leave-it US approach reflected Bush's "little-by-little" strategy of overcoming the WTO Cancún deadlock and the choppy FTAA waters after mid-2003, with the weapons of what Costa Rican José Merino del Río dubs the *unholy trinity of market fundamentalism*: market opening, deregulation, and privatization.[40] Furthermore, with much larger trade flows at stake and growing CA dependence on the US, the United States could raise the ante in a way Canada could not. Canada finds it harder to compromise rhetoric and principles with reality than the US—and, one might add, even CA states. The US approach corresponds curiously with qualities one might find in John Gray's Mars and the Canadian approach with qualities from his Venus:[41] one was couched in self-help, immediate interest gratification, and unabashed usage of disproportionate power potential as instrument, the other was resigned to uplifting collective welfare, long-term interest satiation, and a softer touch of disproportionate negotiation power.

This is not to give Canada's pursuits a platonic twist. As negotiations progressed, they broached Canada's own vested interests: agriculture, textiles, and other areas Canadian policymakers deem essential to preserving a Canadian quality of life threatened by outside infiltration. Very much like CAFTA, CA4FTA negotiations were conducted very secretly,[42] and what makes them more problematic than CAFTA counterparts, are the Canadian preconditions of democracy and human rights consciousness in developmental pursuits. This does not mean the US does not also seek democratization and human rights upliftment. It does; but it does so outside the negotiations playing field, and certainly the CAFTA negotiations. Again, the means-ends interpretation helps distinguish policy orientations of the two countries: Canada may be using democracy, human rights, and preserving the Canadian way of life, what with its own protected markets and sifted agricultural imports, as the means towards the ends of free trade, whereas the US, contrariwise, may be letting the ends of free trade determine such means as democratization, liberalization, and so forth. Vargo, the top US CAFTA negotiator, said more or less the same. CAFTA, she indicated in a February 11 panel discussion in Washington, provides the opportunity "to lock-in these democratic reforms and to deepen regional integration," and reinforce the "indispensable building blocks of a free society," as well as "innovative ways to promote development."[43] Somehow the Cold War attitude of ends determining means remains in this post-Cold War US economic pursuit: Militarily containing the Soviet Union, and thereby communism, would make the world a safer place for democracy, rather than the promotion of democracy pushing communism away.

Results

Not for the first time, Canada ired the G-21 bloc at the Cancún WTO ministerial's Cancún meeting, when its Minister for International Trade, Pierre Pettigrew, in chairing the Singaporean issues working group, triggered the boycott of less developed countries, which culminated in the eventual breakdown. Others have argued, since concluding a FTA with the United States in 1988, then joining NAFTA, Canada is becoming more and more "a corporate state," that is, pushing interests of corporations,[44] and thereby lining up more and more with the United States in international trade conferences.[45] At a January 2002 Montréal meet on bio-safety, Michelle Swenarchuk of the Canadian Environmental Law Association (CELA), observed "Canada's goal was to prevent international regulation of food and feed . . . . We parroted the U.S. line and even spoke for the United States on some topics."[46] However one sees and interprets Canada's late entry into hemispheric integration, its future policy directions may no longer be controlled solely by Ottawa policy-makers.[47]

What, then, does CAFTA mean? In terms of market access, (a) 80% of US exports will immediately become duty-free, 85% in five years, and fully free over ten years; (b) exports of agricultural products and information-based products will get immediate duty-free access; (c) like Costa Rica and El Salvador, Guatemala, Honduras, and Nicaragua will join WTO's Information Technical Agreement (ITA), which makes IT products duty-free; (d) CAFTA will consolidate Caribbean Basin Trade Partnership Act (CBTPA) duty-free concessions to Central America. On the agricultural front (a) over 50% of all US farm exports will immediately enter duty-free; (b) US tariffs on many products are expected to be phased out over fifteen years; (c) better accesses to US farmers and ranchers than in Canada or West Europe; and (d) SPS improvements are expected to occur throughout.

Over the critical textiles sector: (a) if the rules of origin standard is met, textiles and apparel will be duty-free and quota-free immediately; (b) some Central American apparel using fabrics from NAFTA countries will gain duty-free status, hoping to integrate CAFTA and NAFTA; (c) some apparel using fabrics in short US supply may also get duty-free treatment, a determination to be constantly made; and (d) limited third-country contents will be allowed in CAFTA apparel.

In one other area, services, large market accesses were also agreed upon. Dismantling distributional barriers and loosening lock-in dealer protection regimes go hand-in-hand with market accesses in such other services as (a) telecommunications, (b) financial, (c) wholesaling, retailing, and franchising, (d) express delivery, (e) energy, (h) transport, (i) construction and engineering, (j) tourism, (k) advertising, (l) architects, engineers, accountants, and other professionals, and (m) environmental. Clearly the depth and breadth of service sector openings are astounding for countries barely on the threshold of the developmental ladder: How these will spiral into a race-to-the-top for citizens when such huge proportions remain at or below the margin remains to be seen, and pose a stupendous question-mark![48] Perhaps these inherent constraints contributed to Canada's diminishing enthusiasm, which more real disagreements eventually disrupted.

PPP, THE IMPLEMENTATION DYNAMICS, AND NEGOTIATION THEMES

With dissimilar structures and diverse goals, PPP is an agreement being implemented in topsy-turvy fashion, CA4FTA negotiations moved from enthusiasm to a deadlock, and CAFTA is on third-base awaiting ratification before reaching home-plate. All of them seek liberalization through the broader Washington Consensus, based on secret negotiations and evasive information. Canada and the US also have related FTAA aspirations, while Mexico is more concerned about securing its impoverished south from unstable Central American spillovers and increasingly uncompetitive Río Grande *maquilas* through relocation to the south. After outlining purposes, implementation dynamics are assessed, before extracting some themes for subsequent trilateral comparisons.

PPP: Purposes, Progression, and Projects

Originally, PPP spelled out eight purposes: highway construction; establishing an inter-connected electric grid; developing telecommunications; enhancing human development, particularly by extending educational opportunities and formulating a regional health program; encouraging sustainable development; promoting tourism; preventing natural disasters; and expanding trade. These translated into 5,565m (or 8,977km) of highways, 1,130m (1,830km) of electric lines connecting newly-built dams and gas-fields with factories, and 6 development zones for a string of these factories, or *maquilas*.[49] All in all, 65m affected people live across seven Mexican states and eight countries, representing one-hundred linguistic groups. Mexican President Vicente Fox Quesada who proposed PPP on September 5, 2000 as president-elect, indicated it would work "hand-in-hand" with FTAA, Central American free trade agreements, and multilateral agencies. Yet, it was not until March 12, 2001, that he spelled out the details of his broad developmental formulas, even then pushed by the *Zapatista* caravan descending upon Mexico City only the day before to protest the programs. Although 9/11 jolted his vision, in 2002, he still increased funding from $420m in 2001 to $697m in 2002,[50] while the IADB chipped in with $20b over 25 years.[51] Interests and investments dipped since,[52] Not until 2004 would Mexican interests be perked again, although Mexico never actually abandoned PPP. In the interim, multilateral agencies assumed greater proprietorship.

Over 80% of the Mexican and IADB funds were to be spent on regionalizing the infrastructure, with coordination divided among the regional countries. Just to illustrate, roughly 9,000km of highways to be created or improved were placed under Costa Rican coordination under the International Network of Mesoamerican Highways (RICAM) at a cost of $3.5b. Two major arteries connecting Puebla in Mexico with Panama were dubbed the Pacific and Atlantic corridors, the former through the Tehuantepec Isthmus in Oaxaca, the latter through Tabasco and Quintana Roo. Designed to serve in part as dry canals,[53] they sought to reduce traffic in transporting goods between two oceans — Atlantic and Pacific — since the Panama Canal was insufficient for the purpose, increasingly obsolete and costly, and no longer under direct US supervision. Neither was a new idea, to be sure, but each served new conditions: Panama Canal alternatives were needed, *maquila* relocation had to be facilitated, Central American incorporation into a technologically-transformed global economy was crucial to tapping new markets, harnessing cheap labor, and exploiting local resources more efficiently, and hemispheric integration was essential in an age of fiercely competitive blocs. Augmenting these tasks were also about 2,000km of electric lines, planned at a cost of $409m under the Central American Electricity Interconnection System (SIEPEC), and placed under Guatemalan coordination. Meant to transmit hydroelectric power from 25 new dams, largely in Chiapas, Mexico,[54] and along the border with Guatemala, these transmission lines supplement gas pipelines and new highways in the creation of six *maquiladora* zones.[55] All of these sought the strategic goal of an integrated western hemispheric towards making the region globally competitive in the technologically transformed post-Cold War era.

Coordination teams cemented the eight countries. Derived from the cascading modular multilateralism and hemispheric diplomacy models of Richard Feinberg, these revolved around one country being assigned as key coordinator of a specific arena—as Costa Rica and Guatemala just alluded to were for highways and electricity, respectively. Others were also created, and the policies touched by them diversified. For example, from infrastructure development the shift to education was rapid—indicating not just the developmental thrusts of the various countries, but also the Washington Consensus-based underpinnings of them all, and the inevitable multilateral planning, coordination, and financing.[56] A previous chapter noted how these plans, coordination, and finances were being mobilized even during the Cold War, for example, in Mexico's Chiapas Plan.[57]

PPP was a bold venture increasingly less in Mexico's control.[58] Nevertheless, the policy-making approach was modified even within the country. It not only conjoined leaders in all the eight countries, but periodic and regular meetings were also made part of the PPP. Monthly meetings were to be held under coordinators of each arena of all country representatives, who would then report back higher-up in the decision-making echelon to sub-secretaries or vice ministers who, in turn, would inform secretaries/ministers, ultimately reporting back to the various presidents. This process was consistent with Feinberg's hemispheric diplomacy model emphasis on decentralized functioning. Plans included meeting once a month, even as late as in 2003, when eleven such meetings took place.

Of course, the entire structure collapsed once Fox distanced himself from PPP, steadily through 2002 but more rapidly through 2003. He never fully disassociated himself from PPP, but the supervisory agency he created dissolved, and PPP returned to the foreign secretariat. His disengagement was prompted by both external and domestic developments: PPP was one part of his deeper integration into NAFTA, especially with the US. When this was nipped in the week before 9/11 over immigration by Bush, 9/11 exaggerated policy differences between Mexico and the US, threw Fox into a stalemate in his country's legislature, and thereby the evaporation of domestic funds for development. Amidst this domestic resource constraint and initiative stagnation, the US stepped up its own Central American drives, while Canada also engaged in its own explorations. Mexico was left too politically strapped to continue: Central American leaders found their time and attention better served with CAFTA and CA4FTA than PPP. In domino effect, the entire PPP negotiation structure froze with Fox's disengagement: Ministers did not receive the presidential summons to meet their counterparts across the regions, so the vice ministers did not have the clearance for any further meetings, and all the way down, bringing PPP to a standstill. In turn, Feinberg's CMM and HD models, purportedly proving viable with PPP, also succumbed to its glaring neglect of fitting in US asymmetry.

Further crippling the initiative was grassroots opposition by societal groups, individuals, and common citizens.[59] PPP had the effect of mobilizing many of them, whether in Tehuantepec, across the Usumacinta River with Guatemala, or in Nicaragua. Local groups connected with transnational counterparts, creating the Keck-Sikkink transnational advocacy networks (TAN).[60] They also held several meetings, on a regular basis, thus diffusing the protest gospel. For example, the First International Public Forum met in Tapachula, Chiapas during May 2001, the Second met in Guatemala in November that year, the Third in Nicaragua during July 2002, and the Fourth in Honduras in 2003. The 250 NGOs and 1,000 people attending the First Forum snowballed into 350 NGOs and 3,000 people by the Third, indicating the growing momentum. Other meetings also impeded PPP: on biodiversity in Chiapas during June 2001, on hydrocarbons, in Petén, Guatemala during March 2002, and various indigenous congregations, as at San Cristobal de Casas under Bishop Felipe Arizmendi.[61]

It was not buried, however, for a number of reasons. First, some projects were underway already, and they were fulfilling domestic Mexican needs. Second, Mexico's fears of *maquilas* migrating out of the country remains a real threat, and needs immediate attention. Third, once CAFTA was signed, it was only logical to bring Mexico back in the regional trade pursuits, since it serves a critical passageway, not just across both oceans, but between Central and North America as well.[62] Besides, it is also a part of FTAA, and therefore even more needed after CAFTA to drive FTAA home. Finally, both sides remained armed to push their goals, corporations and multilateral agencies to enhance the Washington Consensus, grassroots groups and individuals to prevent its implementation.

THEMES FROM
NORTH AMERICAN–CENTRAL AMERICAN EMBRACE

A number of themes help understand PPP, from conception to implementation, as another dimension of the emerging North American-Central American embrace. Three convey the gist of this development: wages and industrial migration; developed versus developing country relationships; and the society-state-supranational nexus. Before turning to each, a couple of caveats: First, PPP is not the only context within which these themes originate, proliferate, or find prominence; and second, none of these themes reflect any causal or consequential relationship with PPP. Viewing them as reflecting independent situations adjusting to PPP, another independent situation, helps to extract a fuller North American-Central American picture.

Wages and Industrial Migration

Mexico is not the only North American country with nationalized industries, and PPP does not address the generic nationalized industry problem per se: SEMATECH is a public US sector information industry company, as is health in Canada; and PPP does not touch agriculture, the traditionally sheltered industry. What PPP does, and only for Mexico, is to compensate declining industries, given increasingly attractive global production networks, before they either migrate to another country or become nationalized because they provide too many jobs or produce a critically needed product. After Mexico abandoned import substitution industries and began liberalizing several public sector industries, it no longer has any significant manufacturing plant providing too many jobs or producing critically needed products—in other words, nationalized industries are few and far in between across the country.[63] The thrust of PPP, then, is to prevent industrial migration, and a long string of *maquila* plants stand in line by the exit door given the spiraling operational costs. What it proposes is to relocate these plants where possible in Mexico, and where not possible, to relocate them in countries with which Mexico enjoys relative free trade. The south of Mexico and Central America are locations where shifted industries would remain competitive. In a nutshell, PPP seeks to keep North American products in North America, and where this is difficult, to extend North American frontiers to Central America.

Central American states utilize the opportunity to build infrastructure, create jobs, diversify from agriculture, and integrate into global manufacturing, rather than agricultural, streams. This is a transfer of least relevance for Canada, useful for the United States, since it is the largest market of *maquila* products and home of corporations in need of low-wage workers, but critical for Mexico since its macroeconomic foundations depend on stable microeconomic performances. At the same time, it is fitting to Central American states, many of which recently concluded a variety of free trade deals and possess an ample labor supply to comply with.

The interesting negotiations questions against this background are not about *if* or *how*, but *what* and *where*—not about whether to invite *maquilas* or how to incorporate them in the social fabric, though they are important issues, but about what can be done to invite them and where to locate them with minimal disruptions across such traditional societies. In turn, these plants complement the free trade agreement with the United States more than the one with Canada. How these questions are resolved is theoretically significant since countries benefiting from future *maquila* migration may benefit from Central American experiences, but the relevant theories have less to do with negotiations than industrial restructuration. In the final analysis, they contribute to regional integration, particularly seen from sectoral rather than state perspectives, and therefore industrial strategies are just as useful a source of knowledge about regional integration as state-level negotiations. This is an underlying PPP contribution we can not expect from CAFTA or CA4FTA, but which impacts both.

Developing-Developed Country Syndrome

Related to the industrial theme is the relative development dimension. Low-wage industries ambiguously denote a developing or underdeveloped country. Yet, Mexico hosting *maquila* does not rank in the same category as, for example, Guatemala hosting *maquilas*: The gulf of difference between both gets lost in semantics. Similarly, *maquilas* exiting Mexico does not connote Mexico necessarily moving up in the developmental ranks: Mexico is not the United States by a wide margin even as it bids *maquilas* bye bye. PPP's contributions are twofold in this respect.

First, it compensates for certain inabilities of free trade agreements. FTAs seek to generally align policies between signatory countries, and are compelled to do so on as symmetrical and reciprocal a basis as far as is practicable. In other words, they cannot, by definition, negotiate industrial relocation from high-wage to low-wage arenas: Not only is there an asymmetry, reciprocity proves meaningless, and policy alignments are unrealistic, if not impossible, but also the more relaxed environmental safeguards, low wages, and worker exploitation *maquilas* taken for granted, cannot be admitted into pure FTAs. In this sense, PPP provides a backdoor entry to regional integration.

Second, the syndrome justifies integrative initiatives between developed and developing countries, a necessary offshoot of the furious regionalized initiatives underway today. NAFTA first broke the DC-LDC barrier within the annals of regional integration, and ever since we have noticed how the Association of South East Nations (ASEAN) brought Myanmar into the fold from the backwoods and the European Union dittoing the same with certain East European countries, such as Slovenia. Yet, no theoretical argument explained these developments. If PPP is seen as representing a half-way or interim regional integration characteristic, we may have less to blush about in explaining cases like Myanmar or Slovenia within orthodox regional integration paradigms.

Neither of these contributions even comes close to proposing Central American states have nothing but an escalation of progress into full-fledged regional integration ahead of them. Ultimately, PPP legitimizes the interface of free trade agreements, regional integration, and less developed countries: Whereas FTAs and regional integration hitherto represented DC characteristics, PPP bends and reshapes them to admit and adjust LDCs too.

Society-State-Supranational Nexus

Both CAFTA and CA4FTA negotiations were conducted under a glass ceiling, keeping as much of a distance from societal groups as possible, hobnobbing with business counterparts, and utilizing multilateral agencies at every available opportunity. PPP must do the same but without the glass ceilings: Projects designed for implementation have to be implemented, *maquilas* necessitating low-wage workers have to enter civil society to recruit them, and in spite of the exploitation likely to follow, and questions demanding answers cannot be couched in deception or by evasion, since the answers the questions seek are less verbal than visual. Consequently, PPP permits the complete linear relationship between society and supranational entities through the state which FTAs and regional integrative arrangements provide only in segments and not necessarily without ups and downs. PPP not only faced more grassroots opposition but also generated greater transnationalized countervailing forces than either CAFTA or CA4FTA. At the same time, it received more supranational developmental funding than either CAFTA or CA4FTA: Those funds finance projects more than principles, yet in spite of sputtering more than CAFTA and CA4FTA, PPP carries a more accomplished track-record than either of the other. How we explain this without accounting for the supranational support and in spite of vociferous opposition from below ultimately depends on the model we utilize and the arguments it is premised upon.

CAFTA-CA4FTA-PPP COMPARATIVE ANALYSIS

Comparing all three North American approaches enhances the contributions of PPP peculiarities assume greater resonance. These approaches are examined under the microscope along at least five comparative dimensions: the negotiation structure; developmental gap between parties; cultural styles as they impact negotiations; policy-making preferences; and exogenous affiliations.

Negotiation Structure

Negotiations were structured differently, at least along three dimensions: fulcrum of decision-making, degree of FTAA structural influence, and timing. CAFTA, CA4FTA, and PPP involved *top-down* and largely clandestine negotiations, even though public involvement is a pre-requisite for Canadian trade negotiations. As it turned out, the center of gravity of the *top* was higher in Mexico than in Canada or the US: It was closer to the chief executive, involved more government officials from the upper echelons than in Canada or the US, and necessitated a newly created agency responsible directly to the president; whereas for Canada, government officials represented established government agencies, operating with greater independence of the chief executive; and though the US Trade Representative (USTR) remained the dominant negotiating authority in the United States, not only does the position necessitate greater collaboration with the chief executive than in Canada, but Zoellick also worked in tandem with Bush more effectively than others in his position with their president before him. In terms of authority, the US was sandwiched between Mexico's maximum presidential engagement and initiative and Canada's minimum.

CA4FTA reflected the three-tiered FTAA-recommended negotiations structure more fully than either PPP or CAFTA, which sprang more from political premises than bureaucratic. As Feinberg's hemispheric diplomacy model shows, the three tiers include: technical teams representing each negotiating group, consisting of lower-level government officials; vice ministers or under-secretaries, who either serve as chiefs of negotiations or work in conjunction with them, at a higher level; and at the top, ministers or secretaries. Details are filtered up to the prime ministers/presidents once they are sorted out. As observed, PPP reflected a top-down structure, with the presidents making and scrutinizing the decisions, delegating them down to other government officials. On the other hand, CAFTA was somewhere in between, with powerful top-down pressures but also the FTAA-stipulated modalities operating all the time.

Recognizing PPP was project-based and not policy-shaking, it was still concluded very quickly, taking only six months from the September 2000 proposal to implementation from March 2001, whereas CAFTA took one full year, and CA4FTA remains stalled. PPP not only serves Mexican policy interests, but also capitalizes on geographical contiguity between Mexico and Central American states. Canada started from scratch, but was located too far away anyway, while for the US size compensates for contiguity. CA4FTA negotiations got off amidst considerable optimism and with lofty goals, but bred increasing frustrations, while PPP and CAFTA were dealt with pragmatically and without any conditional attachments to principles.

Development Gap

Invoking CA countries in a northern embrace raises questions about the developmental gaps, not only with Mexico, but even more with Canada and the United States. In and of itself, this constrains policy implications more than the negotiations themselves. After all, Mexico was a LDC when it joined NAFTA, but profited immensely more than Canada during the ten years of NAFTA.[64] Developed countries DCs face more constraints, as if by definition: The more developed a country becomes, the more stringent the standards it hypothetically imposes on imports, especially if these are agricultural or involve environmental and labor considerations. Indeed, the ninth CA4FTA round, held in Ottawa during July 2–5, 2003, was expected to be the last, but floundered over market access precisely because different development standards imposed negotiations gaps. When the first round was held in San Salvador during December 2001, for example, Salvadorean Minister of Economics, Miguel Lacayo, predicted a final agreement by mid-2002 and implementation by 2003. Neither came true as negotiations faced incremental barriers. In part because it was oblivious of environmental, labor, or sanitary/phytosanitary constraints, and in part owing to cultural dissimilarities I discuss next, PPP was, more or less, a done deal from the start. One exception to DC standards imposing constraints is politics: CAFTA talks eschewed several policy and developmental differentials in order to conclude a rapid agreement precisely because the US prioritized a political opportunity.

Cultural Considerations

Very much like the developmental gap argument, cultural compatibilities factor into negotiations but can be subordinated to political considerations. Even if culture is interpreted loosely to simply refer to adjustment to any specific environment, shades of differences still manifest themselves.

No matter how westernized Central American leaders may be, some of their cultural traits connect better with Mexico than Canada or the US, as for example, a similar language, diet, religion, even clothing. Yet, these were not the reasons why PPP was concluded and implemented faster than the others: Negotiators themselves were closer to Canadian and US styles of dressing and negotiations. Whereas CAFTA ignored cultural issues to produce a political document, CA4FTA, as with all Canadian trade negotiations, is more culturally sensitive since culture is a protected Canadian sector, while Mexico's shift from nationalism towards liberalism dilutes somewhat its historically emphatic cultural salience. Nevertheless, PPP brings together countries with strong presidential systems of governance, histories of one-party rule, patriarchal values, and corporatist patterns of interest intermediation, while Canada's parliamentary system not only invokes multiple party preferences, but also places checks and balances on executive authority and is permeated by all sorts of societal pressures on policy-making,[65] and the US presidential system is closer to the Mexican pole of authority than the Canadian in spite of checks and balances.

Consequently, prior to the CA4FTA negotiations, Canada was mandated by a 1999 Cabinet Directive to conduct an environmental assessment of trade agreements, while the Export Development Act (EDA) of December 2001 requires Export Development Canada to monitor if corporations contribute to social development or promote social leadership. Counterparts of the kind are rare in Mexico, indeed, across Central American states, and if they exist, receive only lip service, while an increasingly authoritative US presidency has to date skillfully navigated environmental waters to avoid impediments, such as safeguards. This is not to say, the environment does not factor into trade policy-making: It does in the US, but is subordinated; and in Mexico's treatment, is even more lax.

Policy-making Inclinations

Policy-making inclinations of the dominant country in each negotiations also differed. Canada's approach promoted universal values even if negotiations are about real-life conditions; Mexico's PPP stemmed from localized concerns amidst global economic restructuration; and the US sought CAFTA to accelerate FTAA. All three carry elements of development: Canada emphasizes poverty alleviation, debt reduction, disaster safeguards, and so forth; Mexico relocates *maquiladoras* to, or builds highways and electric grids across, its southern states and into Central America; and the US hopes to extend these *maquilas* into Central America as a step towards firmly integrating the western hemisphere. Whereas Mexico's inclinations reflect US interests, since *maquiladoras* feed the huge US market, Canada's more ambivalent approach, partly market-driven, partly emphasizing non-market forces, elevates the environment and the non-material human condition. Different inclinations do not necessarily mean contradictions, but impact negotiations differently.

Exogenous Affiliations

Exogenous affiliations were not only critical in the negotiations, but also left behind different impacts. Examples of exogenous affiliations include broadening Canadian, Mexican, or US interests beyond North America, engaging, no matter how reluctantly or enthusiastically, with hemispheric or multilateral organizations, adjusting to global competitiveness, and Canada and Mexico tip-toeing US interests. As previously discussed, they have elicited different Canadian, Mexican, and US responses. For example, all three engage multi-lateral organizations, Canada and the US more forthrightly than Mexico: Canada sees in multilateral organizations an alternative to excessive US influence, even though the World Bank, IMF, and IADB tip-toe US preferences; Mexico is more ambivalent and apprehensive turning to them to deepen US attachments, but also remaining cautious owing to a long history in which they were seen as tools of an interventions US; and multilateral engagements are part and parcel of US trading interests.

SIMILARITIES, DIFFERENCES, & IMPLICATIONS

What are the similarities and differences in negotiating the agreements?

Similarities

At least five similarities are drawn. First, clandestine deliberations are preferred to negotiations in the public domain, in the process violating the democratic underpinnings of trade liberalization—and undermining the bases of Feinberg's hemispheric diplomacy model. The US executive branch in fact violated a US District Court order to make documents from trade negotiations more public by January 17, 2003, since trade agreements impact domestic public health, labor, and environment.[66] Pressures were exerted in Canada too to open the deliberations to the public.[67] PPP has repeatedly been chastised for being conducted privately, and at the expense of particularly indigenous groups.

Second, venue rotation enhanced inclusiveness. Each member was made to feel a little extra responsible, creating one of its few claims to symmetry in the negotiations. Interestingly, trans-regional awareness and knowledge also flowed symmetrically, with Central American state officials learning much more about each of their three northern neighbors than ever before, and likewise, North American officials learning new intricacies about Central American states to add to their stock of knowledge.

Third, for the first time, all three North American countries were on the same level regarding FTAA in these negotiations than ever before. Canada embraced the hemispheric idea only recently, while Mexico saw it during the 1990s as a step towards preserving Mexican interests in Washington. This was a hard-won but inevitable US victory, since it alone championed the hemispheric cause, first after World War II in response to a global communist threat, then after the Cold War in response to global economic competition.

Fourth, all three North American reflected the central themes of the Washington Consensus, especially privatization and marketization, not only of industrial goods but for Canada and the US of also many agricultural products. Not only that, they also found Washington Consensus subscribers across Central America—a region too riddled in conflict until very recently to even permit the wherewithals of trade liberalization to establish roots.

Finally, the negotiations enhanced a greater sense of a North American identity. Three countries worked towards similar goals, albeit differently, reflected similar multilateral agendas and negotiation structures, and converged upon similar positions in other trade negotiations, such as the WTO's ministerial meeting in Cancún. Engaging Central American states strengthened this sense of regional convergence, itself a new diplomatic development.

Differences

Equally significant are some of the differences, six of them. First, whereas CA4FTA had parallel environmental and labor agreements, much like NAFTA had, CAFTA did not, although both issues belong as one of the nine original negotiation clusters, and PPP proceeded without any consideration of them. Mexico, in turn, is more openly accused of jeopardizing the environment with PPP than is either Canada with CA4FTA or US with CAFTA.

Second, whereas the United States unabashedly included NAFTA's Chapter 11 provisions into CAFTA, Canada, and Mexico did not,[68] indicating the greater US willingness to allow corporations to challenge foreign governments than Canada or Mexico. Perhaps the most controversial clause is the right of foreign business enterprises to sue governments, much as Metalclad successfully did against the Mexican government for US$16.4m over the San Luis Potosi trash disposal controversy. Charles M. Gastle sees Chapter 11 as representing *frontier justice* for two reasons: It invokes very intrusive means and methods of free trade dispute settlement; and the secretive tribunals remain aloof to appellate review.[69]

Third, although actual bargaining was very secretive in all three sets of negotiations, public consultations received greater priority in CAFTA than in CA4FTA and PPP. Having said that, all three governments manipulated the public, not just through clandestine negotiations, but also through diversionary tactics, concealing information and deliberately casting false red herrings. For example, the Canadian Department of Foreign Trade and International trade (DFAIT) invited public views by February 2, 2001 on a variety of topics,[70] while in Ottawa a roundtable during May 30–31, 2002 of all CA4 members emphasized Canada's development-driven approach to build infrastructure and make agriculture more competitive; yet the public knew less about

CA4FTA than Mexicans of PPP, even though that is not saying much. Americans, by contrast, knew more of CAFTA than any of their North American counterparts of their own state's Central American trade negotiations, but still received information piecemeal.[71] On the flip side, CAFTA and PPP mobilized the grassroots more than CA4FTA, even though this was in terms of opposition.

Fourth, even though not perfectly symmetrical, CA4FTA or PPP negotiations did not carry any Canadian or Mexican damoclean sword over Central American states like the CAFTA negotiations did, particularly after the Cancún WTO ministerial meeting failed in September, 2003. Central American states participating in the Cancún G-21, such as Costa Rica, El Salvador, and Guatemala, were asked in no uncertain terms by the United States to not only drop out of G-21 but also fulfill some very drastic reforms they were previously hesitant to.

Fifth, the interventionist US TCB-based developmentalist approach contrasts with Canada's humanitarian developmental and Mexico's restructuration developmental approaches. Whereas Canada and Mexico prioritized infrastructural development for the public at large, such as highways, electricity, water supply, farm modernization, and so forth, TCB focuses on selective and eclectic infrastructures promoting commerce.

Sixth, although Canada, Mexico, and the US intentionally rely on multilateral organizations for Central American purposes, in particularly the International Bank for Reconstruction and Development (IBRD) and the IADB, the roles these organizations play and the relationships they have with the three countries are diammetrically opposite. Canada sees these as vehicles of de-emphasizing direct US influences, Mexico reluctantly relies on them, seeing them as necessary evils, while the US sees them as either extensions of US policy-making or agencies whose natural inclination is to flow in the same direction as US policy interests, but behind the United States. Consequently, they augment both developmentalist and TCB purposes. Given their location, proximity to US policy-making machineries, and dependence for resources on private banks, as overwhelming proportion of which are US registered, it is not surprising TCB commitments increasingly outweigh developmental counterparts. Certainly this has been the Central American experience, with more TCB allocations than development, and the latter being forced by either natural calamities, such as Hurricane Mitch, or the abject inability of the Central American countries to meet their international debts. Central America is not an even playing field if the United States is involved, at least not for Canada or Mexico, which reiterates the original question if Canada or Mexico is there out of an independent quest to build its own constituency, or simply follow the US flow in utilizing Central America as a stepping stone towards a FTAA, and ultimately towards reconstructing the WTO. As will become evident, Canada's ambiguous position remains as far from the US as possible on this score, Mexico's as close to the US.

Implications

What do these imply for negotiations? Four observations follow. First, size matters. Given Canada's paltry Central American engagements over trade, services, and investments, compared to the US, but simply owing to a much smaller Canadian economy than the US, it is simply not in a position to either challenge the US or to offer Central American states any viable alternatives to the United States. Even as they have doubled over the 1995–2002 period, Canadian engagements cannot register improved performances for ever or over the long-haul: The items of trade and the types of potential investment available are just not there in absolute terms; and if the US is brought in, the relative prospects are even worse off.

Second, as the capitalist approach becomes the trademark of all three countries, its human face gets differentiated exposures, with more salience in Canada's policy priorities than in Mexico's or US counterparts. How significant this is in an age of anomie-cultivating globalization, liberalization, and democratization one cannot always say with certainty, but in negotiating with identity-conscious Central Americans, it does leave a more meaningful personal touch than a cash-nexus attitude of other FTAs.

Third, Canada's arguably inductive response to Central America, by contrasting with the deductive Mexican and US responses, leaves it with more symbolic appeal but less negotiation substance, while the reverse is true of the United States. Yet, with the human factor absent or neglected in all three, negotiations serve a bureaucratic function than anything else.

Finally, should liberalization, regionalism, and FTAs ever collapse, Canada is likely to face fewer costs and the US would be up to its neck in expenses, with Mexico somewhere in between—reiterating the parallel relationship between commitments and costs. Nevertheless, the size of the US economy powerfully deters any unfavorable US outcomes.

NOTES

1. See my own "After Cancún: G21, WTO, and multilateralism," *Journal of International and Area Studies* 11, no. 2 (December 2004):1–16.

2. "Canada's interest in the FTAA," Louise Elliott observed in November 2002, "has always surpassed that of the United States . . . ." See "Canada moves on bilateral

trade negotiations in wake of FTAA summit," *Canadian Press*, November 3, 2002, from: http://www.geocities.com/ericsquire/articles/ftaa/cp021103.htm

3. "The unintended consequences of a US-Central American free trade agreement," *Fraser Forum* (June 2003):13.

4. Donald R. Mackay, "Challenges confronting the Free Trade of the Americas," *FOCAL Policy Paper*, June 2002, 5.

5. The salient CAFTA examples: telecommunications and electric industry workers, led by Fabio Chavez Castro. See Richard Lapper, "Costa Rica may derail US free trade plans," *Financial Times*, October 13, 2003, from: http://news.ft.com/servlet/ContentServer?pagename=FT.com/StoryFT/FullStory&C=StoryFT

On encompassing interests groups, see Mancur Olson, *The Rise and Decline of Nations: Economic Growth, Stagflation, and Social Rigidities* (New Have, CT: Yale University Press, 1984), ch. 1.

6. This is one common theme in news reports of the rounds. The 6th Round in New Orleans, as reported in *The Advertiser*, Lafayette, Louisiana, "will be conducted in secret as the city tries to boost its foreign trade presence out in the open." See "Secret CAFTA talks continue," *The Advertiser*, July 29, 2003, from: http://www.theadvertiser.com/business/html/CC6EB14B-1B61-4322-8F1A-D4D379735605.sht Katherine Stecher makes the same argument for transparency in the 7th Round in Managua. See op. cit. The Canadian Council for International Cooperation agrees fully. See Esperanza Moreno, "Secret deals breaks trail for FTAA?" Oneworld.net, July 16, 2004, from: http://www.oneworld.net/article/view/76972/1/

7. Oxfam, "CAFTA:an undemocratic negotiation process," http://www.oxfamamerica.org/advocacy/art5543.html

8. Elliott, op. cit.

9. Alongwith Costa Rican Investment Board (CINDE), a temple of neoliberalism. See José Merino del Río, "CAFTA: A perspective from Costa Rica: A treaty tied by chains," February 20, 2003, from: http://www.americaspolicy.org/commentary/2003/0302caftacr_body.html

10. This is not to say nothing has been written about what has been called balancing behavior. Arthur Lall, among others, raises this possibility in DC-LDC negotiations. See *Multilateral Negotiations and Mediation: Instruments and Methods* (New York: Pergamon, 1985).

11. See Vanessa Ulmer, "CAFTA negotiation session 3:March 31–April 4, El Salvador," Carnegie Endowment of International Peace, *News Summary*, from: http://ceip.org/files/news/CAFTA-summary-3.asp

12. Katherine Stecher, "CAFTA:a shot-gun wedding," *NicaNet:the Nicaragua Network*, from: http://www.nicanet.org/alerts/cafta_negotiations_2.htm

13. Jenalia Moreno, "Worker rights a tricky issue:illegal conditions a concern," *Houston Chronicle*, October 22, 2003, from: http://www.chron.com/CDA/ssistory.mpl/business/2171778

14. From US Trade Representative, "Sugar:putting CAFTA in perspective," *Trade Talks*, from USTR homepage: http://www.ustr.gov

15. From Rob Hotakainen, "Sugar:a sticky election issue," *Sacramento Bee*, September 5, 2004, from: http://wwwsacbee.com

16. "Briefing on the U.S./Central American free trade agreement," *Yahoo!* News, CAFTA Coalition, June 2003, from:

17. Oxfam, "Agriculture under CAFTA," from: http://www.oxfamamerica.org/advocacy/art=5542.html

18. "Will WTO stand affect CAFTA," *High Plains Journal*, September 10, 2003, from: http://www.hpj.com/edit1/WillWTOstandaffectCAFTA.CFM

19. "Congressmen urge caution in FTAA negotiation," *The South Florida Business Journal*, September 25, 2003, from: http://www.bizjournals.com/southflorida/stories/2003/09/22/daily37.html

20. John De Santis, "Shrimpers go global:economic stress leads to unlikely alliances," *The Houma Courier*, July 23, 2004, from: http://www.houmatoday.com/apps/pbcs.d11/article?AID=20030723/NEWS/307230321/1026

21. "US places duties on shrimp sales," *BBC News*, July 29, 2004, from: http://news.bbc.co.uk/1/hi/business/3937851.stm

22. Kristi Ellis, "CAFTA talks hinge on 3 major sectors," *Trade Observatory*, October 2, 2003, from: http://wwwtradeobservatory.org/news/index.cfm?ID=4850

23. Lynn Chatowetz, "CA trade reps meet in Washington for free-trade talks," *Honduras This Week Online*, September 16, 2002, from: http://www.marrder.com/htw/2002oct/business.htm

24. Doug Palmer, "U.S. eyes post-Cancun trade deal with Central America," *Yahoo! News*, October 17, 2003, from: http://story.news.yahoo.com/news?tmp1=story&u=nm/20030929/pl_nm/trade_cafta_dc_1

25. How the first two are being undermined already with the spread of *maquila* plants is discussed by Mark Engler, "CAFTA:free-trade vs democracy," *Foreign Policy in Focus*, January 29, 2003, from: http://www.globalpolicy.org/globaliz/econ/2003/0603CAFTA.htm

26. From Sharon O'Regan, "Integration in Central America," *Focal*, May 19–20, 2004, from Focal web page.

27. CBI: Caribbean Basin Initiative; GSP: Generalized System of Preferences, adopted in the GATT's Kennedy Round talks 1964–67.

28. US Embassy, Guatemala, "Transcript of final press conference, IV Round of CAFTA negotiations," Guatemala City, May 16, 2003, from: http://www.kampala.usembassy.gov/guatemala/wwwh.caftaguae02.html

29. From El Salvador's TCB experiences. See Government of El Salvador, "National action plan for trade capacity building:El Salvador," December 2002, 16, from http://www.sice.oas.org/geograph/central/plan_sal.asp Similar reports were required by the United States to furnish TCB funds from all Central American states. See, in addition, Government of Costa Rica, US-Central American Free Trade Agreement, Integral Cooperation Agenda, "Conceptual porposal for a nationa action plan:Costa Rica," December 2002; Government of Guatemala, Ministry of Economics, "National action plan for trade capacity building in Guatemala:a proposal by the Government of Guatemala in the framework of the US-CAFTA," December 2002; Government of Honduras, US-Central American Free Trade Agreement (US-CAFTA), "National action plan for trade capacity building:Honduras," June 2003; and Government of Nicaragua, "Operational

program for the national action plan for institutional strengthening," December 2002. All from the USTR webpage.

30. From Emad Mekay, "U.S. trade:Central American free trade deal a dud, activists say," April 10, 2003, from: http://www.tradesobservatory.org/news.index .cfm?ID=4285

31. AFL-CIO: American Federation of Labor-Congress of Industrial Organizations.

32. From Mark Engler, "The trouble with CAFTA," January 16, 2004, *The Nation*, from: http://www.thenation.com/doc.mhtml)i=20040202&s=engler

33. Kate Mendenhall and Margaret Reeves, "Support banana workers:bring justice to the table," *Global Pesticide Campaigner* 14, no. 1 (April 2004). From: http://www.panna.org/resources/gpc/gpc_200404.14.1.06.dv.html

34. Jim Lobe, "Coke benefiting from child labor in sugar cane fields," *OneWorld United States*, July 16, 2004, from: http://us.oneworld.net/article/view/87896/1/ Also see Human Rights Watch, "Turning a blind eye:hazardous child labor in El Salvador's sugarcane cultivation," June 2004, from: http://hrw.org/reports/2004/elsalvador0604/

35. Carnegie Endowment for International Peace, Global Policy Program, Trade, Equity, and Development, Audley, "Environment and trade:the linchpin to success for CAFTA negotiations?" *Issue Brief*, July 2003.

36. Clearly evident in CAFTA's "leaked" environmental chapter, which is substantively so lax in enforcement as to make NAFTA's more detailed environmental agreement appear a bible. See "Leaked CAFTA environmental chapter," *Quest for Peace*, from: http://www.quixote.org/quest/advocacy/fair_trade_cafta_environment_ chapter.htm

37. Eric Green, "US sees CAFTA promoting Central American democracy, prosperity," Washington File, February 11, 2003, from: http://usinfo.state.gov/regional/ar/ trade/03021101.htm; and ————, "Central American nations call for US ratification of CAFTA," Washington File, July 14, 2004, from: http://usinfo.state.gov/ xarchives/display-html?p=washfile-english&y=2004&m=July&x=

38. USTR, 2003.

39. "Initial strategic . . . , 2003."

40. "CAFTA:a perspective from Costa Rica," *Americas Program* (Silver City, NM: Interhemispheric Resource Center, February 20, 2003).

41. From *Men are from Mars, Women are from Venus: A Practical Guide for Improving Communications and Getting What You Want in Your Relationship* (New York: HarperCollins Publishers, 1992), 13–20.

42. This was clearly an impediment in conducting my research. The Government of Canada's Department of Foreign Affairs and International Trade (DFAIT) provides the most restricted, obsolete, and dry information on the subject, as anyone searching any links from its website will discover. Try: http://www.dfait-maeci.gc.ca/tna-nac/ menu.en.asp

My experiences are not unique. No less authorities than the American Policy Group (APG) and the Canadian Council for International Cooperation (CCIC), which are usually supportive of policy-makers in Ottawa, made a CA4FTA statement in May 2003 with the following opening words: "The Government of Canada should demonstrate its commitment to transparency and civil society." Later in the report, it points out how Canada was instrumental in the 2001 FTAA trade ministerial to releasing negotiation documents and in recognizing "the need for increasing participation of the different sectors of civil society in the hemispheric initiative." This was clearly not done under CA4FTA, even though APG and CCIC made this a key request. See "The proposed Canada-Central America free trade agreement," Statement, May 2003, from: http://www.ccic.ca/devpol/americas_policy_group/apg25_ca4fta_pettigrew_statement.htm

A May 30–31, 2002 roundtable report on CA4FTA sponsored by the Canadian Foundation for the Americas (FOCAL), went even further: "Trust," it argued, "will improve with more dialogue and debate . . . and with better collection and sharing of accurate, transparent information" (1). Otherwise, it continued, "a public backlash may be the outcome" (6). When one recounts the attitudes expressed in the EKOS Survey, this does not appear a far-fetched outcome. See FOCAL, "Evolution of Central America's political development & economic integration," *Roundtable Report*, May 30–31, 2002, Ottawa, Canada.

43. From Eric Green, "U.S. sees CAFTA promoting Central American democracy prosperity," *Washington File*, February 11, 2003, from: http://usinfo.state.gov/regional/ar/trade/03021101.htm

44. Murray Dobbin is one. See "Canada is a world-class trade bully," *National Post*, November 14, 2001, editorial, from: http://www.tradeobservatory.org/news/index.cfm?ID=3110

45. Canada's responses to 9/11 and the war in Iraq show an entirely different policy approach, one emphasizing distance and minimal neighborliness.

46. From Dobbin's article, op. cit. One must keep in mind CELA is a traditional foe of FTAs. Even during the NAFTA environmental negotiations, it was up in arms. See Barbara Hogenboom, Mexico and the NAFTA Environmental Debate: The Transnational Politics of Economic Integration (Utretcht, Netherlands: International Books, 1996).

47. The same somber conclusion seems to be driving Greg Anderson's "Hemispheric integration in the post-Seattle era," *International Journal* LVI, no. 2 (Spring 2001):205–33.

48. From US Trade Representative, "Free trade with Central America:summary of the U.S.-Central America Free Trade Agreement," December 17, 2003, from USTR webpage: http://www.ustr.gov

49. Figures from Wendy Call, "Resisting the Plan Puebla-Panama," Citizen Action in the Americas, *Americas Program* (Silver City, NM: Interhemispheric Resource Center, September 2002). As of March 2004, however, PPP highways envisioned or constructed totaled 9,450km. See Vince McElhinny, "Update on PPP Mesoamericana transport integration initiative," March 11, 2004, from: http://www.interaction.org/idb

50. Mark Connolly, "Plan Puebla Panama," *The Ecologist*, June 2001, from: http://www.theecologist.org

51. Call, "Resisting the Plan Puebla-Panama."

52. Until it was revived at the March 2004 6th meeting of the Tuxtla Mechanism for Dialogue with Central American presidents (with four of them being absent), only

$78m was allocated in the Mexican budget for PPP in 2004 . See Miguel Pickard, "The Plan Puebla Panama revived:looking back to see what's ahead," *Americas Program* (Silver City, MD: Interhemispheric Resource Center, June 8, 2004).

53. Mexico, Presidencia de la República, *Plan Puebla Panamá: Capítulo Mexico: Documento Base* (Mexico, DF: Presidencia, 2001), 136–41; and Mario Rodriguez, "The PPP's megahighways & electrical grids:who benefits?" *Plan Puebla Panama: Battle Over the Future of Southern Mexico and Central America,* ed. Network Opposed to the Plan Puebla Panama (NoPPP), 16–18, no publisher information or date given.

54. Miguel Pickard, "PPP:Plan Puebla Panama, or private plans for profit? A primer on the development plan that would turn the region from southern Mexico to Panama into a giant export zone," September 19, 2002, from: http://www.corpwatch.org/issues/PID.jsp?articleid=3953

55. Call, op. cit.

56. Calling the PPP area a "multinational enclave," Alejandro Alvarez Béjar traces the contestation between indigenous groups and international capital to the Miguel de la Madrid administration of the mid-1980s. See "The Plan Puebla-Panama:development of a region or a multinational enclave?" Paper, Mexico City: UNAM, no date, no other information.

57. For a map of the projects, see "Center of plant diversity:the ameritas," from: http://www.nmnh.si.edu/botany/projects/cpd/mamap.htm

58. See the polemic, "The Interamerican Development Bank and the Plan Puebla Panama," March 2003, from: http://www.nadir.org/nadir/initiativ/agp/free/colombia/idb_plan_puebla.htm

59. Ryan Zinn, "The Lacandon Jungle's last stand against corporate globalization:Plan Puebla Panama and the fight to preserve biodiversity and indigenous rights in Chiapas," *CorpWatch,* September 26, 2002, from: http://corpwatch.radicaldesigns.org/article.php?id=4148

60. Margaret E. Keck and Kathryn Sikkink, *Activists Beyond Borders: Advocacy Networks in International Politics* (Ithaca, NY: Cornell University Press, 1998), esp. ch.1.

61. Call, op. cit., 2002.

62. According to the North American Forum of Integration (NAFI), these highways create corridors right up to Canada: A Pacific Corridor from Tijuana, through I5 to Vancouver, thence through the Alaskan Railway further north; the Central Western Corridor through Chihuahua and Denver to Edmonton; the Central Eastern Corridor connecting Montréal and Toronto, through Detroit, with Texas and Mexico City, either through Monterrey or Tampico. The PPP projects would easily connect with these, bringing Central America directly into the North American heartland. See NAFI, "Trade corridors," from: http://www.fina-nafi.org/ang/corridors.html

63. Sebastian Edwards shows Mexico's remarkable privatization rate was the fastest across the hemisphere. See *Crisis and Reform in Latin America: From Despair to Hope* (Washington, DC: International Bank for Reconstruction and Development, 1995), 183–99.

64. Government of Canada, Department of Foreign Affairs . . . , 2003b; and "Free trade on trial," 2004

65. Americas Policy Group, 2003; and *Fondación canadienne pour les Amériques*, 2002.

66. Squire, 2002.

67. "The Canada-Central . . . ," 2003; and "The proposed Canada-Central . . . ," 2003.

68. Not necessarily because it lost a NAFTA Chapter 11 case against the Virginia-based Ethyl Corporation and had to pay $20m for prohibiting an environment unfriendly gasoline additive. Its International Trade Minister, Pierre Pettigrew, was not enthusiastic about corporations suing countries. (Scoffield, 2000).

69. Gastle, 2002.

70. Government of Canada, DFAIT, 2001.

71. *Fondación canadienne pour les Amériques*, "Evolution of Central American political development & economic integration," Roundtable Report, May 30–3, 2002.

Chapter Five

Gatekeeping in Vain?
Balancing Inside-Out &
Outside-In Forces

INTRODUCTION: FOUR ATTENTION LEVELS

Far from being islands, insulated from the public and confined merely to the negotiators, FTAs ultimately generate domestic and external consequences, creating winners, losers, and a wide range of in-betweeners—outcomes we normally associate with democratic elections. Yet, whereas democracy is constantly played out in the legislature, for instance, FTAs, as became amply clear with Central America in this study, carry more than a fair share of exclusive engagements, restrictionist policy-making, and ambiguity bordering on deliberate duplications. How do we account for exogenous vectors—spectators, sideliners, supporters, and societal naysayers—within any negotiation framework under such circumstances?

On one level, before the FTA becomes a treaty, it must be ratified, with specific components impacting vested interests undergoing public scrutiny. Questions then arise as to how open the Central American trade negotiations have been, which groups perceive future benefits, costs, or remain more indifferent than committed, whether these make a difference to the policymakers's outcomes or not, and what theory or paradigm helps interpret all of the above dynamics coherently.

Shifting to a second level, how the Central American states position themselves also demand attention. With at least five of them, what is the convergence-divergence balance, if it is important in the first place? And if it is, how uniformly distributed are the expected benefits and costs? And if not, then why not, given the wide developmental disparities between them and the dissimilar historical baggage each brings to the negotiating table? Behind the questions lies a unique historical moment for these states: They not only seek external trade arrangements, but do so amidst an enormous domestic transformation from authoritarianism towards representative government. Costa Rica's supposed exceptionalism barely camouflages several windows of opportunities and transparencies still struggling to open up. Do these qualify Central America to play in the big leagues, or even find willingness among themselves to do so with self-confidence? Whatever the findings, are there lessons to be drawn for other similarly positioned countries?

Attention is also demanded at a third supranational level, where multilateral agencies, like the Inter-American Development Bank (IADB) and International Bank for Reconstruction and Development (IBRD), as well as broader regional trading compacts, such as the Free Trade Area of the Americas (FTAA) exert influence or seek engagement. Special attention is paid the FTAA for a number of reasons. First, it is the goal towards hemispheric integration once FTAs across Central America are completed. Second, FTAA issues parallel their multilateral counterparts: they specify the goal of trade openness, methods whereby this may be attained, disciplines for the various categories of trade openness, connections with and concerns about non-traded products, services, or situations, as for example, labor, the environment, health and phytosanitary standards, and so forth. Third, FTAA provides in part the negotiation structures, not just in terms of Feinberg's cascading modular multilateralism (CMM) and hemispheric diplomacy (HD) models, but also the blueprint for treating trade openness technicalities. Finally, because of all of the above, FTAA also provides a preview of multilateral outcomes of regional trading arrangements, in particular because CMM is premised upon plurilateral engagement and a generalizable domestic-foreign nexus.

At a fourth level are the three A-teams: Canada, Mexico, and the United States. How have negotiations with so-called little leaguers boosted their own interests? To what extent are those interests statist, regionalistic, hemispheric, or multilateral? Why did the negotiations produce different results? Does it really matter if those results are so diametrically different when the North American gravitational pull has historically and increasingly been towards the United States? Most critically, though, how are they coordinating pressures from below, imperatives from above, constraints from within, and tradeoffs from outside while preserving the democratic fabric which must simultaneously serve as a model for other transitional countries south of Mexico?

Accordingly, this chapter comes in five sections. The first profiles societal responses in the three A-team countries, distinguishing supporters from opponents, and how their responses can be captured by any paradigm and interpreted theoretically. Shifting attention to Central American dynamics, the second section identifies both catalyzers and roadblocks, as well as convergences and divergences between the countries. The next port of call involves the supranational context, seen through FTAA lenses, and how Central American negotiations reflect or diverge from the idealized FTAA model. The fourth section addresses the gatekeeping issue, how the three A-teams, that is, the three North American countries, coordinate pressures from below and mandates from abroad, while pursuing their specified goals. The chapter concludes by summarizing relationships between models and trade-related developments in the fifth section.

BLOWING IN SOCIETAL WINDS

Social groups in all three countries were aware of the negotiations, expressed their points of view, and followed the progress, in spite of the glass ceiling separating them from actual negotiations. That the groups were ignored raises questions about the nature of multilateral negotiations amidst democratization —an issue left for the conclusions of this chapter and of the manuscript. Table 5.1 identifies a cross-section of supporters, opponents, and mixed groups, while some of their responses or positions are specified in Table 5.2

Interpreting tables 5.1 and 5.2 simultaneously not only informs us of the specific groups and their various positions, but also exposes us to the diversity of groups constituting supporters, opponents, and those in between, enabling us to survey a fairly representative cross-section of the broad FTAA picture of positions, and connecting those positions with specific arguments. One notices at the outset the wider array of mobilized groups in the United States than in Mexico and more dramatically so than in Canada, alerting us to at least one paradox and confirming at least one trading pattern. The paradox is simply the desire of trade negotiations to seek greater transparency not being matched by commensurate transparency in the negotiation processes themselves. The trading pattern confirmed relates trading size to negotiated outcomes: The larger the relative size of trade, the greater the impact this has, compared to other trading partners, on completing negotiations—thus reifying the Darwinian principle of the fittest ultimately surviving longer than others.

As may be expected, supporters include businesses and groups reflecting corporate interests and a paradoxical political bipartisanship. Whereas business groups are driven by considerations of comparative advantage and profits through market access, political parties also bring external competitiveness to bear on domestic considerations. Consequently, whereas the former will argue, for instance, how the jobs created by foreign exports offset any immediate environmental costs, the latter will similarly preserve domestic labor and/or environmental standards in adjusting to cheaper imports but re-

Table 5.1. Free Trade Supporters, Opponents, and Mixed Groups

Countries	Supporters	Opponents	Mixed Groups (Reflectors)
Canada	• Business groups • FUNPADEM (Sharon O'Regan) • Bipartisan support	• Canadian Council of International Cooperation (ex-CEO Esperanza Morena) • Americas Policy Group (Allison Crosby, Suzanne Rumsey as co-chairs)	• FOCAL
Mexico	• Business groups • Bipartisan support: PAN; PRI	• Center for Economic & Political Investigations of Community Action (CIEPAC) • Convergence of Movements of the People's of the Americas (COMPA) • Mexican Network of Action Against Free Trade (RMALC)	• Issues not sufficiently disseminated across the entire state as to permit definitive identification
United States	• PPI (Gressner) • American Apparel & Footwear Association • US Association of Importers of Textiles & Apparels (Brenda Jacobs) • Business Coalition for US-Central American Trade (Calman Cohen) • Bipartisan support	• Carnegie Endowment for International Peace (Sandra Polanski, Director, Trade, Equity, & Development Project) • Millikin & Co. Textiles • Louisiana Shrimp Association • National Farm Coalition (Dena Hoff) • Oxfam • Sierra Club	• Agriculture • Textiles

main indifferent to labor/environmental standards in exporting countries, perhaps even consciously violating them. All well and good, but the business positions postpone labor/environmental costs into an unknown future when deterioration may become irreparable, since any measurement of labor standards worsening can only be accurately assessed *a posteriori* while environmental damages are generally incremental and cumulative; and party interests assume both a large and ever-growing national pie and unbounded democratization abroad, both reflecting unrealistic articles of faith.

Table 5.2. Central America & Group Positions

Countries	Positions of Supporters	Positions of Opponents	Positions of Mixed Groups
Canada	a. new business opportunities b. offsets US domination c. supports Canada's leadership role d. since agreement is inevitable, going with the flow as early as possible brings home the fruits much earlier e. consistent with foreign policy principles	a. hemispheric agreement by stealth b. public interests constrained c. investors empowered over people d. indigenous groups, women affected negatively e. human rights affected negatively	a. not fully developed: premature b. both supporters and opponents not strident enough since engagement opportunities are limited; thus both supporters and opponents incorporate arguments from the other side
Mexico	a. State development encouraged (brings fruits to the south) b. adjustment to global restructuration c. prevent future Zapatistas d. part of Mexico's southern shift e. leadership opportunities	a. tantamounts to corporate exploitation b. rain forests destroyed c. indigenous lifestyles disrupted, indigenous people dislocated d. *maquiladorization* and women exploitation e. distorted nationalism	a. not yet well-defined, given the zero-sum orientation of supporters and opponents: awaits clear formation of such groups
United States	a. comparative advantage (textiles) b. not a race to the bottom (Ed Gressner) c. reduce barriers (Calman Cohen) d. if not the US, others may step in, creating lost opportunity e. consistent with US history (Monroe Doctrine)	a. latter-day mercantilism b. pushes CA farmers to drug production c. boosts emigration d. anti-cumulation e. undemocratic f. public hearings not meaningful g. corporate capacity to sue government increases	a. both agriculture and textiles share similar predicament: some winners, some losers, converting both sectoral FTA responses into industry specific determinations, and industrial FTA responses into firm-specific determinations

The third group may be too strapped to exert any immediate policy impact, but carries enormous long-term consequences. If an industry, like agriculture or textiles in the specific Central American cases, is divided over free trade arrangements, policy-makers get the opportunity to divide and rule domestic interests for immediate purposes, which over the long-haul actually weakens existing log-rolling or corporatist structures in the legislature, breeding post-pluralist variations which decisively shift the free-trade policy-making advantage to free-trade policy-makers in the executive branch.[1] Although grass-roots or domestic opposition may remain a permanent part of the free-trade landscape, executive branch officials face the million dollar question, not whether to pursue free trade, but how and to which groups to reward, punish, ignore, or incorporate in the process.

Pinpointing Bridges and Blockers

Opposition groups are clearly more visible, vocal, and replete with arguments: They fear they have more to lose than supporters have to gain. A country-wide assessment specifies the positions of what Fen Osler Hampson dubs *bridges* and *blockers* in multilateral negotiations.

In spite of Canada's minimal contacts, oppositional forces and firepower are disproportionately larger. Speaking for the Canadian Council of International Cooperation (CCIC), former CEO Esperanza Morena raised at least five objections: (a) the stealthy approach to negotiations; (b) how existing public policy interests become illegitimate without a public or legislative mandate; (c) corporate empowerment over people and human concerns; (d) motley groups such as natives and women becoming further marginalized; and (e) environment and human rights becoming further endangered.

One finds several parallels in the positions of the Americas Policy Group (APG), as articulated by its co-chairs, Allison Crosby and Suzanne Rumsey. At least five supportive positions may be extracted from the various Canadian groups: (a) new business opportunities created, both in trade and for investors; (b) by diversifying trade and investment dependence on the US, long-term US domination may be eased; (c) Canada's hemispheric leadership drive, most robustly demonstrated at the Québec FTAA summit, would be strengthened; (d) with the US building hemispheric FTA interests, the earlier this inevitable embrace is made, the lower the costs for Canada; and (e) a Central American FTA would be consistent with Canada's underlying post-World War II foreign policy principles of promoting development, democratization, and humanitarianism.

Mexico's opposition stems more from the grassroots than Canada's urban-rooted groups, with the United States falling somewhere in between, reflecting both ends of the spectrum. Indigenous Mexican groups clearly lead the assault on PPP, and by transnationalizing their cause, they inflict more extensive damages on PPP than any opposition network in the US against CAFTA or in Canada against CA4FTA. Their arguments are many, and have stoutly prevented any PPP progress. These include: (a) FTAs favor corporations, and lead inevitably to corporations exploiting people; (b) *maquiladorization* breeds labor and women exploitation; (c) massive environmental damages would follow the infrastructural projects and dam constructions; (d) not only would indigenous people be dislocated, but their lifestyles also disrupted; and (e) a one-size-fits-all Mexico City development pattern, rather than strengthening Mexican nationalism, may actually weaken it by eliminating local socio-cultural political-economic patterns of attitudes and behavior.

On the flip side, arguments supporting PPP as part of the broader Washington Consensus are equally abundant: (a) Mexican development would be enhanced, as the relatively impoverished southern states are brought into the developmental mainstream; (b) with the migration of northern *maquilas*, economic disruptions would be avoided by relocating *maquilas* in the south, which would also help Mexico adjust to global restructuration processes; (c) by developing the south, future rebellions, like the *Zapatista* uprisings, would be prevented; (d) Mexico's southern shift would conceivably help dampen its northern US attention, thereby reducing US dependence and promoting trade diversification; and (e) leadership possibilities may arise in the south to replace a history of mutual suspicion, indifference, and alienation.

More societal reactions in the United States than in Canada and Mexico reflect the greater societal engagement in the FTA negotiations, the larger US economic size, and the greater potential damage this size entails for US society. At least seven arguments against CAFTA are discernible: (a) given the enormous economic disparities, many see CAFTA as a modern form of beggar-thy-neighbor, or mercantilist, policy approach; (b) Central American farmers would be so squeezed out of their routine production, they may be driven into producing cocaine or other narcotic production; (c) in turn, emigration pressures would be fueled; (d) threatened textiles producers strongly oppose cumulation, whereby other third countries would find gateways through Central America into US markets; (e) the negotiations were not only not democratic, but also promoted non-democratic Central American patterns of behavior to persist; (f) public hearings were wasted opportunities, as nothing substantive emerged; and (g) incorporating NAFTA's Chapter 11 make foreign governments hostages to US corporations, thus prolonging the Latin American ghost of US neo-imperialism.

US protestors, interestingly, align their opposition to personally-felt rather than principle-deviating conditions, paying as much attention to the perceived

FTA impacts in boosting drug shipments and illegal migrants to the United States as to FTAs constituting mercantilism and undermining democracy. There are reasons why. Narcotics and illegal emigrants capitalize on the most porous boundaries between DCs and LDCs anywhere in this world, raising alarms epitomized by Samuel P. Huntington's fear of a less Anglo-Saxon and more Hispanic US society evolving.[2] One part of the mercantilist argument from incorporating NAFTA's Chapter 11 divides Central American states into leaders, who pay lip-service to this threat, and the general public, who feel more fearful of this threat. Given their transitional statuses, Central American states cannot benefit from such domestic divisions when both democratization and liberalization necessitate majority policy support. Ironically, the only country where the Chapter 11 threat is making some noise is one where no corporations are likely to wield it against the government: the United States.

Since democracy is the adopted form of government across the entire North and Central American spectrum for the first time, how the social pulse, by impinging the political market, affects ratification, remains the ultimate test. Canada's efforts may be the farthest from ratification processes, Mexico's have been sufficiently subdued to contemplate any legislative showdown, all the more so since they do not constitute a treaty in need of subsequent ratification, and the US, by concluding negotiations, stands closest to a ratification. Of course, this post-negotiations phase came closer to reality with Bush's November 2 electoral victory, but apprehensions of not having the win-set circulated in relevant circuits at the time.[3] Group heterogeneity ensures a close call regardless. Much like the relatively safer NAFTA treaty necessitated carrots and sticks in October and November 1993, CAFTA is unlikely to get clear sailing even with Bush's victory and a handsome Republican congressional majority.

Unlike CA4FTA, CAFTA is also engaged in other post-negotiations functions. One is to extend membership to the Dominican Republic, and eventually Panama.[4] The other is to reconnect with FTAA, a rendezvous with whose destiny also draws closer and closer every day, but, in addition to the Brazil-led revolution against it during 2003, may also be hastened by the November 2004 Bush victory.

At least five common issues springing from the above country-specific discussions warrant at least a minimum of attention: (a) the positions reflect more group-specific interests than partisanship; (b) at least two claims seem to be unfounded: the more a country trades with Central American states, the more the issues of contention, or conversely, the less a country trades with Central American states, the fewer the issues of contention; (c) asymmetry on the negotiations table is matched by asymmetry in the network of societal influences; (d) societal influences in these particular negotiations more or less streamline influences in other trade negotiations; and (e) influence articulation reflects greater democratization than negotiations themselves.

Turning to the first argument, group-specific interests come across more vividly than political party platforms, indeed attempts to link the two, if they exist in the first place, play a secondary role to projecting the group's position. Speaking for the US National Family Farm Coalition, Montana farmer Dena Hoff may have been speaking for a Democrat or a Republic, American, Canadian, or Mexican counterpart. Trade deals, she ventured, mean "more farmers off the land," since they "have to have a price above product [cost]."[5] How influential such group positions were in the 2004 US elections may be a moot point; but by and large, group-specific interests precede broader interests in both priorities and articulation. Even protests against CAFTA by Nicaraguan farmers, for example, are more against liberalizing maize, beans, and US agrobusinesses than against the United States.[6] Again, with a little bit of politics, it could be directed into an anti-US demonstration, since the US farmer receives fifty-times more of a subsidy than his Nicaraguan counterpart, who, with a miserable income of less than $2 per day, lives much at the margin than his US counterpart, and which negotiations don't always acknowledge or portray. Similarly for fair-trade US supporters who search to reduce the gap between worker's wages and their quality of life or preserve the environment: Their consumption of coffee, for example, might have the Guatemalan farmer's welfare in mind, but have driven retail corporations out of the fair-trade deal as prices spiral beyond manageable levels. Although Starbucks, Dunkin Donuts, as well as Procter & Gamble, which produces Folger's, joined TransFair USA, promoting the fair-trade themes, Starbucks and Dunkin Donuts later dropped out owing to spiraling costs.[7]

Behind this unevenness lies an unusual but logical bipartisanship across North and Central America: The agreements or negotiations find support from contesting parties. Canada's Liberal Party is directly involved in the negotiations, but the Conservatives initiated regionalizing trade under Brian Mulroney in the first place; Mexico's PAN proposed PPP, but borrowed several PRI projects or initiatives from the 1980s and 1990s; and even though the US Republicans are gung-ho about them, it was Bill Clinton's Democratic Party which gave FTAA and NAFTA the decisive initial push. Political parties may still be struggling to plant their roots across democratizing Central American states, but the free trade and regional integration pursuits are seen by the dominant mainstream parties as offering win-win possibilities.

Second, even though the US trades the most, of the three countries, with Central American states, and Canada the least, this does not necessarily mean greater US and lesser Canadian group mobilization against the agreement. Other factors explain why there are more US and fewer Canadian groups mobilized: More media networks cover US negotiations than Canadian; US negotiations have been more media-conscious, without being fully open, than Canadian negotiations; and the US routinely stirs more emotions than any other country, including Canada, over negotiations. That it also trades more with Central American states than Canada and Mexico does not explain why, in comparison to its negligible trade, Mexico generated widespread PPP opposition, and sometimes in collaboration with societal groups inside Central America. Transnational groups further blur the relationship between traded volumes and societal opposition:[8] Issues like the environment and human rights do not become the property of any specific country, as the joint AFL-CIO and Central American trade unions call to preserve workers rights, debt relief, humane immigration, and transparency in negotiations indicated.[9] Barbara Hogenboom brings this out more vividly with the NAFTA environmental side-agreement negotiations.[10]

Third, asymmetry on the negotiations table is mirrored by influence group networks in at least two ways: (a) Just as the US dominated the CAFTA negotiating agenda by pre-announcing the conclusion date and inducing a recalcitrant Costa Rica back to the table within a month of refusing to sign, US interest groups also adopt a patronizing approach to their Central American counterparts, setting the pace, speaking for them, in short, stealing the show in supposedly symmetrical gatherings. Take for example, the following statement: "These are the kinds of barriers that do not promote an expansion of commerce between Central America and the United States." If made by a Central American group leader, it would command less attention, not just in the media, but also by counterpart US groups. Since it was made by Calman Cohen of the Business Coalition for US-Central American Trade, and because he had Central American service markets in mind, it certainly caught Central American attention—evident most vividly in Costa Rica's return to the negotiation table in January 2004. (b) A second asymmetry, also revealed by the same comment, is the monopoly exerted over Central American media by elites either conducting or supporting the negotiations, which contrasts with the typically two-way exchanges in the US media over any issue being negotiated. Grassroot groups are more handicapped from aggregating and articulating their preferences across Central America than, for example, in Canada and the US, but to some extent also Mexico. A climate of poverty, absence of organizational resources, and historical instances of political closure and suppression do not help level the negotiations playing field, especially if it is too skewed to begin with. Nevertheless, pockets of resistance are there, especially among the various indigenous groups, get virtually ignored *carte blanche* in the negotiation process.

Fourth, the nature and themes of Central American negotiations streamline their counterparts in more general trade negotiations. Unless they are held in

islands or desert locations, we are very familiar with how protestors of all
stripes can hijack WTO ministerial meetings, evident in Seattle in 1999 and
coming on down to the Cancún deadlock in August-September 2003. The issues are similar: agriculture, environment, labor, anti-capitalism, anti-big
business, exploitation, all of the above, or some of the above. CAFTA and
PPP faced similar ghosts, not just during any specific negotiations or congregations, but throughout the duration of overall negotiations or policy implementation. The only difference seems to be the citizenship diversity of the
participants: With CAFTA and PPP, they are almost entirely from the participating countries, with WTO from anywhere. Even as both supporters and opponents rally to trade negotiation venues, those intent on injecting confusion,
chaos, and/or anarchy, that is, free-riders of the interplay of supporters and
opponents, complicate matters for secular reasons. By and large, even though
only a handful of issues increasingly hijack trade negotiations these days, as
more and more issues become not just economically, but also socially and
environmentally sensitive, the likelihood of turbulence accompanying trade
negotiations no matter how big or small in participation also grows. Perhaps
this is a function not only of democracy, but also of democratic expansion
across the world, in itself worthy of further assessment.

Finally, no matter how secretly conducted the negotiations, they have acti-
vated civil society groups in some very unexpected locations, capitalizing on,
reflecting, and enhancing democratization. Barring Costa Rica, Central
American states, and even Mexico, are more exposed to all four winds today
than, say, ten years ago; and although this development would have happened
regardless of trade negotiations, given the relaxation of political structures,
trade negotiations nevertheless play a significant catalyzing role. Even
though they are never unlikely to even the playing field, trade negotiations increase public awareness, become educational, and promote non-economic integration across all kinds of barriers and boundaries. These may be taken for
granted in experienced and developed countries such as Canada and the
United States, but they still remain relatively new in Mexico and absolutely
eye-opening across many segments of Central America. What's inside the
opened can may be determined, in part, by what kind of a can is being
opened.

LITTLE LEAGUERS IN GULLIVER-SIZED GAMES

How capable are the Central American states of fitting in and fulfilling free
trade arrangements with the three vastly larger North American economies?
Of course, this depends on how enthusiastic they remain about joining, to

what extent they satisfy certain internationalized rules indirectly affecting such engagements, their capacity to adopt measures directly affecting performances, and whether they have the goods and services to perform under these circumstances. Tables 5.3, 5.4, and 5.5 summarize discussions. As a caveat, since comparable data for Belize, Dominican Republic, and Panama could not always be found in time, emphasis is on the remaining Central American states.

Based on earlier discussions, although supporters and opponents abound in every country, especially dividing policy-making elites and the masses in the countryside, factories, and urban slums, tables 5.3, 5.4, and 5.5 hazard a rough overall impression on enthusiasm, engagement, policy adjustments,

Table 5.3. Central American Responses

	B	CR	DR	El Sal	G	H	N	P
1. On PPP	I	I	I	I	I	I	I	I
2. On CA4FTA		E		M	M	M	M	
3. On CAFTA		M	E	E	E	E	E	E
4. On FTAA	E	E	E	E	E	E	E	E
5. On ILO Principles								
a. freedom of work		Yes	No	Yes	Yes	Yes	Yes	
b. forced labor		Yes	No	Yes	Yes	Yes	Yes	
c. against discrimination		Yes	Yes	Yes	Yes	Yes	Yes	
d. on child labor		Yes	Yes	Yes	Yes	Yes	Yes	
6. On Structural Reforms								
a. stabilization		1978			1987–91	1992	1991	
b. trade liberalization		1986		1989	1988	1990	1991	
c. tax reforms				1993	1994	1994	1992	
d. financial reforms		1988		1990	1991	1991	1990	
e. privatization					1990			
f. labor reforms								
7. Labor distribution (1970)								
a. traditional agriculture		18.6		28.0	37.0	40.3	26.0	
b. modern agriculture/ mining		24.4		30.0	23.2	24.1	26.5	
c. manufacture		15.1		17.6	14.6	14.0	19.2	
8. Convergence-Divergence Balance (CD-Balance)		C	C	C	C	C	C	C

C Legend: I = indifference, E = enthusiasm, M = mixed

Sources: Jorge Nowalski and Keynor Ruiz, "CAFTA/TLC hacia una apertura comercial laboralmente justa e incluyente," *CAFTA/TLC: Reflexiones sobre el futuro*, ed. Jorge Urbina, et al., Colección Prospectiva #5, Centro Internacional para el Dessarollo Humano (San José, CR: Lara Segura y Asociados, 2003), 44; Rosemary Thorp, *Progress, Poverty and Exclusion: An Economic History of Latin America in the 20th Century* (Washington, DC: Inter-American Development Bank, 1998, published by Johns Hopkins University Press, Baltimore, MD), 162, 174, 228–29; and The World Bank, *Entering the 21st Century: World Development Report, 1999/2000* (Washington, DC: World Bank, published by Oxford University Press, New York, 2000), 230–39.

and performance capabilities. In terms of enthusiasm towards PPP, CA4FTA, CAFTA, and FTAA, Table 5.3 offers some slightly mixed observations. Five issues at the least stand out.

First, owing to the US, CAFTA elicits more enthusiastic responses from all Central American countries except, to some extent, Costa Rica, whose mixed inclination paralleled its eventual CCRFTA embrace. More telling was the shift of other Central American states in CA4FTA talks from greater enthusiasm towards a mixture of confusion and indifference. PPP ranked somewhere in between, reflecting increasingly more indifference by 2004 than earlier, not only because the original endogenously-generated enthusiasm had petered out, but also because CA4FTA and CAFTA usurped a lot of that enthusiasm at various stages. Given their limited administrative infrastructures, Central American countries may find putting all FTA eggs in the US basket may still compensate for neglecting the other two, although the panglossian world of doing well with all three integrative efforts, which was the original expectation, may have been tempered by real-life developments, such as Mexico's refrain from PPP between 2001 and 2004, as well as Canada's topsy-turvy Latin interests sliding into its pessimistic phase just when CA4FTA negotiations were to enter their golden moments.[11]

Second, another interesting interpretation stems from Costa Rica's variance: By running into problems with CAFTA but not PPP or CA4FTA, Costa Rica's relatively more developed regional status suggests the level of development as an influential factor in FTA negotiations. While noting Costa Rica's different experiences for future references, other less developed countries in Central America may heed Otto von Bismarck's crisp observation of free-trade being a policy of strong states. If eventually true of the United States in North America and across Central America, the aphorism also suggests free trade cannot benefit all states seeking free trade—a caveat acquiring greater significance given the multilaterally-driven adoption of free-trade rules, regulations, and disciplines.

Third, the adoption of a variety of ILO's work-related conventions may be deceptive. On the one hand, every country adopted these several conventions,[12] save El Salvador, though it is unlikely to remain a laggard, at least in adoption, for long. On the other, these conventions are not compatible with *maquilas* and a variety of other work-related labor practices common to transitional countries:[13] Working hours, child labor, adequate remuneration, and so forth, are not just flouted, but since the alternative seems more to be unemployment than corporate censure, the likelihood of these malpractices and violations being contested also remains low. Taking the case of Central America's strongest *maquila* industry, in Honduras, Ralph Armbruster-Sandoval finds each shift typically runs 10–12 hour rotations, instead of the stipulated

8 hours/day. "Inside the factories," he further observes, "workers are not allowed to talk with each other. Bathroom breaks are timed and regulated. In some cases, women have been forced to take birth control pills. Pregnant women have also been fired without receiving their legally guaranteed benefits . . . . Many factories are also extremely hot and poorly ventilated, making breathing very difficult. Asthma, bronchitis, and other respiratory-related illnesses along with fainting spells, have been widely reported. Stress related problems, such as insomnia, loss of appetite, spasm, and diarrhea, are also quite common."[14] He might as well have added the lack of infrastructures to deal with these ailments, such as hospitals or health controls. It is interesting how the US automobile industry, especially GM's Linden plant in New Jersey, reflected many of these same restrictions even after the New Deal had established minimum thresholds and safeguards.[15] The implications should not be discussed: corporate culture threatens labor standards everywhere, more so in LDCs than in DCs, suggesting FTAs are unlikely to more than marginally uplift social, working, and possibly environmental conditions across Central America—one reason why Canada is unlikely to generate enthusiastic or deep-rooted trading interests in the region compared to the United States, and because of the United States, Mexico.

Fourth, all countries embraced several other policy reforms directly impacting performances, and in spite of having the appropriate administrative infrastructures in place. This may tantamount to naught if the period of infrastructural development is protracted, or riddled with confrontation, challenges, or other uncertainties. On the other hand, small disruptions could create large, future consequences, rippling from one policy-making domain to another.

Finally, the striking convergence, evident particularly in the different types of reforms being undertaken, is not surprising since policy-makers in all five countries believe in the same free-trade philosophy, thereby making the US a leading partner. There also appears to be a parallel civil society pattern in the five countries: There is more ambivalence than enthusiasm, and reflecting deep and blatant opposition groups to the deals.[16] Domestic divergence between leaders and the masses is as common across Central American as across North American states.

Turning to tables 5.4 and 5.5, some indicators show other FTA building blocks, particularly related to policies and performances, stoutly and steadily falling into place across Central America. Five observations support this conclusion.

First, not only are Central American countries individually and collectively concluding other FTAs, as Table 5.5 indicates, but also PPP, CA4FTA, and CAFTA have useful and necessary supplementary arrangements leading

Table 5.4. Central America's Transitional Country Profile

Dimensions	Costa Rica	El Salvador	Guatemala	Honduras	Nicaragua
1. *Destination of exports (2002, in %)*	US:51.8 CA:14.2 EU:11.1	US: 65.4 CA: 25.2 EU: 2.9	CA: 39.0 US: 30.0 EU: 10.7	US:47.8 CA: 20.2 EU: 6.1	CA: 36.6 US: 32.9 EU: 13.3
2. *Sources of FDI (2001, in %)*	US: 57 Can: 15 CA: 6	US: 30 Can: 8 CA: 12	US: 70 Can: 2 CA: 17	US: 46 Can: 20 CA: 11	US: 40 Can: 15 CA: 17
3. *FDI receipts in comparative context (1990–99, in %)*	42.3	17.3	18.1	10.4	12.0
4. *Volume of FDI received (1990–99, in US$b)*	3.51	1.43	1.5	.86	.99
5. *Types of economic engagements (in %)*					
a. micro-enterprise	50	30	20	15	15
b. self-employed	50	70	80	85	85
6. *Sectoral breakdown of microenterprises (in thousands & relative %, 1997)*					
a. commercial:	55 (35%)	185 (42%)	252 (45%)	156 (43%)	68 (47%)
b. manufacture:	38 (24%)	109 (25%)	134 (24%)	116 (33%)	29 (20%)
c. services:	65 (41%)	145 (33%)	173 (31%)	86 (24%)	47 (33%)
d. total:	158	438	560	359	143

Source: Jorge Nowalski and Doris Osterlof, CAFTA/TLC: Potencial competitivo de los sectores productivos de Centroamérica, Colección Prospectiva #7, Centro Internacional para el Dessarollo Humano (San José, CR: Lara Segura y Asociados, SA, 2004), 36 and 41; and Nowalski and Keynor Ruiz, "CAFTA/TLC hacia una apertura comercial laboralmente justa e incluyente," CAFTA/TLC: Reflexiones sobre el futuro, ed. Jorge Urbina, et al., Colección Prospectiva #5, Centro Internacional para el Dessarollo Humano (San José, CR: Lara Segura y Asociados, 2003), 34–35.

Table 5.5.   Central America in FTAs

Free Trade Agreements (members with year)

- Costa Rica–Mexico: 1995
- Nicaragua–Mexico: 1998
- Northern Triangle (Guatemala, El Salvador, Honduras)–Mexico: 2001
- El Salvador–Panama: 2003
- Costa Rica & El Salvador–Chile: 2002
- Costa Rica–Canada: 2002
- Costa Rica–CARICOM: Ratification underway
- Costa Rica, Guatemala, Honduras, Nicaragua–Panama: Underway
- Central America–European Union: Underway
- Guatemala, Honduras, Nicaragua–Chile: Underway

towards FTAA. For example, Central American countries have been strengthening their own FTAs, with intra-regional trade accounting for a minimum of 14.2% of Costa Rican exports and a maximum of 36.6% for Nicaragua, both figures from 2002, as Table 5.4 shows. FTAs have also been extended to outlying partners, such as Dominican Republic and Panama, and explore the region south of Panama too, for example, with Chile. Not only is this developing the regional trading bloc philosophy in the original hemispheric playground of regionalism, but also boosting intra-regional trade volumes, rules, and disciplines. Table 5.4 also shows similar interlocking foreign direct investment (FDI) patterns for the region: The second column indicates a low of 6% of Costa Rica FDI originating in Central America to a high of 17% each of Guatemala and Nicaragua originating in Central America.

Second, Central American trade is not nearly as swallowed up by the United States as Mexico's has been under NAFTA: They do have a minimum of healthy or a maximum of robust trading/investment relations with the European Union countries — a factor shaped as much by historical exchange networks as a contemporary imperative under furious globalization and competitiveness forces. Table 5.4 indicates a low of 2.9% of Salvadorean exports going to the EU, to a maximum of 13.3% of Nicaragua's. Yet, the puzzle whether, by not being as hopelessly and irreversibly locked into the US trading orbit as Mexico, Central American states enhance their bargaining positions with the United States, continues to remain just that: a puzzle, suggesting, regardless of the volume of trade conducted with the United States, bargaining may remain subordinated to the dynamics of attaining an overall outcome. On the one hand, with limited options, Central America may become the prototype of other regional arrangements involving the United States; and although Brazil provides a FTAA counterpart, the more interesting issue is how long Brazil can continue defying core US trading interests. On the other, a conjoined Canada-Mexico-US approach to Central American states, as in the form of a FTAA-track drive, would probably go a long way to deemphasize the length, breadth, and depth of European engagements. In sum, Central and Latin American states are poised to line up behind the United States in any transatlantic skirmish, much to their expected detriment.

Third, Central America appears to be capitalizing on one of the few virtues less developed countries have: reliance on microenterprises as a trigger and engine of growth. Microenterprises receive inevitably more encouragement in FTAs between DCs and LDCs, and according to Table 5.4, their contribution is a function of how developed the LDC is. In the more developed Costa Rica, for instance, they account for 50% of all economic engagements, involving a total of 158,100 people, 41% in services, 35% in commerce, and 24% in manufactures. At the other end of the spectrum, microenterprises represented 15% of all economic engagements in both Honduras and Nicaragua, employing 359,000 and 143,700 people, respectively. In both countries, commerce engaged the largest share of those workers, with 43% and 47%, respectively, while in the second place, manufacture accounted for 33% in Honduras and services 33% in Nicaragua. Although Guatemala had the largest number of microenterprise workers, with 560,000, they accounted for only 20% of economic engagements, with 45% in the commercial sector, 31% in services, and 24% in manufacture; and El Salvador, with a second microenterprise total employment ranking of 438,131 accounting for 30% of all economic engagements, also had the commercial sector leading the others with 42%, services with 33%, and manufactures with 25%. What Barrington Moore calls the bourgeois impulse,[17] often seen as the turning point in the transition from a traditional society towards modernization, is clearly visible and active across Central America, springing not much from the agricultural sector, as Moore found across Europe, but from urban-rural microenterprises.

Fourth, Mexico's *maquila* history could inspire Central American further. Established under the 1965 Border Industrialization Program, Mexico's twin-plant industries made several notable contributions towards economic development until NAFTA was adopted thirty years later: By providing jobs, it hastened urban migration, liberated rural women who dominated the workforce, elevated the technological base, for example, from textiles to semi-conductors, and added significantly to the net national production base. Of course, a longer list of problems were generated, but the positive developments may encourage more than discourage Central American policy-makers in tip-toeing the same developmental route. After all, *maquila* plants fuel the microenterprise upsurge in the region.

Finally, with Central American states showing strong signs of rallying intra-regional arrangements, exploring all North American avenues of extension, and keeping extra-hemispheric options valid and potent, they certainly cannot be dismissed as little leaguers in a big-fish game: True, there are several vulnerabilities of small-sized economies in this form of expected transactions, such as agriculture being squeezed out of its importance and various societal standards sustaining, at best, ambiguous performance levels, but the expected gains from big-league trade currently dwarf potential losses to be ignored. That itself remains a catalyst of further future policy reforms in the directions of the Washington Consensus, FTAA, and WTO. Central America's past may rapidly be subordinated to new cleavages, social structures, and nature of foreign integration—all irreversibly replacing authoritarianism, corporatism, and old forms of direct discrimination but not necessarily by democracy, fully-functioning pluralism, and a discrimination-free society. Likely patterns may be a hybrid of both with subtle forms of discrimination masking authoritarian and corporatist tendencies within a half-baked democracy and deformed liberalization.

One indication of this is the growing interest of Central America's 2–4m migrants settled in the United States. A delegation representing them traveled to Guatemala City during the 4th Round of CAFTA to platform for including immigration in the agreement, as well as principles affecting the rural sector, where many of the delegates originated, as well as consumer protection, transparency, public participation, and more detailed negotiations.[18]

SUPRANATIONALIZING MARKET FUNDAMENTALISM OR LOCALIZING SUPRANATIONALISM?

Empirically and theoretically FTAA comes across more as *Fit This Ambiguous Agreement* than a Free Trade Area of the Americas! Table 5.6 sheds comparative light between FTAA and the Central American integrative pursuits, while Table 5.7 does likewise between FTAA and WTO. In the final analysis, FTAA mirrors WTO methods and negotiations disciplines better than Central American integrative pursuits engaging North American countries do FTAA. Yet, WTO methods and negotiations disciplines do percolate through FTAA to Central American pursuits, although reverse percolation is much harder to establish, more difficult to comprehend, and vastly different in nature. FTAA is clearly the star organization. As "the most comprehensive trade and investment regime in the world," FTAA is more than a bridgehead between the multilateral and regional levels; and by transplanting rigid WTO disciplines across Central America, it becomes "NAFTA on steroids."[19] It is the terminal point of both CAFTA and CA4FTA, and PPP finds its legitimacy in precisely the FTAA network of plurilateralism, bilateralism, and issue-specific coordination. Yet, unless FTAA can fall in line behind the US, that is, shed the current FTAA-Lite synonym, it may be overtaken by a NAFTA-Plus, that is, a NAFTA-CAFTA combination imposing take-it-or-leave-it terms to the remainder of Latin America. Brazil may then feel the pinch.

The FTAA negotiating structure, established at the 1998 Santiago Summit of the Americas, influenced both CAFTA and CA4FTA. Table 5.6 spells out the mandate and scope of 9 FTAA negotiations committees, what the follow-up rules and disciplines are, and how Central American integrative efforts reflect them. At least five observations follow.

First, the mandates and scopes are more suitable for DCs than LDCs, implying the giant leap traditional and transitional Central American countries must make to fulfill them. No one realistically expects any Central American country to survive external competition or retain even fragments of its sovereignty: The liberalization theme behind every single negotiating committee essentially comes at a time when no Central American country possesses any competitive industry, whether in agriculture, service, or investment, when with so many pressing financial needs, it can not engage in significant subsidization, and when no country possesses the administrative infrastructure and trained personnel to monitor intellectual property rights or engage in dispute settlement proceedings. Even the more advanced LDCs, such as Brazil, China, or India, have problems with some of these negotiating committee issues, for example, the controversies over the Singapore issues continue to derail WTO-sponsored meetings. That Central American states can do any better involves a leap of faith without adequate footing.

Second, although the rules and disciplines associated with each negotiating committee is modeled on the WTO, as evident in Table 5.7, FTAA actually goes beyond—indicating in the process the unwritten US competitive liberalism goal of reconstructing WTO through FTAA and other FTAs concluded by the United States, what Thomas Palley of the Open Society Institute calls "divide and rule."[20] Behind the Cancún WTO breakdown lay a series of discipline-related disagreements between DCs and LDCs;[21] and FTAA could represent an alternate approach of coopting LDCs through FTAs before revisiting these same unchanged WTO disciplines. If this reading is correct, then not only is FTAA the moment's potential star trade agency, but CAFTA is also performing a critical role, one-sided though it may be, over which Central American countries have no voice, Canada has no choice but to tiptoe through CA4FTA, and Mexico is already part and parcel of the unfolding drama through its NAFTA membership—making NAFTA the first critical US-based FTA upon which CAFTA must be positioned in order to make FTAA a done deal by the previously announced US goal of 2005. As previously noted, with CAFTA falling in line, FTAA members will find bargaining chips to exchange with the United States, following their NAFTA and CAFTA members behind the US banner.

Table 5.6. FTAA Negotiations Disciplines & Central American Integrative Efforts

FTAA Negotiating Committees Mandates and Scope	Proposed Rules and Disciplines	Connections with Central American Integrative Efforts
1. Agriculture: tariff, non-tariff barriers, & subsidy elimination; social functions of agriculture (food security, protect workers, prevent hunger) neglected	Modeled on WTO: land reform not recognized, but full-fledged liberalization as uncompromised goal	CAFTA fulfills these, CA4FTA did not, PPP focus on other issues
2. Services: All services to be given universal coverage, unhindered entry foreign corporations under fundamental rights framework	Modeled after GATS rules of WTO, but goes further: market access MFN & national treatment equalized for foreign & local providers; public sector elimination	Same as above
3. Market Access: curtail use of public instruments for development	Complete 10-yr liberalization	Same as above
4. Investment: Protect investors and permit challenges of government	Complies with WTO, and goes beyond: exempts foreign investors from controls	Same as above
5. Intellectual Property Rights: full protection, under safeguards	Modeled on WTO's TRIPS, but goes beyond: restricts farmers from saving seeds for future use; indigenous knowledge given only limited protections	Same as above
6. Government Procurement: open to foreign corporations; transparent rules and non-discrimination	Full compliance with WTO, but goes beyond by using national treatment to open markets for foreign corporations	Same as above
7. Competition Policies: prevent especially public sector oligopolies/ monopolies	Full compliance with WTO, and goes beyond by enforcing supranational watchdogs	Same as above
8. Subsidies, Dumping, & Countervailing duties: deepen WTO disciplines to eliminate these	Unclear fulfillment: US subsidizes strategic sectors	Same as above
9. Dispute Settlement: institutionalize rules; safeguards	One area in which multilateralism lags behind regional (NAFTA) arrangements	Builds upon NAFTA Chapter 11

TABLE 5.7.   FTAA Negotiating Committees & WTO Agreements

Negotiating Committees	WTO Agreements
1. *Agriculture*	• Tariffication from 1995 • Reduction of tariffs (1995–2000 for DCs, and 1995–2005 for LDCs): includes market access, domestic supports on many, and export subsidy elimination
2. *Services:* covers all types, from banking and telecommunications to tourism and professional services to cross-border supply, consumption abroad:	• GATS: MFN in all type; national treatment in specified sectors; transparency in regulations
3. *Market access*	• Modalities by May 31, 2003 • Stocktaking in WTO 5th ministerial meeting, Cancún, September 2005
4. *Investment*	• Doha Development Agenda (1996): liberalizes or fulfills (a) trade and investment (b) competition policy, (c) transparencies, and (d) trade facilitation; to be fulfilled by January 1, 2005 • TRIMs: Trade Related Investment Measures Agreement • Agreement on Implementation of Article VI of GATT 1994
5. *Intellectual Property Rights* includes copyrights, trademarks, industrial designs, patents, trade secrets, geographical indications, and integrated circuit layout designs	• Agreement on Trade-Related aspects of Intellectual Property rights (TRIPS), 1986–94 • Principles: national treatment, MFN, balanced protection • DCs to fulfill by 1996, LDCs by 2006 in all areas, except pharmaceuticals (by 2016)
6. *Government Procurements*	• Agreement on Government Procurement: ensures transparency
7. *Competition Policies*	• Doha Development Agenda (1996): liberalizes or fulfills (a) trade and investment (b) competition policy, (c) transparencies, and (d) trade facilitation; to be fulfilled by January 1, 2005
8. *Subsidies, Dumping, & Countervailing Duties*	• Anti-dumping Agreement expands GATT Article VI (Agreement on Implementation of Article VI of GATT 1994) • Agreement on Subsidies and Countervailing Measures • Agreement on Safeguards (terminate export subsidies by 2003, all others by 2002)

TABLE 5.7. (*Continued*)

Negotiating Committees	WTO Agreements
9. *Dispute Settlement*	• Trade Policy Review Boards (to improve transparency): supranational watchdog review every 2 yrs for DCS, 6 yrs for LDCs • Dispute Settlement Board (all WTO members): creates panels, goes through 2 stages, roughly 15 months; allows appeals

Third, if the above interpretations hold, then the 9 negotiations committees together make corporations not just the judge, jury, and executioner of all trade policies, but also US-corporations as judge, jury, and executioner more specifically.[22] They implicitly subordinate all governments but the United States, making particularly LDC governments vassals of their corporate interests. An earlier section mentioned how NAFTA's Chapter 11 allows corporates to sue governments; but as the various negotiating committees indicate, corporations get multiple entry points into the government: privatizing public sectors (3rd,7th), government procurements (6th), protecting property rights (5th), and adjudicating differences (9th). Since US corporations dominate all indices, for example, the Fortune 500, as well as the unholy market fundamentalism trinity of market opening, deregulation, and privatization, they are likely to benefit more than any other corporations,[23] and conceivably more than ever before since the market access holy grail is investment-driven rather than trade-driven. In fact, trade is serving as an investment instrument, as evident, for example, on the trade-related investment measures (TRIMs) emphasis.

Fourth, not only does the United States benefit more than any other country from this trinity, but it also alone receives special treatment. For example, the 8th negotiating committee seeks to eliminate all forms of subsidies, dumping, and countervailing duties—but it does not touch strategic US sectors which are also subsidized. Many of these are defense-related, for example, SEMATECH, but the underlying point is still the uneven playing field created. US exceptionalism continues in the 21st Century just as it did with the GATT agriculture waiver from 1955.

Finally, perhaps the most profound tension is structural: With emphasis on openness and privatization, the unholy market fundamentalism trinity erroneously carries connotations of an even playing field, when the FTAA mandates, scopes, rules, and disciplines clearly indicate US-sponsored FTAs are of the few, by the few, and for the few, with the few representing elites and corporations, and not of the many, by the many, or for the many, where the many represent the public. Camouflaged by technical terminologies, these agreements are indictments not even written in laymen's parlance for commoners to comprehend.

Collision with CMM & HD

These observations automatically collide with Richard Feinberg's CMM and HD models built from the Miami Summit of the Americas in 1994. What are some of the similarities and differences?

Similarities

Among the similarities, at least three are obvious. First, both are built upon the unholy market fundamentalism trinity. Full-fledged openness is envisioned over 10–15 years in just about every economic sector outside the United States, necessitating the elimination of public sector investments and the uncontrolled encouragement of private enterprises. Second, the three legs of CMM—issue-specific coalitions, bilateralism, and plurilateralism—remain, though prioritized differently. Greater emphasis is placed not only on bilateralism as the route towards plurilateralism, but US-based bilateralism as the model, rather than the original assumption of plurilateralism breeding more plurilateralism, while issue-specific coalitions, though not eliminated, remains to symbolize a symmetric playing field. Finally, elite-centricism serves a central function, evident not only in the negotiators and policymakers themselves, rallying around the core Washington Consensus themes, but also in the consensus-based negotiations and negotiating camaraderie across the table.

Differences

More profound are the differences. Three of them illustrate the changing trading atmosphere between Miami 1994 and Central America's integrative efforts in 2004. First, negotiations have moved right across the spectrum, from openness and inclusiveness towards private, secret, and exclusionary deliberations. Even societal groups, a fundamental part of Feinberg's HD, complain about being left out, while the CMM's issue-specific coalitions, which used to trigger symmetrical negotiations then, are no longer performing any triggering role. One reason why may be the smaller Central American FTA setting compared to the broader hemispheric counterpart, but this also reiterates the paucity of issues, competencies, administrative agencies, and disciplines available for Central American states compared to their hemispheric counterparts—an issue touching the second big difference.

Second, by 2004, not only have negotiations become more secret and exclusive, they have also narrowed the issue agenda. Feinberg found upwards of twenty agenda issues in 1994, treated with roughly symmetrical importance. Today, the emphasis is on direct and specific, trade and investment issues. Lip service is paid such indirect and general issues as the environment and labor rights. In fact, these cannot be prioritized, at least in Central America, since the integrative efforts are premised upon *maquiladoras*, which cannot operate if environmental and labor issues become symmetrically concerns. No attention is paid other issues of social concern, such as education, women participation, narcotrafficking, and so forth—even though they played so cohesive a role ten years ago.

Third, the place and positioning of FTAA in the larger picture is vastly different today, thereby altering its role and functioning, as well as membership obligations. This shift is not just because negotiations have become more private and the issues have narrowed. Its relationship with NAFTA explains the shift. In its genesis, FTAA emerged as a parallel body to which it was hoped NAFTA would one day merge. Certainly that was the spirit one could deduce when Chile was considered a fourth NAFTA *amigo* in 1994 and 1995. That did not happen, Mexico faced a crisis, but more importantly, Mexico's recovery spoke volumes of future shifts. That recovery demonstrated the indispensable US role, and the opportunity to damn the torpedoes and fully root the unholy market fundamentalism trinity: Bail-out plans provided the mechanism to both dismantle stubborn public sector enterprises and denationalize controls over natural resources. That NAFTA performed better than expected in the initial years demonstrated the magic of the ever-fleeting *maquiladora* industry for a market economy: It confirmed Mexico's time in the sun was brief, and replacements were needed, and this Central America supplied for a number of other coincidental and circumstancial reasons. More important was the institutional lesson: NAFTA-fying FTAA was more practical than a FTAA with plurilateral premises. The difference was more critical: FTAA had over twenty agenda issues, emphasized symmetry, and in short, sought a nirvana in the irreversibly uneven hemispheric playing field; and by contrast, NAFTA had passed the litmus tests of prioritizing untrammeled trade and investment over all other issues, legitimizing asymmetry, and not only playing on an uneven hemispheric field but also sustaining the slope infinitely. Environmental and labor issues, among others, fell by the waysides, and business interests were anchored more solidly than ever since World War II. Rather than NAFTA becoming one component of FTAA, it was more fruitful to extend the disciplines of NAFTA into FTAA—disciplines such as Chapter 11 provisions to allow corporations to sue governments, Chapter 19 on anti-dumping and countervailing dispute settlement mechanisms, and many on investment.

FTAA began making the appropriate changes after the 2001 Québec summit, when all 9 negotiating groups initiated discussions on market access from May 15, 2002. From July 15, 2003, countries began submitting revisions of their original offers. Original offers for agricultural and non-agricultural products, services, investment, and government procurements were to be made between December 15, 2002 and February 15, 2003. Clearly one sees a bureaucratically-driven fulfillment of the scheduling,[24] which not only echoes NAFTA patterns but is also acquiring as independent an identity as counterpart European Union patterns are in that region of the world—and, critically, both antedating WTO's treatment of similar issues.

The market access and agriculture negotiation groups illustrate the nature or the procedures behind standardized methods and modalities. Addressing "the entire tariff universe," the market access and agriculture negotiation groups focused on the following issues: establishing the base tariff, specifying the types of tariff concessions, schedules and paces for tariff elimination, the methods to be adopted in making concessions, and the nature of rules of origin, for example, the timetable and modalities to be adopted, identifying non-tariff measures, and how to treat trade distortions.

From a Central American viewpoint, one notices efforts at (a) establishing conformity; (b) prioritizing the unholy market fundamentalism trinity; (c) imposing not only disciplines where none or few existed before; and (d) a bureaucratic and technical series of exercises for which the administrative infrastructures, skilled personnel, and public interests were either low or non-existent.

Finally, the WTO context. Just as Table 5.6 established the direct and substantive FTAA-Central America relationships, Table 5.7 places the FTAA negotiating committees against the WTO agreements specifying the rules and disciplines. Almost all of these are specified in Chapter 2 of *Understanding the WTO*,[25] while Chapter 3 explains dispute settlement.

From Table 5.7 we see (a) every FTAA negotiating committee connected to specific WTO agreements; (b) many of the agreements having completion deadlines, a large proportion of them by January 1, 2005—a date originally set for completing the FTAA, but which was not met; (c) the more liberal time-span for LDCs, as an alternative to becoming marginalized by not completing the agreements in the first place; (d) the increasing inter-relationships between trade and investment, implying diminishing attention to labor, environment, and other social issues—which are explicitly discussed in other chapters of *Understanding the WTO*; (e) greater supranational surveillance over state actions, but also loopholes adventurous countries can take advantage of; and (f) FTAA being fairly well connected to WTO, but Central American integrative efforts lagging in connecting with FTAA, even more so with WTO—suggesting the greater power of working in smaller groups than larger, but also the tighter US control over small-group dynamics over large-group.

BIG FISHES & LITTLE STREAMS

What does the economic integration with Central American states mean for the North American states? Canada, Mexico, and the United States are examined along six dimensions in Table 5.8: identifying their interests, as well as attitudes toward hemispheric, multilateral, NAFTA, Central American arrangements and societal pressures. Interestingly, whatever analytical information is derived gets subordinated to that single salient characteristic of relative economic size which made both CA4FTA and PPP appear so meaningless.

As previously observed, each North American state sought different goals: humanitarianism and hemispheric leadership for Canada, industrial restructuring and southern regional integration for Mexico, and global competitiveness and hemispheric market security for the US. Both external and mundane domestic triggers lay behind Mexican and US interests, whereas Canada utilized a natural disaster to invoke vintage foreign policy principles. Similarly, the scope varied, with Mexico restricting itself to only Central American, although to more states than either Canada or the US, Canada blandly treating Central American states selectively as part of a vague and open-ended notion of the western hemisphere, and the United States explicitly and purposefully identifying Central American states as specific components of a specific hemispheric notion with finite members. One may argue Canada's Central American interests to be symbolic, Mexico's a reluctant adjustment imperative, and the US's as opportunity creation, even though global competition is common to all three as a causal factor.

Different responses produced different attitudes. Towards the western hemisphere, original Canadian enthusiasm masked an opportunity to diversify hemispheric leadership away from the United States even though Canada unwittingly prompted the hemispheric drive by proposing a FTA to the United States at the May 1985 Shamrock Summit. Diminishing prospects of diversified hemispheric leadership eventually reduced Canadian enthusiasm, probably to the level of Mexico, which was cool towards Chile's NAFTA membership aspirations in the first place, and still views the US as its defining and exclusive trading partner after 9/11 as it did before. On the other hand, the US alone carried a business-like approach, viewing the hemisphere

Table 5.8 North American Country Interests Profiled

Dimensions	Canada	Mexico	United States
Nature of State Interests	• Humanitarianism • Hemispherism	• Industrial restructuring • Regionalism in the south	• Global competitiveness • Market security
Attitude towards Western Hemispheric Arrangements	• Ebbing enthusiasm • Goal: diversify regional leadership	• Dimmed enthusiasm • US-based integration still bedrock of hemispheric engagement	• Instrumentalism • CAFTA as means to FTAA • FTAA as means to restructured WTO
Attitude towards Multilateral Agencies	• Accepts WTO as unavoidable framework • Washington institutions essential	• WTO less important than NAFTA • Washington institutions as necessary evils	• WTO needs restructuring • Washington institutions useful surrogates
Attitude towards NAFTA	• Very helpful • Useful to move beyond	• Essential, preferably with bilateral US relations as bedrock	• Increasingly as stepping stone towards hemispheric arrangements
Attitude towards overall Central American integrative efforts.	• Increasingly at a loss	• Frustrated: cannot live with it, future viability necessitates it • Prefers broad Central American leadership: tense history with Guatemala as constraint	• Optimism • Fulfillment
Particularized attitudes toward Central America	• Favorably-inclined towards Costa Rica, and on fairly symmetrical terms		• Unquestionable preference for asymmetrical relations, CA as followers
Attitude towards Societal Pressures	• Keep an explicit distance over negotiations, but long-term inclusion	• Acknowledged under PPP pressure	• Keep a subtle distance, fulfill societal demands, superficially at best

as the instrument whereby the WTO may be restructured along pro-US lines and tones, much as Central American would serve in signing, sealing, and delivering FTAA in accordance to US expectations.

Towards multilateral agencies, and generally towards multilateralism, Canada emphasized their independent presence more than the other two countries, in part because of their appeal as alternatives to exclusive US domination, or at least as vehicles of loadshedding US Latin engagements. By contrast, Mexico found them less relevant than the United States, and indeed sees them as extension of US policy pursuits. As for the United States, both are tools, but of a different nature than for Canada: They help restructure the WTO as it increasingly drifts from the range of US policy expectations, whereas the Washington-based institutions were, and continue to remain, firmly under US control.

Against such temperaments, NAFTA also elicits quite distinctive attitudes. It was necessary for Canada, although Canada was agnostic to looking south beyond the United States between the February 1990 Davos Summit, when Carlos Salinas de Gortari proposed NAFTA, and September 1990, when NAFTA negotiating began in fits and starts. For Mexico it was, and continues to remain, a privileged community, providing the most untainted medium for bilateral US-based transactions. On the other hand, the US increasingly sees it as a stepping stone, initially towards the rest of the hemisphere, and thereafter farther beyond.

Given these posturings and perceptions, all three see a different Central America. Canada is at a loss about Central America, and sees it as a source of either confusion or complications, even though these are the stuff of which hemispheric leadership has often been made. Canada's helplessness matches Mexico's damned-if-I-do, damned-if-I-don't approach, although closer proximity prevents Mexico from despairing as easily, loudly, and comprehensively as Canada. Contrasting the frustrations of both, the US is not just optimistic about its Central American pursuits, but can also point to accomplishments, itself reinforcing the belief one can only get what one wants by going out and grabbing it, and utilizing means both fair and foul.

Fourth, particularized attention differs. Canada's symmetrical approach contrasts with Mexico's first-among-equals and asymmetrical US preferences. History largely shapes these attitudes, with Canada lacking such a history, and therefore its nuances, Mexico's reflecting wariness towards Guatemala, and the US accustomed to leading the way, as always. Because of its democratic claims, Costa Rica is the devil Canada gets along with better, Mexico's challenge is to surmount the Guatemala devil, while the US sees Central America much like it views the entire hemisphere, partners to challenge global devils with.

Finally, all three show some similarity in responding to societal pressures: These are not just undesirable, but also need to be both minimized and kept on the receiving end. Canada does this explicitly, the US implicitly, and Mexico, having been bitten by explicitly shunning these forces, is seeking arms-length compromise. Ultimately, all three need societal-level approval and legitimacy. Canada hopes to get these *a posteriori*, Mexico by having to change its policy posturings, and the US by wheeling and dealing with societal interests amidst the negotiations process, at times in full faith, such as conducting the environmental report, at times superficially, such as by subordinating the report to the political necessity of a done deal within a stipulated time-frame.

SIFTING INFORMATION, FITTING MODELS

Given the various levels of analysis, of all the models discussed in Chapter 2, even though Fen Osler Hampson's multilateral negotiations framework captures more of the critical dynamics from this ever-complicated Central American context than the others, a hybrid model is nonetheless more fruitful. Hampson's multilateral negotiations model not only admits societal actors explicitly, much like Richard Feinberg's hemispheric diplomacy model, but unlike Feinberg's specifies the routes to two contrasting outcomes, isolating bridging and blocking opportunities (rather than coalitions, since the number of participating countries were so few) from each other. One might argue Mark Habeeb's model also creates similar opportunities through the turning points, but very much like Feinberg's counterpart, does not elaborate the nature of the groups: By lumping them into one catch-all category, their models do not distinguish between supporters, opponents, and mixed groups—a distinction increasingly necessitated by democratization and ratification. By distinguishing between such groups and their impacts, Hampson's framework also lends itself to a more effective disaggregation into the various stages of pre-pre-negotiations, pre-negotiations, and negotiations, derived by placing Winham's, Gross Stein's, and Tomlin's combinations together. Habeeb's model permits this through the turning points, but obviously ignores the actors. The post-negotiations phase needs to be added to all these models, and when it is, we can capture Putnam's ratification dynamics, introduce reverse flows, instill greater purpose and study relevance, and ultimately, better explain all of the above in one coherent framework. It is not the most perfect hybrid, but not for any exogenous reason: The negotiations were themselves too secretive, involved too few actors, and therefore hindered adaptation to any single interpretive model. The derived hybrid is worth testing in hemispheric and multilateral negotiations.

Disaggregating influences upon decision-makers helps identify potential bridges and blockers among the groups, and suggests how the inevitable outcomes may resuscitate negotiations if they break down in the first place. Whether societal influences were heeded by policy-makers or not is besides the point, made all the more pointless by the negotiations being so clandestine. That they were made at all provides some societal input. Similarly for potential bridges and blockers: Very few, if any, external bridges and blockers were engaged, but negotiators did face roadblocks without there being any coalitions, and were able in some cases to overcome these, again, without resorting to coalitions. Only Mexico, having paid the price of not doing so, heeded societal pressures over PPP. It had no choice: grassroots opposition virtually brought PPP to a standstill. Finally, the outcomes differed, but distinguishing between those crossing the humps and others ending in a deadlock alerts us to the nature of forward momentum. Even with the most symmetrical negotiations approach, Canada did not grasp this technique at all: Postponing negotiations is a rare, contemporary experience, when at the end of the day compromises increasingly prevail over non-negotiable original positions. As discussed, Mexico's forward momentum sprang from the PPP setbacks, while sheer economic size and what US Trade Representative Robert B. Zoellick dubbed a "can-do" US attitude, kept the momentum sustained from start to finish in a tight schedule.

Without geographical contiguity, Canada's tossings and turnings between its hemispheric/multilateral preferences and domestic resources might be a sign of the times. Jean Daudelin may have hit it on the head in a slightly larger hemispheric context. "Only through American eyes do the Americas, as an integrated whole," he argues, "make strategic and economic sense. For the other countries of the continent, the landscape is never hemispheric . . . . The hemisphere becomes relevant to them strictly *through* their bilateral relationship with the US . . . ." Speaking of Canada's "foreign policy on the fringe," he attributes its hemispheric retreat to being alone in promoting FTAA: Its human security agenda, according to Daudelin, "questions the traditional concept of state sovereignty, to the extent that it submits the latter to a higher principle:security of the people." In his estimation, only Mexico and Brazil, in that order, remain relevant to Canada; and even the Caribbean troika of Bahamas-Barbados-Bermuda ranks far higher not only of Central American states taken together, but also the largest three Latin countries—Argentina, Brazil, and Mexico—taken together. In 2001, Canadian investment in the Bahamas alone surpassed all of these other countries.[26] Caribbean emigration partly explains this anomaly, but by doing so, also exposes why Canada's Latin sheet is so relatively blank.

Both the FTAA methodology and domestic constitutional or legislative requirements set only the parameters of negotiations. FTAA's market access and agriculture methods/modalities highlight the categories of issues to be negotiated through several stages:[27] general principles; submission of timetable and offers; determining scope of negotiations; establishing the base tariff, types of tariff concessions, tariff elimination schedules, and concession-making methods; and identifying rules of origins, timetables, and non-tariff measures. Similarly, domestic ratification processes, electoral calendars, and constitutional commitments, for example, democracy, largely hover on the background of negotiations than on the table as bargaining chips. Ultimately, state interests set the tone, direction, volume, and content of each negotiation, adjusting domestic priorities to fluctuating external circumstances. The larger the gap between the two, the greater the tendency towards subordinating or superficially treating the former, in turn suggesting the increasing attempt by Canada, Mexico, and the US to define an international role for itself.

CONCLUSIONS: WARDENS WITH NO WALLS

With stumbling blocks at each of the four levels of analysis, Central America seems mired in commercial land-mining and without any visible exit option. Turning to the societal level, since the 1999 Seattle WTO ministerial meeting, societal preferences continue to rock trade negotiations, even if they are conducted clandestinely, and in commensurate asymmetrical fashion, with maximum noise in the United States, then Mexico, followed by Central American states, and Canada—in that order. Paradoxically, even though CAFTA was the only fully negotiated agreement completed, its forthcoming ratification process may be the straw to break, not only the Central American, but also the entire Latin American back. Before the US elections, it remained a divisive issue; what transpires after the elections remains unpredictable, but not many groups, particularly supporters, are holding their breath.[28] Even as the fastest FTA concluded, CAFTA's impacts may be most devastating should it fail, not necessarily for the United States, which can easily shift attention to many of its other trading partners, rather for Central America, and significantly at that, while less so, but damaging nonetheless, for Mexico. Canada alone can adopt a "I told you so" posture, even though this may not tantamount to any gains, and constitutes an inappropriate policy approach in such an age of ruthless global competition and in which Canada might be isolating itself.

At the multilateral level, the US has the most to lose since it invokes more rules, regulations, and disciplines from this level. Canada would also be jolted since this is the level it identifies with most, but given its reluctance to retreat from this level, the costs would not be high. Mexico, likewise, may feel the ripples, not the waves, since multilateralism shorn of a US connection becomes a meaningless concept in North and Central America.

Turning to the third level of Central American states, the fall-out or harvest could be the maximum here: Any integrative agreement would represent an advance, and one with the US would be seen as a jackpot, at least by officials. Contemplating life after a failed CAFTA is not a Central American priority at the moment, further exacerbating the expected shocks should it actually materialize. Amidst the tumult, Mexico may find its own *maquilas* headed over the ocean to Asia, rather than across the Sierra Madres towards Central America: They cannot wait for a political agreement to take force. This would inflict greater costs for all countries between the United States and the Panama Canal.

Finally, the North American states. The fulcrum of these negotiations have been expert groups, each facing different dynamics and rate of fulfillment. Among the most salient such groups have been on market access, origin and customs procedures, technical and phytosanitary norms, agriculture, government procurement, services, intellectual property, investment, dispute settlement, and illegal trade practices.[29] For the United States, and particularly with Central America, negotiations were structured in terms of similar issues under eight groups, representing negotiations heads, market access, services and investment, dispute settlement and aspects, intellectual property and government procurement, environment and labor, cooperation, and sanitary/phytosanitary. Both adopted parallel structures addressing similar issues.[30]

Canada's disconnections and disorientation differ from Mexico's fidgety restructuration, and both pale into insignificance against the more purposeful and productive US pursuits. If global competition is the underlying devil, the US is preparing accordingly, Mexico has no choice but to follow suit, leaving Canada out in left-field: All three face the structuration costs, but Canada's lack of innovative responses and sticky feet may not mitigate these costs as US imagination and dynamics may its own costs, and by default, also Mexico's.

Canada may not remain unscathed from these developments: Alone among industrialized countries, it stands to benefit the most in the best case scenario of a united hemispheric plank by doing the least, but contrariwise could lose the most should a hemispheric fortress not eventually emerge, again for reasons beyond its own control. Whether remiss or bliss is better than the steady state in between is a lesson Canada will be well placed to evaluate.

NOTES

1. On post-pluralism, see Delworth Gardner, *Plowing Ground in Washington: The Political Economy of U.S. Agriculture* (San Francisco: Pacific Research Institute for Public Policy, 1995), 163–238.

2. "The Hispanic challenge," *Foreign Policy* (March/April 2004):30–45.

3. See "Labor unions to fight free trade deal," *ABCNews*, December 18, 2003, from: http://abcnews.go.com/wire/Politics/ap20031218_435.html; and Stephen J. Norton, "Net political gain for Bush in dropping steel tariffs?" *CQ Weekly*, December 6, 2003, 2998–3001.

4. As of mid-October 2004, the two countries were in the 5th Round of FTA talks, begun under Mireya Moscoso's administration during April 2004, but continued, with greater "prudence and caution," by newly-elected Martin Torrijos. See Kathy Martinez, "Panama, U.S. launch 5th trade talk round," *Sacramento Bee*, October 18, 2004, from: http://www.sacbee.com

5. Emad Mekay, "U.S. trade:Central American free trade deal a dud, activists say," *Trade Observatory*, April 10, 2003, from: http://www.tradesobservatory.org/news .index.cfm?ID=4285

6. See Eduardo Tamayo, "Nicaragua:marcha contra acuerdo de libre comercio con EE.UU," September 19, 2003, from: http://movimientos.org/show_text.php3?key= 2006

7. Jake Batsell, "Fair trade coffee demand sparks debate on workers wages, lives," *The Seattle Times*, October 7, 2004, from: http://www.seattletimes.com

8. Keck and Sikkink, op. cit.

9. "AFL-CIO and Central American unions release first-ever declaration demanding that trade negotiations address workers' rights and development:trade negotiation expanded 'NAFTA' in Central America begin today," January 8, 2003, from: http://www.aflcio.org/mediacenter/prsptm/pr01082003a.stm

10. *Mexico and the NAFTA Environmental Debate: The Transnational Politics of Economic Integration* (Utretch, Netherlands: International Books, 1996), esp. 141–92.

11. Jean Daudelin explains Canada's most recent Latin disinterest in "Foreign policy at the fringe:Canada and Latin America," *International Journal* LVIII, no. 4 (Autumn 2003):571–90.

12. These include: Freedom to organize, Convention #87 (1948); Rights of unions and freedom to collectively negotiate, Convention #98 (1949); Convention on forced labor, #29 (1930); Convention on abolition of forced labor, #105 (1957); Convention on equality of remuneration, # 100 (1951); Convention on discrimination in employment and workplace, # 111 (1958); Convention on working age, #138 (1973); and Convention on child labor, #182 (1999).

13. "CAFTA tilted against the poor:new benefits for U.S., new burdens for Central America, says Oxfam," December 12, 2003, from: http://story.news.yahoo.com/ news?tmpl=story&cid=669&ncid=669&e=3&u=/usnw/200312

14. "The Honduras maquiladora industry and the Kimi campaign," *Social Science History*, esp edition on labor internationalism, vol. 27, no. 4 (Winter 2003):551–76.

15. Ruth Milkman, *Farewell to the Factory: Auto Workers in the Late Twentieth Century* (Berkeley, CA: University of California Press, 1997).

16. More from Evelyn Iritani, "Latino leaders not united on CAFTA:free trade brings arguments of more wealth or despair,"*Houston Chronicle*, August 27, 2004, from: http://www.chron.com

17. *Social Origins of Dictatorship and Democracy: Lord and Peasant in the Making of the Modern World* (Boston: Beacon Press, 1966), 13–15, and 35–39.

18. Oscar Chacón, "Central American migrants take action on trade and regional integration," *Americas Program* (Silver City, NM: Interhemispheric Resources Center, July 13, 2003).

19. Maude Barlowe and Tony Clarke, "Making the links:a people's guide to the World Trade Organization and the Free Trade Area of the Americas," The Council of Canadians and the Polaris Institute, Ottawa, no date, p. 15; from: http://www.canadians.org

20. "After Cancún:an optimistic case," *Challenge* 46, no. 6 (November-December 2003):30, but see 16–31.

21. See a summary in Ha-Joon Chang, "The future for trade," *ibid.,* 6–15.

22. Gabriel Espinosa, "US investors emerge as CAFTA winners," *Scoop Media* webpage, October 19, 2004, from Council on Hemispheric affairs, Report, no further information.

23. From Merino del Río, "CAFTA". Discussed in Chapter 4 subsection "Power and policy."

24. From FTAA, Foreign Trade Information System, "FTAA: trade negotiations committee:methods and modalities for negotiations," FTAA.TNC/20/Rev.1, October 18, 2002, from: http://www.sice.oas.org/FTAA/M&M_e.asp

25. WTO, *Understanding the WTO* (Geneva, Switzerland: WTO, September 2003; this is constantly updated); previously published as *Trading Into the Future* (Geneva: Switzerland: WTO, 1995). Available from: http://www.wto.org

26. "Foreign policy at the fringe," quotation from 656, subsequent information from 641.

27. FTAA Secretariat, Trade Negotiations Committee, "Methods and modalities for negotiations," TNC/20/Rev.1, October 18, 2002, from: http://www.sice.oas.org/FTAA/M6M_e.asp

28. The themes come across in Jenalia Morena, "NAFTA hurt Latinos, study says:US Hispanics lost jobs, Mexicans saw wages drop," *Houston Chronicle*, August 16, 2004, from: http://www.chron.com/cs/CDA/ssistory.mpl/business/2740054; and Stephen J. Norton, "Ghost of NAFTA haunts future of free trade," *CQ Weekly*, December 6, 2003, 2996–97.

29. Ibarra-Yunez, op. cit., 17.

30. Association of Caribbean States, "Process of negotiations."

Chapter Six

Conclusions:
Running on an Empty Tank?

GOING WITH THE FLOW

As the study shows, only the United States could pursue its Central American trade objectives to the desired end, flying like an arrow to the targeted goal on schedule. Compared to Canada and Mexico in their own pursuits, the US carried more purpose, never let its interest flag, utilized carrots and sticks in its negotiations repertoire, and possessed serious, significant post-agreement plans of which the agreement is a part. In addition to these self-generated characteristics, the United States benefited in no small measure from external developments and circumstances. Greater relative Central American trade dependence on the United States worked as much to its advantage as to attenuating Canadian and Mexican engagements; an unusual camaraderie among like-minded, progressively oriented, and liberalist leaders smoothened the way; although it struggled amidst large post-war reconstruction outlays in Afghanistan and Iraq, the US economy did not take a wrong turn through 2003 and 2004; and Central American states themselves did not slide back into the kinds of acrimonious atmospherics which riddled their twentieth century histories, and in fact, continued working on institutionalizing democratization and liberalization.

Canada and Mexico could not capitalize on positive Central American developments: Canada prioritized principles over pragmatics, is realistically farther away from CA to initiate trade relations then Mexico or the US, which already had trade flows with CA, and probably did not come across as a viable alternative to Mexico or the US to provide CA countries ample incentives; on the other hand, Mexico's greater reliance on pragmatics than principles probably raised more CA alarm-bells than opportunities to exploit, but most of all, was the lack of sufficient will, or to put it more bluntly, interest, in departing from its cherished US-bilateral relations. Unlike its two next-door neighbors, the United States purposefully placed pragmatics over principles without abandoning the latter, and provided the most attractive incentives to CA states. It is a country never too far nor too close to any other country of the world, a characteristic few others have sought to emulate, or if established, fully exploited.

Against that background, the US could do what may prove more difficult for Canada and Mexico to fulfill than moving mountains: eschew negotiating styles, nationalistic stereotypes, and philosophical or principled behavior for the nitty-gritty, practical, and therefore never be completely trapped by peripheral considerations in conducting rational negotiations and transactions — a refined version of the machiavellian maxim of ends determining the means, rather then the reverse Canadian and Mexican preferences of means determining the ends, at least in this case. In the final analysis, should CAFTA be ratified and implemented, two big winners may turn out to be Canada and Mexico, if not from bandwagoning, then reaping the spillover harvest. In turn, a number of empirical and theoretical puzzles and paradoxes emerge.

Puzzles and Paradoxes

At least seven empirical considerations emerge: the unholiness of the unholy trinity of market fundamentalism; increasing incompatibility between multilateralism and democratization; a ratification process going asunder; reconfigured levels of analysis; negotiations developing a split personality; irrelevance and irreverence of models; and ideology becoming a part of the underpinnings.

José Merino del Río's unholy trinity of market fundamentalism is truly unholy: Market opening, deregulation, and privatization constitute the relevant fundamentals, find full embrace in Ottawa, Mexico City, and Washington, DC, drive the economic and trade policies of Canada, Mexico, and the United States, appeal to every Central American country in their socio-political and political-economic transformations, yet assume different shapes, sizes, contours, and colors once policy implementation gets underway—so much so that congruent policy expectations eventually produce divergent policy consequences. One kind of protection or another in every country, North American or Central, dilutes the written agreement or principle so extensively that the trinity itself becomes meaningless without safeguards; and since there are many more safeguards than fundamentals, even at its most resplendent moment, the market economy becomes more defensive, defenseless, and more urgently engaged in rearguard and last-gasp actions than in progressing or finding natural acceptance.

Part of the increasing unholiness may be attributed, and could conceivably be directly related, to the increasing multilateralism-democratization incompatibility: Whereas multilateralism/regionalism reflect policy choices of upwardly-mobile developing/developed countries, the beneficiary of those policies, that is, the general public, shifts in tangential directions under democratization. To be sure, democratization not only permits those policy-shifts but also sustains them; yet paradoxically, below the policy-making levels, it opens up different cans from which the typical citizen prioritizes interests not always consistent with the policy preferences. Environmental safeguards and minimum labor standards convey certain public preferences: the more the development, the greater the need to preserve these; but in turn the costs imposed subtract from the efficient outcomes sought by multilateralism/regionalism, and almost all cases are deflected to other countries. *Maquilas* epitomize this paradox: The typical DC consumer relishes low-cost *maquila* products, but not any *maquila* in his/her backyard. The price of democratization widens this state-society gap, but the ripples touch almost every other shore.

Ratifying multilateral/regional agreements, the third puzzle, is one of them. Although more a US concern presently than Canadian or Mexican—or even Central American—dynamics of the state-society gap unfold most dramatically in the legislature, where the lofty pursuits of policy-makers must touch the reality of plebian concerns. CAFTA, like other regional or multilateral agreements, is not an unalloyed deal, but the more fascinating aspect may have less to do with what the contentious issues are or if the win-set is there, and more to do with how the executive branch cuts a different domestic deal to get an international deal through: This deal is neither democratic in procedure, nor stable enough to outlast the personal influence of any given president; instead, the bribes, pay-offs, and strong-arm methods it is built upon, exposes democracy's soft underbelly and reduces democratization to a political instrument rather than the principle or pillar it is supposed to be. How group heterogeneity eventually produces homogeneity raises more than just democratization eyebrows.

In turn, we confront another puzzle: With the US executive branch ratifying the agreement, consequences will ripple as much in Kansas, for example, as in Kananstakis in Canada, or the Costa Rican highlands—shaking all the neatly assembled levels of analysis we are all so accustomed to. Just within the United States, the executive branch distinguishes itself from the legislature, as we would expect, but the collusion between them also separates them from the public at large, and the public itself disaggregates into those whose bottom-line is determined either by subsidy payments or market competition, or a mixture of both. Thus several levels of analysis emerge just within the domestic level, indicating how much more complex society has become and continues to constantly be. Following the ratification sequence, we also must accommodate ripples in Kansas, Kanansastakis, or Costa Rica. If the executive officials in these locations identify with their Washington counterparts, and the legislators mirror their US namesakes, then the entire society-state-supranational lineage of policy-making levels becomes much more complicated, distorted, and the springboard of continued future flux. No matter how secular the thrust of changes, the americanizing central tendency remains the only visible and constant factor.

As a result, negotiations themselves change fundamentally, highlighting the fifth puzzle. The distinction between top-down and bottom-up decision-making is fairly well known, but what is emerging from multilateral/regional agreements is a subset within the top: The top has its own top-down thrust, such as the president, and a bottom-up component in the legislature—all of these complicating international negotiations. Gilbert Winham, among others, recognized how the exclusive, diplomat-based 19th century negotiations had been steadily replaced by inclusive, management-based 20th century negotiations.[1] By the 21st century, a mixed model seems to be emerging, reflecting both the 19th century exclusiveness and 20th century inclusiveness in a hierarchic relationship—the exclusiveness pertains to the actual negotiations, conducted by professionals, much like the diplomats of the 19th century, and connects with the rest of society—the inclusive component—through the ratification process; and since the ratification process is itself managed by executive branch officials, negotiations assumes a dual face insulated to a large degree from all other vectors, that is, the public.

Nowhere is this changing negotiations nature more vividly evident than in the FTAA's CMM and HD models. What Feinberg observed in the 1994 Miami Summit, of issue-specific coalitions, non-governmental influences seeping through to policy-makers, and bands of transnational brother exerting inter-linked pressures, differ fundamentally from CAFTA, CA4FTA, even PPP practices: It is not that coalitions made no sense in such a small group of negotiators, but that how issue-specific coalitions can be entirely discarded in larger instances of negotiations becomes a critical message, and a message with urgency, since negotiating with the United States, itself the largest market for many exporting countries, must, by definition, be coalition-free if it is to succeed. It is plausible a successful CAFTA will make business-as-usual harder for FTAA, and spiraling outwards, even a successful FTAA-Lite would place pressure on WTO and other negotiating bodies. The ultimate disappearance of several negotiation models with fewer specified components may prove more explanatory than the detailed counterparts we are currently loaded with.

Finally, ideology remains a critical part of both conducting negotiations and explaining them. The literature on particularly CAFTA and PPP, though CA4FTA is no exception, is highly bifurcated between very specified supporters and a motley groups of opponents. Supporters by and large reflect the Washington Consensus, a significant post-Cold War ideology often couched with the same Cold War temperament of defenders of democratization and liberalization—the very forces responsible for the collapse of the Soviet Union and breakdown of communism. The complication is significant: Opponents are viewed, implicitly through this may be, as the communists before them. Thus, a large chunk of the criticism against CAFTA and PPP carry the flavor of emanating from "enemies". Unfortunately, many of the probing arguments come from these groups, and they run deeper and wider than "official" lists of possible weaknesses. It is true, the opponents include communists or would-be communists, but to dismiss some of their very valid arguments because of the company is to ignore the fundamentals of Central American society and culture.

IMPLICATIONS: LIBERALIZATION AND
THE VANISHING ACT

Empirical

At least four empirical implications beg attention: the US ratification itself; status quo sustenance across Central America; fate of NAFTA; and prospects of FTAA.

US ratification is not necessarily hinged to the November 2004 election outcomes: Even with Bush's electoral victory and a Republican congressional majority, CAFTA still summoned a touch-and-go vote, very much like the Trade Promotion Authority (TPA) of mid-2002, and indeed necessitated the Clinton-type NAFTA arm-twisting to get the trade agreement through Congress. External shocks, such as oil prices constraining purchasing power, deficits ballooning, or the economy beginning that much anticipated but long abated recession, could still rock CAFTA's future. How the ratification process took place and the alignments to surface were more than routine: At stake were more sensitive agricultural products than with any previous trade agreements, while the side issues of labor, environment, and human rights were simply assumed away since *maquiladoras*, curiously, are very much part and parcel of the free trade agreement.

Maquiladoras shift attention to Central American states which, unlike Mexico on the eve of NAFTA, see *maquiladoras* as the springboard out of underdevelopment. Just as the country leaders wait with bated breath and ink-dipped quills to sign the first post-ratification legislations, labor unions, environmentalists, and human rights activists remain one step away from unsheathing their swords. Be these as they may, Central American state leaders may have to keep their eyes on too many simmering pots: absorbing rural resentments, curbing rapid urban migration, arresting gangsterism, keeping emigration from running out of control, preventing narcotrafficking from becoming institutionalized, and preserving law and order—and these while still keeping the lid on endemic protracted conflicts. In the best case scenario of CAFTA working its way through these obstacles, there will still be pressures of a polarized and unequal society becoming more polarized and unequal. In the worst case scenario of all these obstacles taking a wrong turn simultaneously, not even the United States can come with a rescue plan.

Third, NAFTA would have to be re-oriented, adjusting not just to CAFTA, but also assuming a long-term southern tilt: with CAFTA ratified, pressures for FTAA will not be far behind. Even as NAFTA enters its most critical third five-year phase, when sensitive products are to be fully liberalized, no attempt is underway to discuss the sequel of a customs union, common market, and common currency. The US is too preoccupied elsewhere, and is unlikely to return to its southern neighbors at least during the remainder of Bush's second term. Even if it does, chances are dim domestic policies will be altered to satisfy external trade liberalization. Mexico needs these to reciprocate any US concessions, and Canada's disinterest may be hard to overcome.

Fourth, the FTAA presents two prospects. On the one hand, it is likely to gather further momentum as it rolls south with a ratified CAFTA, thus presenting recalcitrant Brazil with a possible fait accompli to which it would have to accede. On the other, it would have already pushed Canada and Mexico reluctantly over the hemispheric Rubicon by irreversibly turning both to forging economic relations south of the US, and in this sense, both CA4FTA and PPP would become redundant pursuits: Canada's hemispheric relations would more likely be through FTAA and Mexico's PPP would align even more with Washington-based multilateral institutions. These converging patterns would reflect precisely the Washington Consensus in spirit and in substance.

Theoretical

At least four issues demand reconsideration: US ratification as a regional collective good; homogenizing nationalistic negotiations styles, and in the process boosting both liberalization and democratization; formulating hybrid models to suit the increasingly complex negotiating dynamics; and reinventing hegemonic properties to fit the competitive atmosphere of unipolarity and/or monopolistic behavior.

Turning to the first issue, the US ratification process is slowly merging as a collective trading good in external relations: Executive branch intervention not only makes ratification possible, but also, by making it possible, creates trading partners abroad whose search for US market access becomes the quid pro quo for opening their own markets, no matter how selectively. The net result is greater world-wide liberalization and a significant transformation in the US serving as a global collective gook: Under GATT/WTO, the US served as a collective good more by providing the necessary condition of trade conditions: military security amidst the Cold War. Since the Cold War, the US, by increasingly becoming the market of the world, is increasingly supplying the sufficient condition of trade relations.[3] With this shift, the US is also beginning to collect rent for the collective good it supplies. From this perspective, ratification serves as the instrument of global trade liberalization through rent collection.

Second, access to the US market is not only liberalizing global trading patterns more effectively after the Cold War than during it, but also homogenizing nationalistic negotiations styles around the US pattern. Through the competitive liberalization approach to brick-by-brick WTO reconstitution, the US utilizes national action plans and trade capacity building measures as both incentives and instruments. These have the effect of creating relevant institutions where either none existed before, or if they did, they were too fragile or weak and in need of consolidation; and in the process, the new institutions take US counterpart institutions as models, thus streamlining liberalization. This is of enormous significance, since nationalistic agencies are not only disbanded, but the new institutions carry long-term future mileage: They make the shift towards liberalization irreversible, without guaranteeing they will coexist in harmony with counterpart institutions in other countries. Compared to the more nationalistic past across all of the hemisphere during the Cold War, this carries the potential of improving relations between countries, even as the gap between state and societal preferences within each state widens.

Third, as was abundantly clear in this investigation, all of the above developments necessitate hybrid negotiation models: No single paradigm can capture all the dynamics any more; and not just the constant shifts but also increasing complexities virtually necessitate component flexibility, capacity to accommodate two-way flows, facilitate multiple exit options, and cater to multiple negotiating partners. These are not minor paradigmatic adjustments: How each model can latch on to or dock with competing models may become as critical to its explanatory viability as its internal consistency and coherence.

Finally, just as accessing the US market is creating unipolar tendencies paralleling the simultaneous militaristic monopoly of the US, hegemonic theories need to be reinvented. In the same way as the nature of the US as a collective good became more rent conscious, hegemony too needs to be reconsidered in a competitive system without any viable countervailing force but without also constitution a hierarchic system. The fine line between hegemony and hierarchy is at stake: Whereas the former assumes competition and the latter does not, the only visible prospect for competitiveness in the global market today comes in the shape of rival trading blocs, meaning, without ganging up, there is very little hope of challenging the US; yet, if the US, through the FTAA, establishes an effective hemispheric bloc, other trading pockets of the world may face similar pressures of being either steamrolled or likely to be absorbed by the FTAA as the rest of the western hemisphere faces with a ratified CAFTA. Otherwise, only exogenous, military countervailing forces can balance the global market as after World War II.

NOTES

1. Gilbert R. Winham, "Negotiation as a management process," *World Politics* 30, no. 1 (October 1977):87-114.
2. Ricardo Roett,
3. On both conditions, see Robert Gilpin, *U.S. Power and the Multinational Corporation: The Political Economy of Foreign Direct Investment* (New York: Basic Books, 1975), esp. ch. 1.

Bibliography

"A 'Basin' Marshall Plan." *New York Times*. March 3, 1982.

Abell, John D. 2004. "Coffee production and sustainable development:San Lucas Tolimán, Guatemala." *LASA Forum* 35, no. 2 (Summer):5–7.

Actividades de la presidencia. 2004. "Firma presidente Vicente Fox la incorporación de Colombia al Plan Puebla-Panamá. November 19.

"AFL-CIO and Central American unions release first-ever declaration demanding that trade negotiations address workers' rights and development:trade negotiation expanded 'NAFTA' in Central America begin today." January 8, 2003. From: http://www.aflcio.org/mediacenter/prsptm/pr01082003a.stm

Aguilar Zinser, Adolfo. 1983. "Mexico and the Guatemalan crisis." *The Future of Central America: Policy Choices for the U.S. and Mexico*. Eds., Richard R. Fagen and Olga Pellicer. Stanford, CA: Stanford University Press, 161–86.

Alvarez Béjar, Alejandro. "The Plan Puebla-Panama:development of a region or a multinational enclave?" Paper, Mexico City: UNAM. No date, no other information.

Americas Policy Group and Canadian Council for International Cooperation. 2003. "The proposed Canada-Central America free trade agreement:a statement." May. From: http://www.ccic.ca/devpol/americas_policy_group/apg25_ca4fta_pettigrew_statement.htm

Anderson, Greg. 2001. "Hemispheric integration in the post-Seattle era:the promise of and problems for the FTAA." *International Journal* LVI, no. 2 (Spring):205–33.

Armbruster-Sandoval, Ralph. 2003. "The Honduras maquiladora industry and the Kimi campaign." *Social Science History* 27, no. 4 (Winter):551–76.

Association of Caribbean States. "Process of negotiations to establish the free trade agreement between Central American and the United States of America." Mimeo. No author, no date, no publisher.

Audley, John. 2003. "Environment and trade:the linchpin to success for CAFTA negotiations?" Carnegie Endowment for International Peace, Global Policy Program, Trade, Equity, and Development. *Issue Brief*. July.

Barlowe, Maude and Tony Clarke. "Making the links:a people's guide to the World Trade Organization and the Free Trade of the Americas." The Council of Canadians and the Polaris Institute, Ottawa. No date. From: http://www.canadians.org

Barry, Jeffrey Z. and Bert Brown. 1975. *The Social Psychology of Bargaining & Psychology.* New York. Academic Press.

Batsell, Jake. 2004. "Fair trade coffee demand sparks debate on workers wages, lives." *The Seattle Times.* October 7. From: http://www.seattletimes.com

Bélanger, Louis and Gordon Mace. 1999. "Building role and region:middle states and regionalism in the Americas." *The Americas in Transition: The Contours of Regionalism.* Eds., Mace, Bélanger. Boulder, CO: Lynne Rienner, 153–74.

Brady, Linda. 1991. *The Politics of Negotiations: America's Dealings with Allies, Adversaries, and Friends.* Chapel Hill, NC: University of North Carolina Press.

"Briefing on the U.S./Central American free trade agreement." *Yahoo! News.* CAFTA Coalition. June 2003.

Brysk, Alison. 2000. *From Tribal Village to Global Village: Indian Rights and International Relations in Latin America.* Stanford, CA: Stanford University Press.

Burki, Shahid. 1997. "A fate foretold:the World Bank and the Mexican crisis." *Mexico 1994: Anatomy of an Emerging-Market Crash.* Eds. Sebastian Edwards and Moisés Naím. Washington, DC: Carnegie Endowment for International Peace, 247–58.

Burton, John. 1986. "The procedures of conflict resolution." *International Conflict Resolution: Theory and Practice.* Eds., Edward E. Azar and Burton. London: Longman, 92–116.

"CAFTA tilted against the poor:new benefits for U.S., new burdens for Central America, says Oxfam." December 12, 2003. From: http://story.news.yahoo.com/news?tmpl=story&cid=669&ncid=669&e=3&u=/usnw/200312.

"CAFTA:a perspective from Costa Rica." *Americas Program.* Silver City, NM: Interhemispheric Resource Center, February 20, 2003.

Call, Wendy. 2002. "Resisting the Plan Puebla-Panama." September. From: http://www.americaspolicy.org/citizen-action/series/02-ppp_body.html

"Canada and Costa Rica sign free trade agreement." April 23, 2002. From: http://pm.gc.ca/default.asp?Language=E&Page=newsroom&Sub=newsrelease&Doc=canad.

"Canada's Martin plans to keep up with U.S.'s trade agreements." January 13, 2004. From: http:// quote.bloomberg.com/apps/news?pid=10000082&sid=au3.DIqR1ys4&refer=canada

Canadian Gazette. 2001. "Canada-Central American Four free trade agreement negotiations:consultations on trade negotiations with the Central American countries of El Salvador, Guatemala, Honduras and Nicaragua." January 6. From: http://www.dfait-maeci.gc.ca/tna-nac/ca-gazette-notice-6jan01.en.asp

Caribbean Latin American Action. 2003. "Strengthening the third border:2003 trade & investment forum overview." CAFTA and foreign investment—a public/private sector partnership. CLAA trade & investment forum, Guatemala. July 22–23. From: http://www.clas.org/caftaforum_over.html

Carlsen, Laura. 2001. "NAFTA Minus." The Americas This Week. *The Americas Program.* Silver City, NM: Interhemispheric Resource Center.

"Center of plant diversity:the Americas." From: http://www.nmnh.si.edu/botany/projects/cpd/mamap.htm

Chacón, Oscar. 2003. "Central American migrants take action on trade and regional integration." *Americas Program*. Silver City, NM: Interhemispheric Resources Center, July 13.

Chang, Ha-Joon. 2003. "The future for trade." *Challenge* 46, no. 6 (November-December):6–15.

Chatowetz, Lynn. 2002. "CA trade reps meet in Washington for free-trade talks." *Honduras This Week Online*. September 16. From: http://www.marrder.com/htw/2002oct/business.htm

Citizen's Trade Campaign. 2004. "With FTAA stalled, U.S. engages in NAFTA extension piece by piece." April 27. From: http://alcacmi.org/or/2004/04/4292.shtml

Coatsworth, John H. 1994. *Central America and the United States: The Clients and the Colossus*. New York: Twayne Publishers.

"Congressmen urge caution in FTAA negotiation." *The South Florida Business Journal*. September 25, 2003. From: http://www.bizjournals.com/southflorida/stories/2003/09/22/daily37.html

Connolly, Mark. 2001. "Plan Puebla Panama." *The Ecologist*. June. From: http://www.theecologist.org

Daudelin, Jean. 2003. "Foreign policy at the fringe:Canada and Latin America." *International Journal* LVIII, no. 4 (Autumn):571–90.

de Leon, Sergio. 2004. "Guatemalans commemorate massacre victims." *Yahoo! News,* July 21. From: http://story.news.yahoo.com/news?tmpl=story&cid=589&ncid=734&e=2&u=/ap/200407

De Santis, John. 2004. "Shrimpers go global:economic stress leads to unlikely alliances." *The Houma Courier*, July 23. From: http://www.houmatoday.com/apps/pbcs.d11/article?AID=20030723/NEWS/307230321/1026

De Walt, Billie R. 1985. "The agrarian bases of conflict in Central America." *The Central American Crisis: Sources of Conflict and Failure of U.S. Policy*. Eds., Kenneth M. Coleman and George C. Herring. Wilmington, DE: Scholarly Resources, Inc., 43–54.

Dobbin, Murray. 2001. "Canada is a world-class trade bully." *National Post*. November 14. Editorial. From: http://www.tradeobservatory.org/news/index.cfm?ID=3110

Domínguez, Jorge I. 1997. *Technopols: Freeing Politics and Markets in Latin America in the 1990s*. University Park, PA: Penn State University Press.

Druckman, Daniel.1986. "Stages, turning points, and crises:negotiating base rights, Spain and the United States." *Journal of Conflict Resolution*, vol. 30 (June):327–60.

Edelman, Marc and Rodolfo Monge Oviedo. 1995. "Costa Rica:non-market roots of market-access." *Free Trade and Economic Restructuring in Latin America*. Eds., Fred Rosen and Deidre McFadyen. New York: Monthly Review Press for North American Congress on Latin America.

Edwards, Sebastian. 1995. *Crisis and Reform in Latin America: From Despair to Hope*. New York: Oxford University Press, for The World Bank.

———. 1997. "Bad luck or bad policies? An economic analysis of the crisis." *Mexico 1994: Anatomy of an Emerging-Market Crash*. Eds., Edwards and Moisés Naím. Washington, DC: Carnegie Endowment for International Peace, 95–124.

EKOS. 2003. "Canadian attitudes toward international trade:survey findings." May 6.
    From: http://www.ekos.com
Ellis, Kristi. 2003. Trade Observatory. October
Engler, Mark. 2003. "CAFTA:free-trade vs democracy." *Foreign Policy in Focus*. Jan-
    uary 29. From: http://www.globalpolicy.org/globaliz/econ/2003/0603CAFTA.htm
——. 2004. "The trouble with CAFTA." *The Nation*. January 16. From: http://www
    .thenation.com/doc.mhtml)i=20040202&s=engler
Eschbach, Cheryl L. 1991. "Mexico's relations with Central America:changing prior-
    ities, persisting interest." *Mexico's External Relations in the 1990s*. Ed., Riordan
    Roett. Boulder, CO: Lynne Rienner, 172–77.
Espinosa, Gabriel. 2004. "US investors emerge as CAFTA winners." *Scoop Media*
    webpage. October 19. From
Esteban Carranza, María. 2000. *South American Free Trade Area or Free Trade Area
    of the Americas? Open Regionalism and the Future of Regional Economic Integra-
    tion in South America*, The Political Economy of Latin America. Aldershot, Hants,
    UK: Ashgate Publishing Co.
"Farming in Mexico:from corn wars to corn laws." *The Economist*. September
    25–October 1, 2004, 50.
Feinberg, Richard E. 1997. *Summitry in the Americas: A Progress Report*. Washing-
    ton, DC: International Institute of Economics.
——. 2003. "The political economy of United States' free trade arrangements." Pa-
    per. Berkeley APEC Study Center (BASC). University of California, Berkeley,
    March 21–22.
——. 2003. *Bilataeral Trade Agreements in the Asia-Pacific: Origins, Evolution and
    Implications*. Conference paper. Berkeley APEC Study Center. University of
    Berkeley, Berkeley. March 21–22.
Flynn, Matthew. 2001. "Fox strives to spread maquiladoras south." *Updater*. August
    7. From: http://www.us-mex.org/borderlines/updater/2001/aug7ppp.html
Fondación canadienne pour les Amériques (FOCAL). 2002. "Evolution of Central
    American political development & economic integration." Roundtable Report,
    May 30–31. Ottawa.
Free Trade Area of the Americas. Foreign Trade Information System. 2002. "FTAA:
    trade negotiations committee:methods and modalities for negotiations."
    FTAA.TNC/20/Rev.1. October 18. From: http://www.sice.oas.org/FTAA/
    M&M_e.asp
——. Secretariat. Trade Negotiations Committee. 2002. "Methods and modalities
    for negotiations." TNC/20/Rev.1. October 18. From: http://www.sice.oas.org/
    FTAA/M6M_e.asp
"Free trade on trial." *The Economist*. January 3, 2004, 13–16.
Gardner, Delworth. 1985. *Plowing Ground in Washington: The Political Economy of
    U.S. Agriculture*. San Francisco: Pacific Research Institute for Public Policy,
    163–238.
Gastle, Charles. 2002. "NAFTA's Chapter 11 *frontier justice* needs reform." *The
    Lawyers Weekly*. December 6. http://www.tradeobservatory.org/news/index
    .cfm?ID=3967

George, Alexander. 1979. "Case studies and theory development:the method of structured, focused comparison." *Diplomacy: New Approaches in History, Theory, and Policy.* Ed., Paul Gordon Lauren, 43–68. New York: Free Press.

Gilderhus, Mark T. 2000. *The Second Century: U.S.-Latin American Relations Since 1889.* Wilmington, DE: Scholarly Resources.

Gilpin, Robert. 1975. *U.S. Power and the Multinational Corporation: The Political Economy of Foreign Direct Investment.* New York: Basic Books.

Glass, Vicki. 2004. "CAFTA:the Latin American perspective." Washington Office of Latin America (WOLA). *Congressional Briefing.* Letter. January 22. From http://www.wola.org

Gleíjesos, Pierro. 1983. "Guatemala crises and response." *The Future of Central America: Policy Choices for the U.S. and Mexico.* Eds., Richard R. Fagen and Olga Pellicer. Stanford, CA: Stanford University Press, 187–212.

Government of Canada. 2002. "Government response to the report of the standing committee on foreign affairs and international trade: strengthening Canada's economic links with the Americas." Catalogue # E2-474/2002. From: http://www.dfait-maeci.gc/tna-nac/Consult3-e.asp

Government of Canada. Department of Foreign Affairs and International Trade. 2003a. "Initial strategic environmental assessment report of the Canada-Central American Four Free Trade Negotiaions (El Salvador, Guatemala, Hondurras and Nicaragua)." June 18. From: http://www.dfait-maeci.gc.ca/tna-nac(IYT/ea0423-en.asp

———. 2003b. "NAFTA at 10:a preliminary report." Catalogue # E2-487/2003. From: http://www.dfait-maeci.gc.ca/eet/research/nafta/nafta-en.asp

———. 2001. "Consultations on trade negotiations with the Central American countries of El Salvador, Guatemala, Honduras and Nicaragua." January 6. From: http://www.dfait-ameci.gc.ca/tna-nac/ca-gazette-notice-6jan01–en.asp

Government of Costa Rica. Tratado de Libre Comercio entre Centroamerica y Estados Unídos y Agencía Integral de Cooperación. 2002. *U.S.-Central America Free Trade Agreement Integral Cooperation Agenda: Conceptual Proposal for a National Action Plan.* San José, CR: Government of Costa Rica, December.

Government of El Salvador. 2003. "Tratados de libre comercio:Canada:Miami sede de reunion CA4-Canadá plantean lista de exclusiones a Canadá." September 1. From: http://www.minec.gob.sv/default.asp?id=38&mnu=31

———. Tratado de Libre Comercío Centroamerica-Estados Unídos. 2003. *National Action Plan for Trade Capacity Building: Meeting the Challenge of Globalization.* 2 vols, vol. 1: *General Strategy.* San Salvador: Government of El Salvador, July.

Government of Guatemala, Ministry of Economics and ECLAC. 2002. *National Action Plan for Trade Capacity Building in Guatemala: A Proposal by the Government of Guatemala in the Framework of the US-CAFTA.* Guatemala City, December.

Government of Honduras. 2003. *U.S.-Central Free Trade Agreement (US-CAFTA): National Action Plan for Trade Capacity Building: Honduras.* Teguchigalpa: Government of Honduras, June.

Government of Nicaragua. 2002. *Operational Program for the National Action Plan for Institutional Strengthening: Republic of Nicaragua.* Managua: Government of Nicaragua, December.

Gray, John D. 1992. *Men are from Mars, Women are from Venus: A Practical Guide for Improving Communications and Getting What You Want in Your Relationship.* New York: HarperCollins Publishers.

Green, Eric. 2003. "U.S. sees CAFTA promoting Central American democracy prosperity." *Washington File*, February 11. From: http://usinfo.state.gov/regional/ar/trade/03021101.htm

———. 2004. "Central American nations call for U.S. ratification of CAFTA:Central Americans vow to strengthen enforcement of labor laws." *Washington File*. July 14. From: http://usinfo.state.gov/xarchives/display.html?p=washfile-english?y=2004&m=July&x=...

Habeeb, Mark. 1988. *Power and Tactics in International Negotiations: How Weak Nations Bargain With Strong Nations.* Baltimore, MD: The Johns Hopkins University Press.

Hampson, Fen Osler. 1995. *Multilateral Negotiations: Lessons from Arms Control, Trade, and the Environment.* Baltimore, MD: The Johns Hopkins University Press.

Hathaway, Dale. 2002. "The impacts of US agriculture and trade policy on trade liberalization and integration via a US-Central American Free Trade Agreement." Paper. Special Initiative on Integration and Trade, Integration and Regional Programs Department, Inter-American Development Bank, Washington DC, October 1–2.

Heath, Jonathan. 1999. *Mexico and the Sexenio Curse: Presidential Successions and Economic Crises in Modern Mexico.* Washington, DC: Center for Strategic and International Studies.

Hirschman, Alfred. 1981. *National Power and the Structure of Trade.* Berkeley, CA: University of California Press.

Hogenboom, Barbara. 1996. *Mexico and the NAFTA Environmental Debate: The Transnational Politics of Economic Integration.* Utretch, Netherlands: International Books.

Hornbeck, J.F. 2004. "The U.S.-Central America Free Trade Agreement (CAFTA):challenges for sub-regional integration." *Congressional Research Service.* Report. Order code: RL31870. April 25, 32.

Hotakainen, Rob. 2004. "Sugar:a sticky election issue." *Sacramento Bee.* September 5. From: http://wwwsacbee.com

Huck, Eugene R. 1991. "Early United States recognition of Colombian independence and subsequent relations to 1830." *United States-Latin American Relations, 1800–1850: The Formative Years*, ed. T. Ray Shurbutt. Tuscaloosa, AL: University of Alabama Press, 197–227.

Human Rights Watch. 2004. "Turning a blind eye:hazardous child labor in El Salvador's sugarcane cultivation." June. From: http://hrw.org/reports/2004/elsalvador0604/

Hussain, A. Imtiaz. 1994. *Politics of Compensation: Truman, The Wool Bill of 1947, and the Shaping of Postwar U.S. Trade Policy.* New York: Garland Publishing, Co.

———. 2004. "After Cancún: G21, WTO, and multilateralism."*Journal of International and Area Studies* 11, no. 2 (December).

Ibarra-Yunez, Alejandro. 2001. "Mexico and its quest to sign multiple free trade agreements:spaghetti regionalism or strategic foreign trade?" April. From: http://egade.sistema.itesm.mx/investigacion/documentos/documentos/2egade_aibarra.pdf

Ikle, Fred Charles. 1964. *How Nations Negotiate.* New York: Harper & Row.

Inter-American Development Bank. 2002. "Plan Puebla-Panama:finance commission report of the Plan Puebla-Panama." June 15.

International Bank for Reconstruction and Development. 2000. *Entering the 21st Century: World Development Report, 1999–2000.* Washington, DC: IBRD.

International Monetary Fund. 2001. *Direction of Trade Statistics Yearbook Quarterly.* September 2001. Washington, DC: IMF.

——. 2001. *Direction of Trade Statistics Yearbook 2000.* Washington, DC: International Monetary Fund.

——. 2001. *Direction of Trade Statistics Yearbook, September 2001.* Washington, DC: International Monetary Fund.

Iritani, Evelyn. 2004. "Latino leaders not united on CAFTA:free trade brings arguments of more wealth or despair."*Houston Chronicle.* August 27. From: http://www.chron.com

Jacobson, Harold, Dusan Sidjanski, Jeffrey Rodamar, and Alice Hongassian-Rudovich. 1983. "Revolutionaries or bargainers:negotiators for a new economic order." *World Politics* 35, no. 3 (April):335–67.

Keck, Margaret E. and Kathryn Sikkink. 1998. *Activists Beyond Borders: Advocacy Networks in International Politics.* Ithaca, NY: Cornell University Press.

Kreklewich, Robert. 1993. "North American integration and industrial relations:neoconservativism and neo-fordism?" *The Political Economy of North American Free Trade.* Eds., Ricardo Grinspun & Maxwell A. Cameron. New York: St. Martin's Press, 261–70.

Krugman, Paul. 1995. "Dutch tulips and emerging markets." *Foreign Affairs.* July–August:28–44.

"Labor unions to fight free trade deal." *ABCNews.* December 18, 2003. From: http://abcnews.go.com/wire/Politics/ap20031218_435.html

Lall, Arthur. 1985. *Multilateral Negotiation and Mediation: Instruments and Methods.* Pergamon.

Lapper, Richard. 2003. "Costa Rica may derail US free trade plans." *Financial Times.* October 13. From: http://news.ft.com/servlet/ContentServer?pagename=FT.com/StoryFT/FullStory&C=StoryFT.

"Leaked CAFTA environmental chapter." *Quest for Peace.* From: http://www.quixote.org/quest/advocacy/fair_trade_cafta_environment_chapter.htm

Lederman, Daniel, Guillermo Perry, Rodrígo Suescún. 2002. "Trade structure, trade policy and economic policy options in Central America." Paper. Washington, DC: World Bank, November.

Lobe, Jim. 2004. "Coke benefiting from child labor in sugar cane fields." *OneWorld United States.* July 16. From: http://us.oneworld.net/article/view/87896/1/

Mackay, Donald R. 2002. "Challenges confronting the Free Trade of the Americas." *FOCAL Policy Paper*, June.

Maira, Luís. 1983. "The U.S. debate on the Central American crisis." *The Future of Central America: Policy Choices for the U.S. and Mexico.* Eds., Richard R. Fagen and Olga Pellicer. Stanford, CA: Stanford University Press, 66–97.

Martinez, Kathy. 2004. "Panama, U.S. launch 5th trade talk round." *Sacramento Bee*, October 18. From: http://www.sacbee.com

Martz, John D. 1980. "Democracy and the imposition of values:definitions and diplomacy." *Latin America, the United States, and the Inter-American System. Eds., Martz and Lars Schoultz.* Boulder, CO: Westview Press.

Mayer, Frederick. 1998. *Interpreting NAFTA: The Science and Art of Political Analysis.* New York: Columbia University Press.

McElhinny, Vince. 2004. "Update on PPP Mesoamericana transport integration initiative." March 11. From: http://www.interaction.org/idb or vmcelhinny@interaction.org

Mekay, Emad. 2003. "U.S. trade:Central American free trade deal a dud, activists say." April 10. From: http://www.tradesobservatory.org/news.index.cfm?ID=4285

Mendenhall, Kate and Margaret Reeves. 2004. "Support banana workers:bring justice to the table." *Global Pesticide Campaigner* 14, no. 1 (April). From: http://www.panna.org/resources/gpc/gpc_200404.14.1.06.dv.html

Merino del Río, José. 2003. "CAFTA:a perspective from Costa Rica." *Americas Program.* Silver City, NM: Interhemispheric Resource Center, February 20. From: http://www.americaspolicy.org/commentary/2003/0302caftacr_body.html

——. "CAFTA". Discussed in Chapter 4 subsection "Power and policy."

——. 2003. "Treaty tied by chains," xxxxxxx, February 20, 2003.

Milkman, Ruth. 1997. *Farewell to the Factory: Auto Workers in the Late Twentieth Century.* Berkeley, CA: University of California Press.

Moore, Barrington. 1966. *Social Origins of Dictatorship and Democracy: Lord and Peasant in the Making of the Modern World.* Boston: Beacon Press.

Moreno, Jenalia. 2003. "Worker rights a tricky issue:illegal conditions a concern." *Houston Chronicle.* October 22, 2003. From: http://www.chron.com/CDA/ssistory.mpl/business/2171778

——. 2004. "NAFTA hurt Latinos, study says:US Hispanics lost jobs, Mexicans saw wages drop." *Houston Chronicle.* August 16. From: http://www.chron.com/cs/CDA/ssistory.mpl/business/2740054

Moreno, Esperanza. 2004. "Making a hemispheric agreement by stealth." February 24. From: http://www.encuentropopular.org/pronunciamientos/estadosunidos/pronunciamiento002.h

——. 2004. "Secret deals breaks trail for FTAA?" *Oneworld.net.* July 16. From: http://www.oneworld.net/article/view/76972/1/

Moseley, Edward H. 1991. "The United States and Mexico, 1810–1850." *United States-Latin American Relations, 1800–1850: The Formative Years*, ed. T. Ray Shurbutt. Tuscaloosa, AL: University of Alabama Press, 122–96.

Moyer, Wayne. 1993. "The European Community and the GATT Uruguay Round:preserving the Common Agricultural Policy at all costs." *World Agriculture and the GATT.* Ed., William P. Avery. International Political Economy Yearbook, vol. 7. Boulder, CO: Lynne Rienner, 95–119.

"NAFTA Chapter 11 alarming." *The Charleston Gazette.* June 19, 2002. From: http://www.tradeobservatory.org/news/index.cfm?ID=3592

Newcomb, John. 2001. "Comment on Canada-Central America free trade proposal." January 9. From: http://www.csf.colorado.edu/forums/elan/2001/msg00022.html

"Nicaragua's proposed dry canal:globalization and the Meso-American megapro-jects." From http://www.nadir.org/nadir/initiativ/agp/colombia/puebla/drycanal .htm or http://environment.nicanet.org/dry_canal2.htm

North American Forum of Integration (NAFI). "Trade corridors." From: http://www.fina-nafi.org/ang/corridors.html

Norton, Stephen J. 2003. "Ghost of NAFTA haunts future of free trade." *CQ Weekly*. December 6, 2996–97.

———. 2003. "Net political gain for Bush in dropping steel tariffs?" *CQ Weekly*. December 6, 2998–3001.

Nye, Joseph S. 1971. *Peace in Parts: Integration and Conflict in Regional Organization*. Boston, MA: Little & Brown.

Odell, John. "Latin American trade negotiations with the United States." 1980. *International Organization* 34, no. 2 (Spring):207–28.

Office of the U.S. Trade Representative. 2003. *Interim Environmental Review: U.S.-Central American Free Trade Agreement*. Washington, DC: USTR, August.

———. Office of Trade Capacity Building. 2003. *U.S. Contributions to Trade Capacity Building: Improving Lives Through Trade & Aid*. Washington, DC: USTR, September.

Olson, Mancur. 1984. *The Rise and Decline of Nations: Economic Growth, Stagflation, Social Rigidities*. New Haven, CT: Yale University Press.

Opening Doors to the World: Canada's International Market Access Priorities, 2004, esp. ch. 4, from: http://www.dfait-maeci.gc.ca/tna

O'Regan, Sharon. 2004. "Integration in Central America." *Focal*. May 19–20. From Focal web page.

Oxfam. "CAFTA:an undemocratic negotiation process." http://www.oxfamamerica .org/advocacy/art5543.html

———. "Agriculture under CAFTA." From: http://www.oxfamamerica.org/advocacy/ art=5542.html

Paige, Jeffrey M. 1997. *Coffee and Power: Revolution and the Rise of Democracy in Central America*. Cambridge, MA: Harvard University Press.

Palley, Thomas. 2003. "After Cancún:an optimistic case." *Challenge* 46, no. 6 (November–December):16–31.

Palmer, Doug. 2003. "U.S. eyes post-Cancun trade deal with Central America," *Yahoo!*

News. October 17. From: http://story.news.yahoo.com/news?tmp1=story&u= nm/20030929/pl_nm/trade_cafta_dc_1

Pentland, Charles. 1973. *International Theory and European Integration: Studies in International Politics*. London: Macmillan.

Pickard, Miguel. 2002. "PPP:Plan Puebla Panama, or private plans for profit? A primer on the development plan that would turn the region from southern Mexico to Panama into a giant export zone." September 19. From: http://www .corpwatch.org/issues/PID.jsp?articleid=3953

———. 2004. "The Plan Puebla Panama revived:looking back to see what's ahead." *Americas Program*. Silver City, MD: Interhemispheric Resource Center, June 8.

Pierri, Raúl. 2002. "South America up in arms over US farm bill." *Inter Press Services* (May 10). From: http://www.globalpolicy.org/socecon/bwi-wto/wto/2002/0510safarm.htm

Poitras, Guy. 1995. "Regional trade strategies:U.S. policy in North America and toward the Asia-Pacfic." Paper. International Studies Association, annual convention, Chicago, March.

Polaski, Sandra. 2003. "Central America and the U.S. face challenge—and chance for historic breakthrough—on workers' rights." *Issue Brief*. February. Trade, Equality, and Development Project. Carnegie Endowment for International Peace.

Proyecto, Louis. 1998. "Class and indigenous roots of the Guatemalan revolution." April 13. From http://www.hartford-hwp.com/archives/47/172.html

Putnam, Robert. 1993. "Diplomacy and domestic politics:the logic of two-level games," *International Bargaining and Domestic Politics*. Eds., Peter Evans, Putnam, et al. Berkeley, CA: University of California Press, 431–68.

Raiffa, Howard. 1985. *The Art & Science of Negotiations: How to Resolve Conflicts and Get the Best out of Bargaining*. Belknap Press.

Rockefeller, Nelson Aldrich. 1969. *The Rockefeller Report on the Americas: The Official Report of a U.S. Presidential Mission for the Western Hemisphere*. Chicago, IL: Quadrangle Books, a New Times edition.

Rojas Aravena, Francisco and Luís Guillermo Solís Rivera. 1996. "Central America and the United States," *Latin American Nations in World Politics*. Eds., Heraldo Muñoz and Joseph S. Tulchin. Boulder, CO: Westview Press, 105–128.

Ross, David F. 1985. "The Caribbean Basin Initiative:threat or promise." *The Central American Crisis: Sources of Conflict and the Failure of U.S. Policy*. Eds., Kenneth M. Coleman and George C. Herring. Wilmington, DE: Scholarly Resources, Inc., 140–48.

Scoffield, Heather. 2000. "Pettigrew rejects NAFTA dispute model." *The Globe and Mail*. April 6. From: http://www.tradeobservatory.org/news/index.cfm?ID=1808

"Secret CAFTA talks continue." *The Advertiser*. July 29, 2003. From: http://www.theadvertiser.com/business/html/CC6EB14B-1B61-4322-8F1A-D4D379735605.sht

Sklair, Leslie. 1993. *Assembling for Development: The Maquila Industry in Mexico and the United States*. San Diego, CA: Center for US-Mexican Studies, University of California, San Diego, 1993, 2nd ed. Originally 1989, by Unwin Hyman, Inc., London.

Solis, Luís G. and Patricia Solano. 2001. "Central America:the difficult road towards integration and the role of Canada." *FOCAL Policy Paper*. May.

Squire, Eric. 2002. "Court orders Bush administration must give trade documents to the public." From: http://www.geocities.com/ericsquire/articles/ftaa/iatp021219.htm

———. 2002. "Canada moves on bilateral trade negotiations in wake of FTAA summit." *Canadian Press*. November 3. From: http://www.geocities.com/ericsquire/articles/ftaa/cp021103.htm

Stansifer, Charles L. 1991. "United States-Central American relations, 1824–1850." *United States-Latin American Relations, 1800–1850: The Formative Years*, ed. T. Ray Shurbutt. Tuscaloosa, AL: University of Alabama Press, 25–46.

Stecher, Katherine. 2003. "CAFTA:a shot-gun wedding." *NicaNet:the Nicaragua Network*. From: http://www.nicanet.org/alerts/cafta_negotiations_2.htm

Stein, Janice Gross. 1989. "Getting to the table:the triggers, stages, functions, and consequences of prenegotiation." *Getting to the Table: The Process of International Prenegotiation*. Ed., Gross Stein. Baltimore, MD: The Johns Hopkins University Press, 239–68.

Stewart, Rigoberto. 2003. "The unintended consequences of a US-Central America free trade agreement." *Fraser Forum* (June):13–17.

Striffler, Steve and Mark Moberg. 2003. *Banana Wars: Power, Production, and History in the Americas*. American Encounters/Global Interaction Series. Eds., Gilbert M. Joseph and Emily S. Rosenberg. Durham, NC: Duke University Press.

Tamayo, Eduardo. 2003. "Nicaragua:marcha contra acuerdo de libre comercio con EE.UU." September 19. From: http://movimientos.org/show_text.php3?key=2006

"The Canada-Central American Free Trade Free Trade Agreement." 2003. Letter to Canada's Minister for International Trade, Pierre Pettigrew, from Gerry Barr of Canada Council for International Cooperation (CCIC); Alison Crosby of the Americas Policy Group (APG); and Suzanne Rumsey of APG. May 21. From: http://www.ccic.ca/devpol/americas_policy_group/agp24_pettigrew_letter_ca4fta.htm

"The Interamerican Development Bank and the Plan Puebla Panama." March, 2003. From: http://www.nadir.org/nadir/initiativ/agp/free/colombia/idb_plan_puebla.htm

"The looming revolution." *The Economist*. November 13, 2004:75–77.

"The proposed Canada-Central America Free Trade Agreement." 2003. Statement APG/CCIC. May. www.ccic.ca/devpol/americas_policy_group/apg25_ca4fta_pettigrew_statement.htm

Tomlin, Brian. 1989. "The stages of prenegotiation:the decision to negotiate North American free trade." *Getting to the Table: The Processes of International Negotiation*. Ed., Janice Gross Stein. Baltimore, MD: Johns Hopkins University Press, 18–43.

Ulmer, Vanessa. 2003. "CAFTA negotiation session 3:March 31–April 4, El Salvador." Carnegie Endowment of International Peace. *News Summary*. From: http://ceip.org/files/news/CAFTA-summary-3.asp

United States Labor Education in the Americas Program (LEAP). "Passage of fast track paves way for CAFTA, a step back for worker rights." From http://WWW.usleap.org/trade/FastTrackPass8-02.html.

United States Trade Representative. 2003. "Interim environmental review:US-Central America Free Trade Agreement." August. Washington, DC.

———. "Sugar:putting CAFTA in perspective." *Trade Talks*. From USTR homepage: http://www.ustr.gov

———. 2003. "Free trade with Central America:summary of the U.S.-Central America Free Trade Agreement." December 17. From USTR webpage: http://www.ustr.gov

———. 2004. "U.S.-Central American Free Trade Agreement signed:USTR says focus must now shift to winning approval of agreement." May 28. Press release. From: http://usinfo.state.gov/ei/Archive/2004/Jun/01-149499.html

US Embassy. Guatemala. 2003. "Transcript of final press conference, IV Round of CAFTA negotiations." Guatemala City. May 16. From: http://www.kampala.usembassy.gov/guatemala/wwwh.caftaguae02.html

"US places duties on shrimp sales," *BBC News*, July 29, 2004. From: http://news.bbc
.co.uk/1/hi/business/3937851.stm

Varas, Augusto. 1996. "Soviet Union-Latin American relations:a historical perspective." *Latin American Nations in World Politics*. Eds., Heraldo Muñoz and Joseph
S. Tulchin. Boulder, CO: Westview Press, 237–61.

Whitehead, Lawrence. 1991. "The imposition of democracy." *Exporting Democracy:
The United States and Latin America*. Ed., Abraham F. Lowenthal. Baltimore, MD:
The Johns Hopkins University Press.

"Will WTO stand affect CAFTA." *High Plains Journal*. September 10, 2003. From:
http://www.hpj.com/edit1/WillWTOstandaffectCAFTA.CFM

Winham, Gilbert R. 1077. "Negotiation as a management process." *World Politics* 30,
no. 1 (October):87–114.

World Bank. 2000. *Entering the 21st Century: World Development Report 1999/2000*.
Washington, DC: World Bank, by Oxford University Press, New York.

World Trade Organization. 1995. *Trading Into the Future*. Geneva: Switzerland:
WTO. Available from: http://www.wto.org

———. 2003. *Understanding the WTO*. Geneva, Switzerland: WTO, September.

———. Secretariat. Trade Policy Review Body. 2003. "Trade policy review: Canada."
Report. February 12, #WT/TPR/S/112. From: http://www.sice.oas.org/ctyindex/
wto/canada/tprs112c_e.asp

Zartman, William. 1971. *The Politics of Trade Negotiations Between Africa and the
European Economic Community*. Princeton, NJ: Princeton University Press.

———. 1982. *The Practical Negotiator*. New Haven, CT: Yale University Press.

Zinn, Ryan. 2002. "The Lacandon Jungle's last stand against corporate globaliza-
tion:Plan Puebla Panama and the fight to preserve biodiversity and indigenous
rights in Chiapas." *CorpWatch*. September 26. From: http://corpwatch.radicaldesigns
.org/article.php?id=4148

Zuñiga, David. 2001. "Availability of cheap labor in the south does not compensate for
the absence of proximity with the USA." *La Journada*. November 19. Tr., Adele Oliv-
eri. From www.globalexchange.org/campaigns/mexico/ppp/journade111901.html

Index